Public Administration

PUBLIC ADMINISTRATION

S.A. Palekar

SERIALS PUBLICATIONS
New Delhi

First Published–2003

ISBN: 81-86771-22-0

Published by

Head Office:
SERIALS PUBLICATIONS
4, B.S.S. Hall, Khyber Pass Market,
Civil Lines, Delhi–110054 (India)
Phone: 0091-11-23811659
Fax: 91-11-23812678
e-mail: serials@satyam.net.in

Branch Office:
4830/24, Prahlad Street, Ansari Road,
Darya Ganj, New Delhi-110002 (India)
Phone: 23245225

Printed at: Tarun Offset Printers, (Delhi)

FOREWORD

Public Administration is an important discipline which is of great relevance and significance in a vast country like India, which is also the most populous democracy of the world. It is indeed a good augury that Dr. S.A. Palekar, Reader in Political Science, Gulbarga University has thought it fit to write a book on *Public Administration* examining its contours and concerns. In this meaningful sense, the present study is a welcome addition to the extent literature in public administration.

Schematically, the book is divided into fourteen well-organised chapters dealing with various aspects of Public Administration. These chapters examine the nature, scope and significance of public administration, the distinction between private and public administration, the various theories pertaining to the discipline of public administration, the functions, importance and structure of organizational management, personnel administration, the relevance and significance of bureaucracy, financial administration and the process and control of accountability of public finance, administrative responsibility in public policy making, district administration and good governance. The book also has a select bibliography which will enable the students to consult additional literature in public administration.

On the whole, Dr. S.A. Palekar has written a readable book on Public Administration which will be of interest to students as well as others interested in public administration in a simple, lucid but affective manner. He has succeeded in discussing various issues in public administration in an academic perspective. The author has taken pains to collect a substantial part of literature in public administration, organized it in a rational and functional manner, benefiting a large number of readers interested in the role and place of public administration in India when India has entered into the third millennium.

V.T. Patil
Vice-Chancellor
Pondicherry University
R. Venkataraman Nagar
Pondicherry–605 014

PREFACE

Public Administration is a continues on going process of action and interaction between each one of us. Public Administration not only ensures the daily life of the individual and the community to run smoothly, but much more, in developing countries like India it is an essential instrument of social change. As a result of that the study of Public Administration has assumed a greater significance in modern times.

Hence, the study of Public Administration is introduced at the under-graduate and post-graduate level. The book has been written to cater to the academic requirements of under-graduate and post-graduate students in particular and public in general. The book gives not merely a preliminary understanding of the subject, but also helps to cultivate a deeper interest in the vast and growing literature on Public Administration.

A select Bibliography is appended at the end of the book to enable the students to consult authoritative works for a detailed study of the different problems discussed in this book.

I express my deep sense of gratitude to Dr. Sharanabasavappa Appa for showering his blessings on me. I am very much grateful to Dr. V.T. Patil, Vice-Chancellor, Pondicherry University, Pondicherry, for writing the foıoword to this book. I am also thankful to

Prof. V.B. Coutinho, Vice-Chancellor, Gulbarga University, Gulbarga, for his encouragement.

I am also thankful to the Librarian and the staff of the Gulbarga University Library and the Indian Institute of Public Administration, New Delhi, for their co-operation.

I am grateful to Prof. R. Chandrashekar for his useful suggestions. I appreciate deeply the co-operation given by my wife Vijayalaxmi and my research student P. Umadevi and finally I thank Serials Publications, New Delhi, for publishing this book.

Dr. S.A. Palekar

CONTENTS

CHAPTER—1

Nature and Scope of Public Administration

Meaning and Definition

The word "public" immediately conveys the idea of all such categories of organization which are publicy owned controlled and arranged. It is thus a continuously active, business part of government, concerned with carrying out the intents of the policies of the people's representatives.

Public administration is the management of affairs of the government at all levels national, state and local. It is a branch of the wider field of administration.

In fact the word administration has been derived form the Latin words 'ad' and 'ministiare' which means to serve. In simple language it means the management of affairs or 'looking after the people'. It is a process of management which is practised by all kinds of organizations from the household to the most complex system of the government. To administer is to manage, direct or serve. The term administration has been variously defined by different writers.

- Administration, a long and slightly pompous word but it has an humble meaning for it means to care for or to look after people, to manage affairs."

(E.N. Gladden)

- "Administration is a process, common to all group effort, public or private, civil or military, large scale or small scale. It is a process of work in a departmental store, a bank, a school, a hotel or a city".

(Prof. L.D. White)

- "Administration is the determined action taken in pursuit of a conscious purpose. It is a systematic ordering of affairs and the calculated use of resources aimed at making those things happen which we want to happen."

(Marx, Morestein)

- "In its broadest sense, Administration can be defined as activities of groups co-operating to accomplish common goals."

(Simon)

- "Administration is the organization and use of men and materials to accomplish a purpose."

(Nigro)

- "Administration may be defined as the organization and direction of human and material resources to achieve desired ends."

(Pfiffner)

- "Administration is the capacity of coordinating many and often conflicting social energies in a single organism, so adroitly that they shall operate as unity."

(Brooke Adams)

- "Administration consists in the systematised orderning of affairs and the calculated use of resources aimed at making those things happen

> which we want to happen and simultaneously preventing developments that fail to square with our intentions."
>
> *(F.M. Marx)*

Marshall E. Dimcok defined administration as concerned with 'the what' and 'the how' of the government. The 'what' is the subject matter, technical knowledge of a field which enables the administrator to perform his tasks. This 'how' is the technique of management. The principles according to which cooperative programmes are carried to success. Each is indispensable; together they form the synthesis called Administration.

Therefore, the two essentials of administration are:

(i) Co-operative efforts;

(ii) Pursuit of common objectives.

Hence, Administration is a collective activity, which involves rational organization and management of men and material, and permeates all planned human activities.

Bertram M. Gross thinks that administration may convey the following:

Managing-an organization
Administering-the activities of an organization
Governing-organized human behaviour
Guiding-an enterprise
Co-ording-an undertaking
Integrating—a group of people
Running-people
Directing—the activities of the people
Supervising-subordinates
Controlling-the use of resources

Keith Henderson gives a precise definition of administration as the "arrangements of men and materials in the rational carrying out purposes."

There are three commonalities available which can be utilized to define "administration."

(a) Goals or activities to be accomplished

(b) Limited resources implied in efficiency and effectiveness

(c) The people referred to as "other people"

Administrators are those who work through people, allocating scarce resources, to achieve goals.

Administration and Management

It is relevant here to make a distinction between administration and management. Administration is a wider term encompassing activities like the spelling out of policies and objectives, establishment of suitable organizational structure to conduct and promote an organized task, providing necessary resources for the realization of the objectives, etc. Administration is a variety of component elements which together in action produce the result of getting done a defined task with which a group of people is charged. It is the inclusive process of integrating human efforts so that a desired result is obtained. The role of management, on the other hand, rests confined within the framework of policy, organizational structure resources.

Ordway Tead feels that administration is the process and agency which is responsible for the determination of the aims for which an organization and its management are to strive, which establishes the broad policies under which they are to operate. Management (on the other hand) is the process and agency which directs and guides the operations of an organization in the realizing of established aims.

Public Administration is one of the aspects of the larger field of administration. The public variety of administration is distinct because "it deals with the ends of the state, the sovereign will, the public interests, law and the coercive element in society."

Public Administration has been variously defined by numerous thinkers:

- Professor L.D. White observes, "public administration consist of all those operations having for their purpose the fulfilment or enforcement of public policy."
- Pfiffner observes, "It would seem that administration consists of getting the work of government done by coordinating the efforts of the people so that they can work together to accomplish their set tasks".
- Gladden gives a brief definition of public Administration when he says that "it is concerned with the administration of the government."
- Harvey Walker observes, "The work which the government does to give effect to law is called administration."

Percy Mcqeen says, "Public Administration is administration related to the operations of government whether central or local."

- Willoughby writes, "The term administration may be employed in Political Science in two senses. In its broadest sense, it denotes the work involved in the actual conduct of governmental affairs regardless of the particular branch of government concerned. In its narrowest sense it denotes the operations of the administrative branch only. As students of public Administration we are concerned with the narrowest meaning of the term."

- According to Marshall E. Dimock, "Public Administration is the fulfilment or enforcement of public policy as declared by the competent authorities. It deals with the problem and powers, the organization and techniques of management involved in carrying out the laws and policies formulated by the policy making agencies of government. Public Administration is law in action. It is the executive side of government.
- Waldo defines Public Administration as "the art and science of management as applied to the affairs of State."
- Prof. Woodrow Wilson defined public administration as "detailed and systematic execution of public law, every particular application of general law is an act of administration."
- According to Luther Gulick, "Public Administration is that part of the science of Administration which has to do with Government and thus concerns itself primarily with executive branch where the work of the Government is done."
- According to M. Ruthna Swamy, "When Administration has to do with affairs of a state or minor political institutions like a Municipal or country council, or District Board, it is called, Public Administration."

Herbert Simon says, "By public Administration is meant, in common usage, the activities of the executive branches of the national, state and local governments."

Merson defined Public Administration as by which "the administrator gets things done and just as the science of politics is an enquiry into the best means whereby the will of the people may be organized for the formulation, so the science of public Administration is an enquiry as to how policies may best be carried into operations."

Ridley comes out with a precise and brief description of public administration in these words:

"Public Administration is administration in the Public Sector....It is administration by the state... Public Administration is governmental administration... It is administration by public authorities... Public authorities are authorities which administer according to the rules of public administration. Public administration should be the study of administration, descriptive, theoretical and normative.

F.A. Nigro's definition is a more comprehensive one, which also includes besides the above mentioned aspects, the relationship between public administration and the political and social systems as well. Nigro has defined public administration in the following words:

Public administration:

(a) is co-operative group effort in a public setting.

(b) Covers all three branches—executive, legislative and judicial—and their interrelationships;

(c) has an important role in the formulation of public policy and is thus a part of the political process;

(d) is more important than, and also different in significant ways from private administration;

(e) As a field of study and practice has been much influenced in recent years by the human relations approach;

(f) is closely associated with numerous private groups and individuals in providing services to the community.

Public administration is the non-political bureaucratic machinery of the government for implementing its laws and policies in action, e.g. the collection of revenues, maintenance of law and order, running the railway and postal services, maintaining an army, running schools and hospitals. These are all acts of public administration. Public administration operates within a political context. It is a means by which the policy decisions made by the political decision makers are carried out. Public administration is decision making, planning the work to be done. formulating objectives and goals, working with the legislative and citizen organizations to gain public support and funds for government programmes, establishing and revising organizations, directing and supervising employees, providing leadership, communicating and receiving communications, determining work methods and procedures, appraising performance, exercising controls, and other functions performed by government executives and supervisors. It is the action part of government, the means by which the purpose and goals of government are realised.

To summarise, these definitions identify public administration with;

- The formulation and implementation of public policies;
- The executive branch of government;
- Organizational structures and machinery of administration;
- administrative processes;
- Bureaucracy and its activities;

- Co-ordination of group activity or social relationship; and
- Interaction between organizations and their environment.

Nature

When we analyse the nature of public administration we are faced with a duality of outlook which may conveniently be called the integral and the managerial view.

According to the integral view, 'administration' is the sum total of all the activities—manual, clerical, technical and managerial which are undertaken to realise the objective in view, i.e. the implementation of the policy or policies in a given field.

Thus, the activities of the errand boy, the sweeper as well as the secretaries and the managers in an enterprise, all constitute administration. In the integral view the work of all persons ranging from the lowest to the highest working in an enterprise are taken into account as being part of administration.

On the other hand, the managerial view regards the work of only those persons engaged in performing managerial functions in an enterprise, as constituting administration. It includes only some of the activities concerned with management which unite and control the rest of them as part of a co-ordinated endeavour, and not the sum total of the activities undertaken in pursuance of the goal.

These two views manifest differences. Acceptance of the integral view makes us court the entire personnel of an undertaking as engaged in administration. The managerial view, on the other hand only includes managerial or supervisory activities as constituting administration. The operational activities are not included. We may also say that according to the managerial view, administration is not doing things, but getting them done. An administrator is a functionary who gets things done by other by directing and supervising their work.

Naturally, the scope of Public administration would be different according to these two different view points. Viewed from the integral angle, public administration would include the whole complex of activities undertaken to accomplish any common purpose. In this sense, it would become a heterogeneous mass of activities and operations having no bond of unity except that of the common purpose towards which they are directed. Thus, any thing that goes on, in say, the Post and Telegraph Department, from planning programmes of activities at the top level to the sorting and delivering of mails would comprise public administration. Some writers feel this is a very vague and unscientific view of the subject which would hinder its development into a distinct academic discipline or science. For its scope would become so vast and unwieldy that it does not lend itself easily to study and instruction, except in particular fields which are unlimited in number.

The managerial point of view, on the other hand, postulates that administration is the organization and use of men and materials in the pursuit of common objectives. It, thus, does not includes all the activities of an organization into its ambit but takes out only those activities for its study which involve the techniques of management and are, therefore, common to all sorts of organizations. This raises the subject to the penacle of a science which can be studied as a general science of organization and management. The scope of this subject is, thus, limited to the techniques of management which Luther Gulick has summarised in a meaningless word

POSDCORD, each letter of which stands for one technique of management, namely, Planning, Organization, Staffing. Direction, Co-ordination, Reporting, and Budgeting. So, according to the managerial school, the scope of public administration is confined to these seven processes or activities in an organization.

A.R. Tyagi states "While this point of view regarding the nature and scope of public administration has the advantage of a certainty and definiteness and consequently, making its study more systematic and scientific, it is farther from reality. For in actual practice, it is seen that the administration is concerned not only with managerial technique but also with questions of policy and programmes as well as with actual operations or execution of these programmes. In the second place problems of organization and management are to be found not only in the executive branch of the government but equally in the other branches also. Summoning sessions of the legislature, conducting proceedings of the legislative chambers and passing a legislative bill involve far more intricate problems of management than management of a small post-office situated in the corner of a mohalla. It would, therefore, be more appropriate to say with Dimock and Dimock that as a study, public administration examines every aspect of government's efforts to discharge the law and to give effect to public policy; as a process, it is all the steps taken between the time an enforcement agency assumes jurisdiction and the last brick is placed (but includes also that agency's participation, if any, in the formulation or programmes in the first place); and as a vocation, it is organizing and directing the activities of others in a public agency. In other words, public administration is the whole government in action. Any attempt to limit its scope either with reference to its activities or the branches of the government will misrepresent its true nature and will make its study unrealistic and a very limited use."

The definitions of 'administration' given earlier do not categorically support either the managerial or the integral view of administration. For example, the definitions given by the Marshall. E. Dimock appear to support the integral view of administration. On the other hand, the definitions given by Luther Gulick. Herbert A. Simon, and L.D. White support the managerial view of administration.

It may be pointed out here that neither of these views can be summarily rejected. Exact meaning of administration would depend on the context in which the term is used. Dimock, Dimock and Koeing sum up by observing that "as a study public administration examines every aspect of government's efforts to discharge the laws and to give effect to public policy; as a process, it is all the steps taken between the time an enforcement agency assumes jurisdiction and the last brick is placed (but includes also that agency's participation, if any, in the formulation of the programme in the first place); and as a vocation it is organizing and directing the activities of others in a public agency."

Scope of Public Administration

The controversy over the scope of Public administration has been unfortunate and yet highly rewarding; rewarding because, the controversy generated vigour, provided extra incentive to the students of Public Administration to get deeply involved in research in areas of administration about which material, data and literature was non-existent such a controversy has resulted in great amount of research, producing voluminlous data throwing new light on unresearched fields of Public administration. The last 100 years have witnessed the growth of "a growing discipline". It is bound to grow despite prejudiced reservations of narrow disciplinarians, even from the filed of the social sciences.

Public administration embraces the entire area and all the activity of the government. We in India do not and cannot accept the restricted definition of public administration. So much is the mutual dependence and so intensive is the interaction between the executive, the legislature and the judiciary that public administration must be defined in the broader terms. It covers all the three branches of the government—the executive the legislature and the judiciary. Necessarily, it is to be studied as part of the larger political processes in a country. The scope of public administration is, thus, wide enough. Keeping this in mind one may say that public administration refers to the organization of public affairs and their direction. Several writers have defined the scope of public administration in varying terms and to varying lengths.

There are broadly two views about the scope of the public administration. These are:

1. The POSDCORB View
2. The subject Matter View

1. The POSDCORB View of Administration

This view corresponds with the managerial view of administration and takes into account only the executive branch of the government. The supporters of this view are Henri Fayol., L.Urwick, J.D. Money, A.B. Reiley Percy, Mc Queen and Aluther Gulick.

(a) ***View of Henri Fayol:*** According to him, the main categories of administration are five: (1) Planning (2) Organization (3) Command (4) Co-ordination (5) Control According to him, these are not merely logical steps which successively occur in the administration process.

(b) ***View of L. Urwick:*** He fully endores Fayol's analysis.

(c) ***View of Percy M. Queen:*** He holds that the study of administration deals with Men, Materials and Methods.

(d) ***View of Willoughby:*** He considers Fayol's and his followers view rather too abstract. He divides his well-known work Principles of Public administration into five major sections (a) General or overhead administration (b) organization (c) Personnel management (d) material and supply, and (e) finance.

(e) ***Views of Luther Gulick:*** He sums up the scope of the subject by the letters of the word POSDCoRB by which he means: Planning, Organization, staffing, Directing, Co-ordinating, Reporting and Budgeting.

Planning means the working out in board outline the things to be done, the method to be adopted to accomplish the purpose.

Organization means the establishment of the formal structure of authority through which the work is sub-divided, arranged, defined and co-ordinated.

Staffing means the recruitment and training of the personal and their conditions of work.

Directing means making decisions and issuing orders and instructions.

Co-ordinating means inter-relating the work of various divisions sections and other parts of the organization.

Reporting means informing the agency to whom the executive is responsible about what is going on.

Budgeting means fixed planning, control and accounting.

According to Gullick the POSDCoRB activities are common to all organizations. They are the common problems of management which are found in different agencies regardless of the peculiar nature of the work they do.

According to Ordway, Tead, the essentials of Public administration are (POSIDDOCEM)—(1) Planning (2) Organising (3) Staffing (4) Initiating (5) Delegating (6) Directing (7) Overseeing (8) Co-ordinating (9) Evaluating (10) Motivating.

The POSDCoRB view of the scope of public administration over looks the fact that different agencies are faced with different administrative problems which are peculiar to the nature of the services they render and the functions they perform. The POSDCORB view takes into consideration only the common techniques of administration and ignores the study of the subject matter with which an agency is concerned, Gullick's approach is technique—oriented rather than subject—oriented.

2. The Subject-matter View of Administration

In reaction to the POSDCoRB view, the subject-matter view of administration comes into reckoning.

(a) ***Subject matter means Line Agencies:*** The subject matter of Public administration comprises 'line functions' or services meant for the people. They include law and order, defence, social security, education, public health, justice etc. These services have specialized techniques of their own, which are not covered by the POSDCoRB activities. Here, the techniques of crime detection, prevention of breaches of peace, control of bad characters etc., are much more important that the formal principles of organization, personnel management or finance.

(b) ***Techniques of Administration differ according to Subject Matter:*** Moreover, even the techniques of management are modified by the subject matter of the services in which they have to operate. Consequently, organization in the armed forces has to be very different from that in education. Even the techniques of co-ordination in the two services are different. Emphasis only on the managerial task resulting in the neglect of the subject matter concerned is, therefore, to miss the very heart of administration.

(c) ***Reconciliation of the two views:*** It is by no means necessary to reject either of these views of the scope of public administration. Both represents the whole truth. Just as the human organ has both an anatomy and a psychology of its own so also administration has the common techniques of POSDCoRB as its skeleton and the specialized methods of various, programmes as its muscles and sinews without either of them, it can not function any more than can the body in the absence, of either the bones or the digestive circulatory or the respiratory processes.

Lewis Meriam says, "Public administration is an instrument with two blades like a pair of scissors. One blade may be knowledge of the fields covered by POSDCoRB, the other blade is knowledge of the subject matter in which these techniques are applied. Both blades must be good to make it an effective tool.

Pfiffner has divided the scope of public administration into two categories:

(i) Principles of Public administration

(ii) Sphere of Public administration

In the first category, Public Administration Studies the following problems:

(a) ***Organization.*** Which means "the structuring of individuals and functions into productive relationship." It represents the static pattern of administration which may be called the 'Anatomy' of administration.

(b) ***Management of Personnel.*** Which is "concerned with the direction of these individuals and functions to achieve ends previously determined." It represents the dynamic aspect of administration and may be called its "Physiology".

(c) ***Method and Procedure.*** Which is the technique of administrating, the process of working, ie.., the 'how' of administration.

(d) ***Material and Supply.*** Which are the tools with whose help administrative work is carried out, e.g., pen and ink, cabin or cardboard, tag furniture and so on.

(e) ***Public Finance.*** Without which personnel cannot be employed and work cannot be performed.

(f) ***Administrative Accountability.*** Both in terms of internal control as well as external responsibility to Law courts, legislature and the people.

Viewed from the jurisdictional point of view, the sphere of public administration includes the central government, state government, its regional and local authorities and also the public corporations.

Thus it may be said that Public administration, in sum, includes the totality of government activity, encompassing exercise of endless variety and the techniques of organization and management whereby order and social purpose are given to the effort of vast numbers. It is the study of men, materials and methods in administration.

A more comprehensive account of the scope of public administration has been given by the Walker by dividing it into two parts:

(i) ***Administrative theory.*** It includes the study of structure, organization, functions, and method of all types of public authority engaged in carrying out the administration at all levels, i.e. national, regional, local, etc. Further, it is a study of all problems connected with external control of Parliament and the Cabinet over administration, internal control of administration machinery, judicial control over administration, administrative tribunals, planning, programming and execution of public actions, requirement of personnel and problems connected there with, research information, public relations, etc. The emphasis is to find out certain principles of administrative actions which can be usefully applied in practical administration.

(ii) ***Applied administration.*** It is difficult to give a comprehensive statement as to what the applied administration should exactly include because of the new and fast-growing field of public administration. Walker has made an attempt to classify the main forms of applied administration on the basis of ten principal functions, which he calls as political, legislative, financial, defensive, educational, social, economic, foreign, imperial and local. He elaborates these functions as under:

- ***Political:*** It includes a study of executive legislature relationship, politico-administrative activities of the cabinet, minister—official relationships, etc.,
- ***Legislative:*** It includes delegated legislation, preparatory work done by the officials in drafting of bills for enactments etc.,
- ***Financial:*** It includes a study of financial administration.
- ***Defensive:*** It includes a study of military administration.
- ***Educational:*** It covers all aspects of educational administration.
- ***Social:*** All administration in the social field such as housing, social, food, security and employment etc.,
- ***Economical:*** It covers all administrative activities in the economic field, i.e., industries, agriculture, foreign trade, commerce, public enterprises etc.
- ***Foreign:*** It covers foreign administration which includes international co-operation, international agencies for international peace and prosperity diplomacy etc.
- ***Imperial:*** It includes problems and techniques of imperial domination over other nations, etc.
- ***Local:*** It covers administration of local bodies.

Although there is over lapping in the classification of Walker, it is a good attempt at an exhaustive definition of applied administration. The present administrator is concerned not only with developing the administrative techniques but it has also become important for him to study the ecological and human aspects of public administration. The study of environment in which the administration operates and the study of human behaviour cannot be ignored by the administrator of today. In a more summarized form, we can sum up by saying that applied administration includes the study of administration in the various countries of the world of various departments or services in the progressive states, of organization at various levels, i.e. governmental, local, national and international, of the historical development of administrative methods and techniques and of the problems connected with international organizations.

It may also be remarked that Public administration is only a means to the attainment of the objects of the state itself—the maintenance of peace and order, the progressive achievement of justice, the instruction of the young, protection against disease and insecurity, the adjustment and compromise of conflicting groups and interest—in short, the attainment of good life. The scope of public administration varies with peoples expectations of what they should get from government. A century ago they expected chiefly to be let alone. Now they expect a wide range of services and protection. Throughout the world the demands made by people upon governments have continually increased and in time to come they would further increase. The expansion of government functions inevitably means more administrative agencies, more officials and employees. The administrative system consequently grows and becomes diverse.

Importance of the Study Public Administration

Public administration had its origin in ancient Greece whose philosophers have entertained administratire thought. But the development of administrative thought in those days was not pure and systematic. The systemic study of public administration began only in recent times.

The term public administration came into use in the 17th C. In its contemporary sense it was employed by Washington and Hamilton at the close of the 18th C. Therefore, in its modern form, public administration is not only a new science but also an inexact science. Hence, as in the case of other social sciences, public administration also lacks precision and uniformity in its terms. Many writes have brought into light the true value of the study of public administration. They are: J.M. Pfiffner, R.V. Presthus, Prof. W.B. Donham, C.A. Beard, F.J. Goodnow and many others.

The following arguments brings about the true importance of the role of Public administration in modern society.

1. Public administration is a means of achieving statesmanship and citizenship. Wise statesmanship requires a sound knowledge of the state and its administration. A good citizen is one who takes active part in the administration of his state. He should thoroughly understand the nature of administration under which he lives. The extent of political progress depends upon the quality of citizens. Every adjustment in the governmental organization and every polity of government are, to a great extent, influenced by the public administration.

2. Public administration establishes close relationship with other allied sciences, it is most closely related to politics. It is also closely associated with Economics. Many of the problems which the public administration faces, today, are economic problems. Society (the subject matter of sociology) needs law, order, peace, and security which are maintained by public administration. History supplies many useful lessons which help the modern administrator in his work. Thus the study of public administrative enables

an individual to understand something of other social sciences. Hence it is an important subject.

3. Public administration executes law of the state. Law is essential to society because it safeguards liberty and right of the individual. It regulates the relation of man with his fellow men. It is the basis of human life. But the laws do not administer themselves automatically. It is the administrator who executes law. If law is not properly executed. Life, liberty and rights of the individual cannot be well secured. A good law which is badly executed is dangerous to social progress. Hence the role of public administration in the administration of law is very important.

4. Education and Public administration act and react upon each other. In democracy education claims an important place in the development of human civilization. But the nature and progress of education largely depends upon the nature of the administration prevailing in the country. Dr. Pattabhi says: ("As democratic institutions develop, the character of education prevalent in country tends to participate in the nature of government that rules the land". So in order to understand the system of education. It is necessary to understand the role of the governmental administration.

5. Public administration provides the working knowledge of the administrative systems in the principal countries. It involves "a study of the activities and techniques" of administrative system found in the advanced states of today. The comparative study of the working of different administrative systems is highly useful to establish the merits and defects of one's one administrative working. This is highly essential for the guidance of the leader of the nation. This argument brings into light the valuable role of public administration.

6. Public administration helps the growth of civilization in society. This argument is advanced by W.B. Donham and C.A. Beard. The former writer says" If our civilization fails it will be mainly because of a breakdown of administration". The later writer says that the future of civilization is dependent upon public administration competent to discharge the functions of civilized society". History is full of instances to show that civilization could not progress under inefficient and incompetent governmental administration.
7. Public administration helps the individual to lead (what Aristotle calls) good life. This is the argument of L.D. White. He states: "The immediate objective of the art of public administration is... the attainment of the good life". It provides individual necessary things such as maternity care, child care. Vaccination, education, employment, food, water etc. Which make his life happy. Every thought and action of the individual are greatly regulated by the Governmental administration. It accompanies him at every turn of his life from the craddle to the grave." Thus modern administration is a welfare administration. Individuals look to their administration for every thing they need in life. As white remarkably observes: "Two centuries ago people expected little but oppression. A century ago they expected chiefly to be let alone. Now they expect a wide range of services and protection".
8. Public administration preserves the stability in society and government. It preserves the stability in society because, public administration is permanent. It does not change whenever government changes. As Prof. M. Ruthnaswamy excellently puts it: "Systems of Government may exist today, and cease to be tomorrow, constitution may come and go, but administration goes on for ever". Public administration strengthens the paths of government, purifies its

organization and 'crowns its duties with dutifulness". It is means by which the policies of the government are adjusted and executed. It helps the government in framing the policies. Administration is the means by which the multifarious activities of ever increasing complexity of society' are adjusted. It is "the faculty upon which social stability rests". (Adams). Administration helps also the social progress. To achieve this end. The public administration initiate a number of steps such as: reduction in economic equality, education, equality, planning etc. They make the most efficient utilization of resources at their disposal. It eliminates waste, conserves materials, promotes social welfare, establishes justice and protects society from diseases and insecurity. Thus public administration plays an invaluable role in the social reconstruction.

It is clear from the above discussion that public administration has assumed a great importance both as a subject of study and an activity. There are many factors, which helped the growth of the importance of public administration.

They are:

1. Industrial Revolution;
2. Scientific and technological development;
3. Growth of cities and city life;
4. The concept of welfare state;
5. Planning and Development activities of the governments.

In order to function successfully, public administration must be free, impartial, fearless and broadminded.

Is Public Administration a Science?

Before we proceed to discuss whether Public administration is a science or not, it is necessary to find out the principal features of science. A subject of science like Physics or Chemistry has these features.

1. Experimentation
2. Uniformity in usage of terms
3. Precision and
4. Unity among writers

Of these, the first feature, viz., experimentation is the most important. The science subjects are studied by means of experiment. What is studied in theory or what is explained by a teacher in the class room can be proved by means of experimentation in a laboratory. A chemist for instance can artificially create facts, combine them with different things and study the effects of the combination by repeating the whole process over and again. This is the great feature of a scientific study.

There is no unanimous opinion among the writers whether Public administration is a science or not. There are some writers who considered it a science. F.W. Taylor, F. Merson, C.A. Beard, Cleun Necley, W.B. Donham and Willoughby held such an opinion. Taylor said that administration is already a science and it consists of scientific enquiry. F. Merson is of the View: "Observation and experience have, particularly among last fifty years, provided a mass of ascertained facts upon which the scientist may exercise his deductive faculties.

C.A. Beard believes: "Public administration has developed a body of rules and maxims which experience has demonstrated to be applicable to concrete practice and to working out approximately of forecast". W.B. Donham says that Public administration has its own techniques and abstractions, so it has a claim to the rank of science. Willoughby says that the subject of Public administration is a science because it has a number of principles of its own as any science subject has. He mentions the following principles:

1. Principle of Political direction
2. Principle of Public Responsibility
3. Principle of Social Necessity
4. Principle of Efficiency
5. Principle of Organization
6. Principle of Public Relations
7. Principle of Evaluation and Progress
8. Principle of Research

There are some writers who did not consider Public administration a science. Jacob Winder, M.R. Cohen, Wallance and Finer held such a view. Jacob Winder passed bitter remark when he said that to call public administration a science is "an open invitation to ridicule". To Cohen, Public administration is a subject which had no definiteness, while Finer concluded that it has no principles. Wallace noticed some dangers in calling it a science.

The charges that are levelled against Public administration are:

1. It has no uniformity
2. There are no agreed principle among the writers on the subject nor is there any scope of evolving such principles in future.
3. Its subject matter is irrational elements of human nature i.e. habits, hopes, fears, likes, dislikes etc. which play a large part in the activities of administration.
4. It is impossible to carry out experimentation in Public administration, because we cannot

experiment with human beings. Human motives and values cannot be weighed and calculated like chemical substance. Human phenomena can only be described, but not weighed.

To what extent Public administration is a Science?

To a large extent, the charges levelled above are correct and convincing. These defects stand in the way of Public administration becoming a science. However, we may point out that to some extent, Public administration is a science. Though we may not have the scope for experimentation in Public administration, we can study the subject experimentally. The student of this subject can experiment things in the World which is a laboratory for him. The whole activities of Public administration are experimental in character. Every policy that is made, every decision that is taken and every reform that is introduced by the administration are experimental and provisional till their effects are ascertained. If after a time, the policies do not yield the desired results, they may be repealed and new policy may come into vogue.

The conclusions of these experiments may not be of mathematical precision, but they contain an element of probability. As remarked by Butler; "This probability is the guide of life". Thus, public administration may be considered a science in a limited sense.

Evolution and Growth of the Study Public Administration

Public administration has two aspects. Firstly it is 'an activity'. Secondly, it is 'a subject of study of intellectual discipline'. The history of Public Administration is very long. Its traces as an activity can be found even in the earlier days. Hence it is necessary for us to understand the nature of administrative activity in the ancient and modern times.

Administration as an Activity

Ancient Period—Precisely when or where public administration began no one can say, because no one knows when or where men first thought of themselves as comprising a community as being a public (J.A. Vieg). However, historical evidence is there to show that the earliest governmental authority was noticed in the primitive family. Each family was a government by itself under the control of patria protesta who enjoyed supreme authority. In course of time, there came, into existence tribal government with a King or Rajah at its head. He was assisted by a council of ministers or chiefs. He established a court and resided in a palace. It seems that some tribes had assemblies too.

The next stage in the development of administration was found in the oriental empires. The empires known for administration were:

1. The Sumerian (5000 B.C. to 2750 B.C.)
2. Assyrian (1200 B.C.-606 B.C.)
3. The Babylonian (2000 B.C.-1200 B.C.) and
4. The Egyptian (3500 B.C.-1000 B.C.)

These empires developed systematic administration, law and literature. The provincial governments were manned by governors. Of all the emperors, the administration Hammurabi (1947 B.C.-1905), the King of Babylonia, was famous. It was in his code, written 4000 years ago, the idea of government as a doer of things was established.

The next stage in the growth of administration was noticed in the ancient Greek cities and Roman empire. The former contributed the idea of democratic administration while the latter gave the world a systematic law. The code of Justinian inaugurated a new era in the history of administration. The contribution of ancient India to the field of administration was in no way less than Greece and Rome.

1. ***Medieval period:*** No proper development of administration as an activity could be witnessed in this period. The whole history of this period was dominated by an unending struggle between the Pope and Emperor. The only type of government that existed in medieval Europe, Feudalism, was neither a state nor a government.

2. ***Modern Period:*** At the beginning of the 16th Century there emerged a new type of states called national states. These states consisted of the people who where bound together by certain common factors such as language, religion, customs and habits. At the beginning the nation states were ruled by absolute monarchs. They, personally, directed, supervised and controlled the administration of the state. At the beginning of the 18th C. absolute monarchies were replaced by democratic institutions in many European states. The emergence of Industrial Revolution helped much the growth of democracy in Europe. The growth of science during this period raised many administrative problems. During the 19th Century the concept of socialism increased the functions of the public administration. The demands of social justice, security, and fair play have demanded administrative interference in the fields hitherto deemed to be the exclusive concern of individuals and have forced on administration the stupendous task of the management of the entire life of the community. "In our times (20th C.) the state has assumed the role of a welfare state. Consequently, public administration also has assumed the role of "Welfare administration". The object of the present day administration is the attainment of good life. It has

become a part of the life of man. It attends on the individual at every stage of life—from few weeks before his birth till few days after his death.

Administration as a subject of study

1. ***Ancient period.*** Public administration as a subject of study existed in the ancient period. Its traces could be found even in the oriental empires whose people have speculated on the state and its problems for the first time. But the development of administrative thought in those days was not pure and systematic. It was treated as an independent subject of study. It was mingled with such other sciences like mythology, religion, economics and theology. In ancient India the traces of public administration as a subject of study could be found. The great Hindu epics (e.g. Ramayana and the Mahabharatha) and treatises (e.g. Kautilya's Arthasastra) were full of administrative thought. Much of the modern administrative thought its derived from Arthasastra: So also the great books written by Chinese Writers (eg. Confucius, Mothi and Mencius) Greek Writers (e.g. Plato and Aristotle) contain a lot of administrative thought.

2. ***Middle Ages.*** Administrative thought in this period was unhistorical, unscientific and uncritical. The quarrel between the Pope and the Emperor was the main issue of this time. If the latter part of the Middle Ages Roman Law restored administrative thought to a little extent. At the close of the Middle Ages Machiavelli (an Italian wrote his famous Prince which contained a lot of a administrative thought).

3. ***Modern Period.*** In the modern period, the term public administration came into use only in the 17th C. In its contemporary sense it was employed by Washington and Hamilton at the close of the 18th C. the first book on Public administration came into light

in France in 1812. The author of the book was C.J. Bounin. The study of public administrative has advanced to an extraordinary degree since 1920. The books written by L.D. White and Willoughby were published in 1926 and 1927 respectively. During this period many writers argued in favour of making public administration an independent subject of study.

Recent Trends in Public Administration

(i) Public administration is gradually coming to be recognized as an independent branch of study. It is being slowly separated from political science.

(ii) Many writers are coming to believe that public administration cannot be regarded as an exact science

(iii) The objective of the administration, today, is social efficiency.

(iv) The POSDCORD view of public administration is undergoing a change. Many people are coming to believe that a proper understanding of public administration is possible with the help of other social sciences.

The above trends in the study of public administration are noticeable in the recent books written by Simon, Thompson, Waldo, Applebey and Bernard.

Public and Private Administration

In modern society there are two types of administration: Public administration and Private or Business Administration.

1. ***Firstly,*** there are some writes who point out that there is no any distinction between the public and private administration. Both possess common fundamental characteristics. The writers who hold

such a view are: Henri Fayol, M.P. Follet, J.A. Vieg and L. Urwick. Henri Fayol said: "All undertakings require planning, organization, command, co-opertion and control, and in order to function properly, all must observe the same general principles. We are no longer confronted with several administrative sciences, but with one which can be applied equally well to public and private affairs". J.A. Vieg observes: "It is a serious misconception to assume that business administration and governmental administration comprise entirely separate spheres, complete distinct from each other. The fact is that they have rather more in common than otherwise".

2. ***Secondly,*** there are some writers who point out that there is a lot of distinction between public and private administration. Both differ in their fundamental characteristics. The writers who hold such a view are: Simon, Sir Josia Stamp etc. Simon suggested three, while Josia Stamp suggested four differences between the public and private administration.

In view of the above, it is necessary for us, to make out the distinction and, then, to point out the relation between the public and private administration.

Distinction Between the Public and Private Administration

1. The public administration differs from the private (or business) administration in business like (Siimon). Public administrator endowed with the power of punishment. He is authorised to use compulsion. For example, the Superintendent of Police, the Magistrate, etc., can use coercive power and give punishment to a person who commits breach of law. On the other hand, private administration cannot be bureaucratic. It can no more use coercion or compulsion. It cannot give physical punishment to its employees or customers. Its powerful weapons are: persuasion,

advice and suggestion. It is by these methods only that private administration can improve its business.

2. Public administration is political, while private administration is non-political (Simon). In democracy, the real power belongs not to the administrator, but to the politician. It is the ministers, who are elected by the people, that exercise, the real power. It is legislature, consisting of elected party men, that enacts the laws of the land. Hence, the administrator is constantly directed and guided by the political executive. The duty of the administrator is to execute the policies and decisions made by the political authority. It is in this sense that public administration is called political. 'On the other hand, business administration is free from political guidance or control. There is no scope for any party administration in a private firm or business concern. Its administration is purely non-political. The private administrator executes the policies or decisions made by the Board of Directors or Management who are not politicians.

3. Public administration is characterized by red tape while private (or business) administration is not so (Simon). The public administration takes a lot of time to dispose of a thing. Everything is done through proper channel. The decisions cannot be taken without the consent of the superior officers. All this consumes much time and results in indefinite delay on the part of public administration. On the other hand, there is no scope for such red—tapism in the case of business administration. Its machinery is not vast. Its rules are not so rigid. The number of administrators is limited. Hence the work is done quietly is done quietly without leading to red-tape.

4. Public administration should observe the principle of uniformity, while Private administration need not observe that (J. Stamp). The actions of the

administrator must be uniform. His treatment of the public also must be uniform. He cannot show favoured treatment to one or the other. The factor such as caste, creed, religion or sex cannot receive special treatment at the hands of the public administrator. This is because that the governmental administration is conducted uniformly according to the rules and regulations. On the other hand, the business administration may not or need not observe the uniformity in its dealings with the customers. It may give favoured treatment to particular categories of its customers without incurring blame. The factors such as poverty, caste, religion and sex may receive special treatment at the hands of a private administrator. It is by this method that the business administration improves its business.

5. Public administration is subject to the principle of external financial control, while private (or business) administration has full control over its finances (J. Stamp). In parliamentary democracy, the finances of the government are controlled by the legislature. It sanctions all the demands for revenue and expenditure. The budget estimates of the government are approved by the legislature. Thus the administration has no any voice or control over the purse of the government. It raises revenue or incurs expenditure as authorised by the legislature. Thus there is complete divorce of finance and administration in public administration. On the other hand, the private administration has its full control its finances. The administrator of private business uses his discretion in matters relating to the revenue or expenditure. He does not hesitate to spend more if it yields greater profits to the company. In doing so, he need not wait for the sanction or approval of any external authority. Thus here is no complete divorce of finance and administration in private administration.

6. Public administration is responsible to the people while private (or business) administration is not responsible to the public (J. Stamp). In democracy the people are the sovereign. The administration is responsible to the people or the legislature elected by the people. It is answerable to the legislature for all its actions. The ministers have to answer the questions regarding the administration put by the legislature or the public. "Even the most trivial administrative occurrence or decision may be the subject of question in parliament". On the other hand, the private administration is not responsible to the public. It does not frame its rules and regulations according to the wishes of the public. The private administration is not governed by the principle of responsibility. Appleby points out that governmental administration differs from all other administrative work by virtue of its public nature, the way in which it is subjected to public scrutiny and criticism.
7. Public administration has no profit motive while private (or business) administration has sole object of profit (J. Stamp). The ultimate object of public administration is the attainment of good life. In other words, its sole aim is the promotion of human welfare. The government is governed by the consideration of public welfare. It does not aim at marginal return. The question" Will it promote the social good?" is of paramount importance to the public administrator. On the other hand, the ultimate object of private administration is he attainment of maximum profit. Its sole aim is the promotion of business which can yield larger profit. "The question 'will it pay?' is of paramount importance to the business man, and is generally his sole test in starting an enterprise or not".
8. Public administration is regulated by law, while private (or business) administration is not. The

administration of the government is to be carried on in accordance with law. Even minor things shall be done according to the legal procedure. He cannot do anything in excess of what law permits him. On the other hand, the private administration is not restricted by law. It may frame its own rules of procedure, but it is not followed at all times. It prefers profit to procedure. Thus the difference between public and private administration is this: "The latter can do everything that is not expressly forbidden by the law, but the former cannot do anything unless he is expressly allowed to do so by law".

9. The activities of Public administration are more important, while the activities of private (or business) administration are not so important. The duty of the public administrator is to maintain peace, order and security, execute law, and improve social services. They are essential to society's existence. On the other hand, these activities of public administration are more comprehensive and Vital (e.g., Socialistic and Welfare activities) while the activities of private administration are less Vital. Since the activities of public administration are Vital to Society, its failure has wide Consequences. Huxley puts the point in these words: 'The State lives in a glass house we see what it tries to do, and all its failure, partial or total, are made the most of. But private enterprise is sheltered under good opaque bricks and mortar'.

10. Public administration is monopolistic, while private administration is competitive. Public administration is the monopoly of the state; while private firm can have its own administration. The activities such as peace, law, order and security are sole concern of public administration. They cannot be undertaken by any private administration.

Relation Between Public and Private Administration

Public administration and private administration are related as follows:

1. Both are governed by the same general principles. Private administration, as in the case of public administration, require planning, organization, command, co-ordination and control'. In both we find the same skill and efficiency.
2. Both are governed by the principle of public service. Besides the motive of profit, the private administration has also the motive of public service.
3. Public administration regulates private administration. In modern times the activities of the business administration are regulated by the law.

It is clear, from the above discussion, that public and private administration have the points of distinction as well as similarity between them. Hence we may agree with the opinion that "Public and private administration are the two species of the same genus, but they have special values and techniques of their own which give to each its distinctive character".

CHAPTER—2

Approaches and Relation with Other Social Sciences

APPROACHES

There are several approaches to the study of public administration. To categorize, we, may divide them into normative approach and empirical approach. The former approach concentrates on what public administration should be, while the empirical approach sets its eyes on descriptions and analysis of actual administrative situations. Another classification of approaches is based upon the objects of study the individual scholar seeks to emphasize. From this angle we get the philosophical approach, the legal approach, the historical approach, the case method approach, the institutional and structural approach, the behavioural approach, etc., Some of these approaches are discussed below.

PHILOSOPHICAL APPROACH

This is perhaps the oldest approaches. Examples of this approach are found in Shanti Parva of the Mahabaratha, Plato's Republic, Hobbes Leviathan, Locke's Treatise on Civil Government etc., The philosophical approach is wide ranging, taking within its purview all aspects of administrative activities. Its goal is to find out and enunciate the principles, or ideals, underlying these activities.

LEGAL APPROACH

This approach came after the philosophical one, but in a sense it is the oldest, systematically formulated approach and traces its ancestry to the European tradition of rooting public administration in law. This approach studies public administration as part of law and concentrates on the legally prescribed structure and organization of public authorities. This approach was formulated at a period when the functions of the State were narrowly limited and simple in nature.

HISTORICAL APPROACH

It studies the public administration of the past within particular time spans, organizing and interpreting the information in a chronological order. Indeed, many administrative institutions can be best understood in the light of their past, which is possible by adopting the historical approach.

CASE METHOD APPROACH

This approach began to be popularized in the thirties. A case is a narration of what has actually taken place in administration, keeping intact the context and all relevant dimensions. Ably handled, the case method approach is a sensitive one seeking as it does to reconstruct the administrative realities and give to students a flavour of the administrative process. As Dwigyth Waldo says, "The case approach has been motivated by a commitment to the objectives and methods of the social sciences, to be sure, but it has been shaped also by a considerable sensitivity to traditional concerns of the humanities and by a practical interest in pedagogy as against research."

INSTITUTIONAL AND STRUCTURAL APPROACH

While scholars trained in law have adopted the legal approach to the study of public administration, others were content to describe the organization and functions of public organizations. It must be emphasized here that the description of organizations was formal, i.e. in terms of what they were designed to be like. The greatest limitation of this approach is that one cannot get a true picture of how an organization functions in practice.

BEHAVIOURAL APPROACH

The growing discontentment against the Institutional structural approach crystallized into what has come to be called the behaviour approach to the study of public administration. This approach, which dates back to the forties, focuses on the actual behaviour of persons and groups in organizations. Herbert A. Simon and Robert A. Dahl have been among the pioneers of this approach.

We can say that no single approach may be sufficient in itself. Public administration can, thus, stand to benefit from a mix of approaches. Infact they are complementary to each other, as each approach has its uses and relevance depending upon the focus of a study.

RELATION WITH OTHER SOCIAL SCIENCES

Relation with History and Politics

Public administration is one of the social sciences. It cannot, therefore, set out of the relations in which it stands to the problems, the valuations and connections with the other social sciences. We can no more understand public administration without the knowledge of the allied sciences. In this world of inter-department phenomena nothing can stand in a state of isolation from the rest. Sidgwick remarked that it is for the good of any dependent of knowledge to understand fully its relation to the other social sciences. All the social sciences are like the petals of a flower and are bound together by a thread of unity. Public administration is closely related to other social sciences, viz., History, Politics, Economics, Sociology, Ethics, Psychology and law.

Public Administration and History

Meaning of Public Administration and History: By Public administration we mean governmental administration. L.D. White defines: "Public administration consists of all those operations having for their purpose the fulfilment or enforcement of public policy". History is a record of past events and movements, their causes and inter relations. It is concerned with individual states and concrete situation with actual happenings. Its object is to understand the development of the study of human societies in space and in time. It also includes a study of public administration, its growth and organization.

Relation of Public Administration to History: Public administration is closely related to History. The relationship between the two social sciences may be explained as follows:

1. History provides a ground work for public administration. It owes an immense debt to history for the material it supplies and the lessons that it teaches. In other words history is vast store house of facts and the past experiences of mankind. It is from the past experiences and records that present public administration obtains necessary guidance for the future line of action. History narrates the administrative problems which arose in the past and how they were solved. The public administrator who faces similar problems, today or in future may receive guidance from history in solving them. The lessons of every age, the variety of alternative ways, and every line written in the brittle pages of history, all

these provide "The search light that illuminates the dark regions of the present and the future" of public administration.

For example, the administrative systems of the ancient Greek city states, Roman Empire, the Municipal Administration of Mauryans, the rule of Akbar—all these teach us as to how a stable, unified, administration could be created. Thus history provides the inspiration and guidance to an honest public administrator. It will be the real basis for criticism of the present and modification of the future administration. In modern times every state maintains administrative records for the future guidance of the public administration.

Public administration also has influence on history. Any study of the historical events of any period without the understanding of the administrative systems of that period becomes drab and bone-dry. For example, the emergence of French Revolution (1789) was partly due to the administrative system prevailed under Bourban kings. Hence our study of the historical events in France in the 18th Century would be incomplete without, at the same time, studying the administrative system of that period.

It should be remembered, that all material of history is not useful for the student of Public administration. He selects only those parts with which he is directly connected. For example, the history of arts and science, military campaigns and naval battles, conspiracies and disputes, rise and fall of dynasties are not interested to a student of Public administration. Let us take an illustration. Mauryan period in Indian History is useful to the student of public administration as providing data for creating a strong administration. But the wars and conspiracies of that period are of little value to him.

Differences between Public Administration and History: While both are intimately connected, they also differ fundamentally. Each subject forms an autonomous discipline and possesses an independent area of its own. History and Public administration differ from each other in three respects.

1. They differ in their method. The method of history is narrative and deals with facts in their chronological order. The method of Public administration is reflective and asks to discover general laws and principles.
2. They differ in their scope. History is more comprehensive because it deals with all aspects of the social life. Public administration has a limited scope because it is concerned with only the administration of the government.
3. They differ in their end. The historical facts are more concrete whereas the facts of public administration are more abstract. History deals with the administration of the state as it has been; Public administration deals with the administration of the state as it is and should be.

Public Administration and Politics

Meaning of Public Administration and Politics: By public administration we mean the governmental or State administration. It is the direction, co-ordination and control of the activities of the state with the object of social welfare. In the worlds of White. "Public administration consists of all operations having for their purpose the fulfllment or enforcement of public policy". Politics is a science which deals with State and Government. It is that part of social science which treats the foundations of the state and principles of Government. (P. Janet). It is concerned with the various activities of the Governmental organs, viz., legislature, executive and judiciary.

Relation of Public Administration to Politics: The relation between the two sciences is very close. Many writes have all brought out the relationship between Public administration and politics. We may mention some of those opinions.

1. **J.M. Gaus States:** "A Theory of Public administration means in our time a theory of politics too".
2. **Woodrow Wilson aptly puts:** "The sciences of administration is the latest fruit of that study of the science of Politics which was begun some twenty two hundred years ago".
3. **Dr. M.P. Sharma observes:** Considered as science, politics and Public administration appear to be the two species of the same genus, two branches growing out of the same tree - the social sciences."- These views expressed above give us an idea that public administration and politics will become identical with one another.

Both are Related as Follows

1. From the beginning public administration has been a part of political science. It has been an organ of the state activity. It is only recently that some attempts were made to give public administration an independent status. The writers like Willson, Bluntchli, Good now and some others have argued in favour of making public administration an independent subject.
2. Public administration helps politics in the following respects:
   - *(i)* The administration helps the government in the suggestion and formulation of policy. Without the help of and suggestion of the experienced administrators, it is not possible for

the political head (i.e., Minister) to frame the policy of the government. Not only the Ministers but also the members of the legislature take the help and suggestion in solving most critical problems concerning public policy. Further, the elected representatives have no time to attend to the technical and complex problems relating to the legislation. Hence it is the civil servants who really draft the bills and place them before the legislative assemblies. The function of the legislature is simply to give its stamp of approval. The function of formulating, "independently the great lines of foreign policy and domestic policy" has escaped the hands of both the legislature and the executive.

(ii) The administrative officers supply necessary information required by the legislative and executive organs of the government. The administration "collects, organizes, and makes available" the mass of factual information which regularly piles up in departmental files".

(iii) The administrative officers execute or enforce the laws, policies and decisions approved by the government in the country. It is the function of the administration to find out efficient means and methods of carrying out the governmental decision. Thus public administration begins where politics ends. There is always a working agreement between the political and administrative officers without which government cannot work.

Thus, it is clear from the above discussion, that public administration is inevitably bound up with politics. They are so closely related that politics without public administration has no fruit: public administration without politics has no root. If both are separated, (to borrow the language of Burgess), "one becomes a cripple, if not a corpse and the other a Will-o-the-wisp".

Differences Between Public Administration and Politics

While both are intimately related, they also differ fundamentally. Many writers like Woodrow Wilson, Willoughby, L.D. White, Luther Gullick, Henry Foyol and Urwick have made a sharp distinction between the two sciences. They pointed out that public administration is a separate study different from the politics and it has its well—marked field and principles. This non-political view of Public administration gained ground, first, in the U.S.A. Woodrow Wilson said: "Administration lies out side the proper sphere of politics. Administration questions are not political questions. Although politics sets task for administration, it should not be suffered to manipulate its politics".

The following differences are suggested between the two subjects:

Sl.No.	*Politics*	*Public Administration*
1.	Wider in scope	Narrower scope
2.	Policy-making	Execution of policies
3.	Winning power	Performance of duties
4.	Amateur	Professional
5.	Non-technical	Technical
6.	Partisan	Non-Partisan
7.	Temporary	Permanent
8.	More Public contacts	Fewer Public contacts
9.	More legislature controls	Fewer legislative controls
10.	Conscious of public opinion	Conscious of technical data, rules and procedures.

PUBLIC ADMINISTRATION AND ECONOMICS

Public administration is a subject which deals with the directions, co-ordination and control of the activities of the State. It is concerned with the fulfilment or enforcement of public policy. Economics is a study of mankind in the ordinary business of life. It is a science of wealth. "Economics in the narrower sense may be defined as the study of human relations in so far as they are concerned with the efficiency in the satisfaction of wants". Men enter into economic relations in order to use their different capacities for the more effective realisation of their different wants. The main branches of economics are consumption, production, distribution and exchange.

Relation of Public Administration to Economics

In the early days of human history, public administration and economics were hardly differentiated. Aristolte treated economics as the art of managing household. Both the sciences are related to the following extent:

1. Public Administration Influences Economics in three Ways.

   (i) Most of the economic activities such as production and distribution of wealth are handled by the administration of the state. It implements the economic policies formulated by the government. Modern administration also handles consumption of goods. The techniques of rationing and control are the examples of this. It leads to socially disastrous consequences where the economic activity is free from the administrative activity.

   (ii) Modern state is a welfare state. So most of the problems, which the public administrator confronts are essentially economic. To-day the administrator must have a thorough under

standing of the economic problems. He evaluates his policies in terms of their economic consequences. For example: if a new bridge is to be constructed, the first thing that the administrator does is to find out how much expenditure is involved in it. Further, the modern administrator is busy in handling such economic problems like foreign trade, labour-capital relation, the nationalization etc., The policies relating to such subjects as planning, taxation, currency, industries, labour legislation, state-aid to agriculture are formulated by the administrative officers. Thus most of the functions performed by the private administration are essentially economic.

(iii) The aim of the modern administration is the attainment of good life. To achieve this end, it ensures economic prosperity, employment, trade of the nation.

2. In the second place, economics influences public administration. The economic conditions materially affect the administrative organization. The emergence of the public corporation, administrative law, administrative tribunals are examples of this. The industrial Revolution has brought in many changes in the organization and methods of public administration in England in the 19th C. Every administrative policy is to be evaluated in terms of its economic consequences. Economic development influences the methods of administration in important ways.

Public Administration and Sociology

Public administration is a science which deals with the management of the governmental activities. It deals with direction, co-ordination and control of the activities of the state-local, state and national. Sociology is the science of human society in all its aspects. The task of sociology is to investigate into the behaviour of man in associative processes. In simple language Sociology is concerned with the behaviour of man as a member of society (or a group). It is the study of human interactions and inter relations, their conditions and consequences (Geinsberg).

Relation of Public Administration to Sociology. Both the sciences are closely associated with the one another. Sociology influences public administration in many ways:

(i) The administrative system is always profoundly influenced by social order Public administration derives from sociology the information regarding the origin and development of laws of social control.

(ii) The administration takes into consideration the opinions and reactions of various groups while executing the policies of the state. The successful execution of a policy depends upon the group reactions.

(iii) Sociology gives the knowledge of the rise, function and behaviour of groups. This knowledge is important to public administration.

Difference Between Public Administration and Sociology

The two Sciences differ in three respects:

1. Both differ in their scope. Public administration has a more narrower and restricted field than sociology. Sociology deals with all forms of human associations. Hence its subject matter is wider than that of public administration which deals only with the direction, co-operation and execution of the state activity.

2. Sociology is prior to private administration. Society came into existence much earlier than of public administration.
3. Sociology deals with organized and unorganized, conscious and unconscious activities of men; while public administration deals with organized and conscious activities only.

PUBLIC ADMINISTRATION AND ETHICS

Public administration is a social science. It deals with the management and execution of the governmental activities. Wilson defines: "Public administration is a detailed and systematic application of law". Ethics is also a social science. It is the science of moral order or right and wrong. It is the philosophy of human conduct. Morality is an essential aspect of human life. Human activities are always tested by morality. It is but natural that every individual possesses certain ethical notions in regard to good, right or wrong. Ethics, therefore, investigates the laws of morality and rules of conduct.

Relation of Public Administration to Ethics

Both are related to the following extent:

1. Every activity of the administrative officer is conditioned by ethical standards. The success or failure of any administrative activity (i.e. execution of enforcement of law) depends upon the ethical sentiments of the people.
2. In democracy administration can not survive longer if it runs counter to the people's sense of propriety' The greatness or strength of any administration is tested by ethical values.

Difference Between Public administration and Ethics

1. Both differ in their nature: Ethics is purely an individual sentiment and changes from man to man.

On the other hand public administration is governed by the principle of uniformity.

2. Public administration is governed by the considerations of expediency; while ethics does not take them into consideration.

3. Ethics has a wider scope because it embraces the inner as well as the outer activities of the individual; while public administration has a limited field of study.

Public Administration and Law

Public administration is an art of managing the state activity. It is concerned with the detailed and systematic application of law. Law is a group of rules which is enacted and enforced by the sovereign authority of the state whose violation leads to penalty or punishment. T.H. Green says that law is "the system of rights and obligations which the state enforces".

Relation of Public administration to Law. The two subjects are very closely related to each other. The relationship between the two subjects may be indicated as below:

1. In the first place, law has much influence on public administration. It regulates the activities of the administrative officer. He cannot do any thing contrary to law. He has to act within the frame work of law. He cannot exercise authority beyond what law permits him. If he does it, he is liable for punishment according to law. Further, law enforces the responsibility of the administrator. It safeguards the rights and liberty of the individual against administrative violation. Thus administration works within the frame work of law. Law secures the responsibility of administration.

2. In the second place, public administration has much influence on law. It has a share in formulating the law of the state. It executes or enforces the law of the state. It discovers best principles upon which the basic concept of law are formulated. Most of the Laws contain in them expression of public policy.

Public Administration and Psychology

Psychology is a science of human mind in relation to his behaviour and elucidates what he actually does. Modern public administration is greatly influenced by the psychological sentiments of the people. Public administration in order to be stable and efficient must reflect the mental ideas of the people. Now-a-days, administration is not only studied but also organized from the psychological point of view.

The examples are:

1. Recruitment to the public offices on the basis of psychological tests
2. Formation of various consultative or advisory committees
3. Formation of staff councils etc.

CHAPTER—3

Organization and its Problems

MEANING OF ORGANIZATION

To a common man's understanding, organization means an association or group of men who come together to attain a purpose or an end. The dictionary meaning of the word "organization" is "to organize" or "to frame and put into working order". In Public Administration organization is attributed to three meanings:

1. 'The act of designing the Administrative structure'; (2) 'both designing and building the structure'; and (3) 'the structure itself'. But these meanings have been thought as narrow.

At present the term Organization carries a special meaning in public Administration. It means a plan of action. It is an action by a group of people who work in co-operation. Its aim is the achievement of some purpose or object or goal. This purpose cannot be achieved if the plan of action or programme is not carried out according to well-understood principles. Thus by organization we mean: (i) a plan of action; (ii) spirit of co-operation (iii) a set purpose; (iv) well defined principles of procedure. Thus, in public administration, organization may be defined as a plan of action: carried out by a group of personnel working as a team according to certain principles to attain the purpose in view.

Many writers on public administration have defined organization. Some of the definitions are noted here under:

1. J.M. Gaus: "Organization is the arrangement of personnel for facilitating the accomplishment of some agreed purpose through the allocation of functions and responsibilities."
2. M. Mark: "Organization is the structure developed for carrying out the task entrusted to the chief executive and his administrative subordinates in government".
3. L. Gullick: "Defines organization as the formal structure of authority through which work subdivisions are arranged, defined and co-ordinated for the defined objective."
4. J.W. Schulze: "An organization is a combination of the necessary human beings, materials, tools, equipment, working space and appliances brought together in systematic and effective co-ordination to accomplish some desired objective."
5. Dimock: "Organization is the systemic bringing together of interdependent parts to from a united whole through which authority the co-ordination and control may be exercised to achieve a given purpose."

The examples of organization are many: In India, they are the Panchayat Raj, the Planning Commission, the Atomic Energy Commission etc., In the USA the National Security Council may be cited as an example.

Need for Organization in administration: Modern State is not a police state, but a welfare state. It is doing every kind of service to the people. As a result the state is performing a lot of functions, political, social, economic, cultural and humanitarian. Due to this, its administrative machinery is ever on the increase. As the reeds of society grow, the administrative structure also grows. Thus it is necessary to bring into existence new organization to meet the new situations in society. For example, the new organizations like Community Development and Panchayat Raj Department and Planning Commission were created in India after independence with the object of establishing socialist pattern of society in India. So also the department of Rehabilitation. Food, and Housing came into being to meet specific needs.

Organizations are built in two ways:

(1) From the top downwards (2) from the down to upwards.

According to the first method, the head of the department is appointed first who in turn appoints the subordinate staff and divides his work between them. According to the second method. The lower officer is appointed first and placed charge of the organization. As it develops and expands, the higher strata of the organization are built up and officers of the higher positions are appointed.

PROBLEMS OF ORGANIZATION

Before organizations are built, there are certain problems to be tackled. The success of an organization depends upon the extent to which these problems are satisfactorily solved. The following are the problems.

Hierarchy

In its literary sense, hierarchy implies rule of the higher over the lower. In public Administration, hierarchy means 'Superior Subordinate relationship or pattern of relationship'. L.D. White defines: "Hierarchy consists in the universal application of the superior-subordinate relationship through a number of levels of responsibility reaching from the top to the bottom of the structure. Marx and Reigning state: "The essential function of hierarchy is to provide an integrated scheme of successive control points for the attainment of efficiency, consistency, continuity in the performance of organizations work.

With the help of these two definitions it is easy to draw the following characteristics of hierarchy:

(i) In an organization, there are different levels of authority, each with its own responsibility and authority.

(ii) An official working at a lower level is subordinate and responsible to the authority at a higher level. Thus there would be several control points.

(iii) There is a close relation between one point of control or one level of authority at its lower or higher level. This relation of the superior and subordinate is called in administration by the name hierarchy.

(iv) In simple language, in an organization, which is based on the principle of hierarchy, each official is subordinate to his immediate superior and through him, ultimately, to the head of the organization. So also, the head directs and controls, first his immediate subordinate and through him, ultimately the lowest official, Thus, each authority is subordinate and responsible to his immediate superior.

Marx and Reigning Say that there are two Ways of Control: (1) Descending and (2) Ascending order: In the former, the control is exercised from the top which travels to the bottom through a number of successive points (e.g. Head-Deputy Head- Assistant, Head- Section, Head- lower- lowest). In the second i.e. ascending order) responsibility starts from the bottom to the top through several points (i.e. lowest-lower-section-Assistant-Deputy-

Head). The officials who occupy seats in between the top-most and lower most authority are described by Marx and Reigning as "Middle Management."

The hierachical system has other names too: (1) Scalar process (Mooney and Reiley), (2) Chain of Command (Marx and Reigning) (3) through proper channel.

Hierarchical system gives many advantages to an organization. The important are mentioned below:

1. The work of an organization can be conducted in an orderly manner. Each level of authority knows the work for which he is appointed and attends to it.
2. A systematic control is possible only in a hierarchical system. Every lower authority is subject to the control of his immediate superior:
3. Responsibility for the work of an organization can be fixed, because each authority is responsible for his work to his higher authority.
4. Hierarchy, lastly, provides unity in administration as there is a close relation and co-ordination between different levels of authority.

Supervision and Control or Span of Control

The second problem which confronts organization is supervision and control. It is generally called the span of Control. Before we discuss the problems involved in this, it is necessary to know what is meant by Supervision and Control. By supervision, we mean the authority to watch the work done by others. Reigning defines supervision: From the view point of management, the supervisor is that person in the organization to whom authority for direction of the work of others has been assigned. By Control we mean the authority to verify, examine and find out whether the work done by the subordinates in accordance with rules and regulations. Henry Fayol defines: Control is an act of verifying with the plan adopted, the instructions issued, and principles established.

The supervision and control go together. The action of these two is known as the Span of Control. The question is how many subordinates should be there under one supervisor for effective control? This question is called span of control or as V A Graicunas calls it Span of attention. Thus, span of control means number of subordinates that one effectively supervise. Dimock defines: The span of control is the number and the range of direct habitual communication contracts between the Chief executive of an enterprise and his principal fellow officers."

J.M. Pfiffner gives seven qualities of good supervisor which are given below:

(i) Liking for the people.

(ii) Emotional stability

(iii) Integrity

(iv) Courage and fortitude.

(v) Enthusiasm for the work.

(vi) High ethical standards

(vii) Curiosity and intellectual ability.

Lastly, the question of effective supervision and control depends on the nature of work to be done and time within which it is to be done.

Delegation of Authority

The third problem which confronts an organization is the delegation of authority. It is possible to exercise all authority by one and same official. There would be neither time for the top authority to decide everything nor it is desirable to be so. Hence, in an organization, some authority should be delegated to the lower officials, i.e. the Middle Management. The important decisions can be left to the head, while minor decisions can be left to the middle authority. However, there is no agreement on the quantum of authority to be delegated. Marx and Reigning are in favour of delegating much authority to the middle management. They say that if everything is decided by the top authority, it results in dangerous congestion of work in the upper ranges of organization. "Appropriate delegation of authority is a basic consideration to successful guidance of operations" (Marx and Reigning).

The middle management is a step-child of administration which bears pressure from top as well as bottom. Hence, it should be delegated more authority. The writers suggested periodical conferences between the head and division heads.

The delegation of authority has one advantage. Viz., that it saves the time of higher authorities and enables to utilise the expert knowledge available in the lower ranks. However, it suffers from doubt that the authority may be misused. It may transfer servant in to master.

Centralisation Vs. Decentralization

This problem of organization is closely connected with the delegation of authority. Where, in an organization, all decisions are taken and communicated by the top to the lower, that system is called centralization. As L. D. White says authority transfers from the lower to the higher. "The process of transfer of administrative authority from a lower to higher level of government is called Centralization" (White). On the other hand, where the subordinate staff is authorised to take decisions and implement without referring to the top, it is called decentralization. As L. D. White says the authority transfers to bottom. "The process of transfer of administrative authority from a higher to a lower level of government is called decentralization" (White).

Thus the basis of centralization or decentralization is the distribution of power of decision (H.P. Sharma).

The Advantage of Centralization is that: It creates effective order and control in an organization. The work can be done in a efficient manner. However there are two disadvantages.

(i) It makes top authority more and more powerful and leaves lower weak and anemiatic.

(ii) There is delay in action, redtapism, lack of responsibility on the part of lower officials.

The Advantages of Decentralization are following:

(i) It creates a balance of authority between the top authority and middle management. It removes 'apoplexy at the top an anemia at the extremities'.

(ii) It promotes quicker action, reduces delay, shortens red-tapism, and instills self-respect in the officials.

(iii) It secures economy in operations.

However decentralization has two disadvantages:

(i) The administration lacks efficiency. There may not be possible for an effective control of the work. The fixation of responsibility is difficult.

(ii) Different decision making authorities may not co-operate. It may be difficult to secure co-operation.

One difficulty that arises in every organization is that the head of the organization is finally held responsible for whatever happens in the organization. Hence, he is afraid of distributing widely the power of decision to his subordinates. Dr. M. P. Sharma suggests that neither rigid centralization or rigid decentralization is desirable. A proper balance between the two is always good.

Command and Co-ordination

Finally, we shall discuss the problem of command and Co-ordination.

There should be unity of command in an organization. It means, an employee should receive directions or instructions or orders from one superior or higher authority. Pfiffner defines: "The concept of unity of command requires that every member of organization should report to one, and only one leader". The opposite of unity of command is called diversity of command. Henry Foyol says that unity of command promotes discipline, ensures stability of administration and secures efficiency of work. All these are possible because, an employee receives orders from one superior only and so he can concentrate his attention well. S. Hudson says that the line of command should be straight which is possible when there is only one boss. If there is more than one boss, the result is confusion. From one he may receive policy orders, from another personnel, from a third budget from a fourth supplies and equipment (S. Hudson).

There should be co-ordination in an organization Co-ordination means adjustment of different parts or forces to one another so that they can work in an orderly and united way to achieve the ultimate end. Terry defines: Co-ordination is the adjustment of the parts to each other and of movement and operation of parts in time so that each can make its maximum-contribution to the product of the whole." L.D. White points out that co-ordination is a process by which different forces and influences are brought together to act together. W.H. Newman; "Co-ordination is the orderly synchronisation of efforts to provide the proper amount, timing and directing of execution resulting in harmonious and unified actions to a stated objective. Charles Worth. Co-ordination is "the integration of the several parts into an orderly whole to achieve the purpose of the undertaking". Thus co-ordination, as the above definitions say, is a name given to method by which different works are brought together and make them work in an harmonious way so as to achieve the purpose in view.

The advantages of co-ordination are: (1) Every employee gets a chance to know the work of the other (2) It avoids conflicts and overlapping of work. (3) It makes administration run unitedly and harmoniously.

Co-ordination may be achieved by coercive or compulsory method or voluntary.

CHAPTER—4

Theories of Organization

There are several theories of organization (i) The Classical theory of organization, (ii) The Human Relations Theory, and (iii) The Systems Theory.

I. The Classical Theory Includes:

(i) The Scientific Management,

(ii) The Bureaucratic Theory, and

(iii) The Formal organization Theory.

Scientific Management

The first coherent theory of organization is referred to as 'Scientific Management', which came to be formulated in the beginning of the twentieth century. At that time, the conditions in the factories were rather unplanned. There was nearly complete absence of standardization of methods of work. It was against such a general back ground of managerial unconcern for methods and tools of work that Scientific Management emerged as new philosophy of management. Frederick Winslow Taylor (1856-1915), an engineer by training is regarded as the father of Scientific Management, for it was he who first advocated the systematic adoption of the methods of science to problems or management in the interest of higher industrial efficiency. Taylor himself did not employ 'Scientific Management' to refer to his thoughts. This concept was first used by Louis Brandeis in 1910. From that time onwards Taylor also began using this term. He pointed out: "Management is true science, resting upon clearly fixed laws, rules and principles, as a foundation." He argued that management comprised a number of principles which commanded applicability in all types of organizations, "The same principles can be applied with equal force to all social activities; to the management of our homes; the management of our farms; the management of the business of our tradesmen, large and small; of our churches, our philanthropic institutions, our universities and our governmental departments".

The overall goal of Scientific Management is higher industrial efficiency, Besides, several specific objectives are embodied in Scientific Management. It for instance, seeks standardization of working conditions—The second objective of Scientific Management is standardization of work methods. What is the best procedure for doing a job is an example of standardization of work methods.

Scientific Management is also called the 'physiological organization.' It theory is concerned with only that range of human behaviour which relates to production.

The Bureaucratic Theory of Organisation

The term 'Bureaucracy' lends itself to two usages; it refers to the tasks and procedures of administration, as well as is used as a collective word for a body of administrative officials. The word 'Bureaucracy' was first coined by Vincent de Cournay (1712-1759), an economist of France. But it was in the nineteenth century, conditions of increasing state intervention, that the term came into regular use among European Writers. It was, however Max Weber (1864-1920) who founded the modern sociological study of bureaucracy, freed the term from pejorative connotation, and emphasized the indispensability of bureaucracy for the rational attainment of the goals of an organization.

Following are the characteristics of bureaucracy as enumerated by max weber:

1. Officials are appointed on the basis of a contract.
2. They have a money salary, and usually pension rights. The salary is graded according to position in the hierarchy. The official can always leave the post, and under certain circumstances it may also be terminated.
3. The officials post is his sole or major occupation.
4. The official may appropriate neither the post nor the resources which go with it. The Characteristics of bureaucracy were: precision, continuity, discipline, strictness reliability. These characteristics made it technically the most satisfactory from of organization.

The Formal Organization Theory

The Formal organization Theory, also known as the Mechanistic Theory or the Structural theory, is the dominant on in the field and has been enunciated most notably by Henri Fayol, Lather Gulick, L.F. Urwick, J.D. Mooney, A.C. Reiley, Mary Parker Follent, R. Shelton, etc., These writers argue that administration is administration regardless of the kind of work being under taken or the context with in which it is performed. They then proceed to identify the important elements in the process of administration as well as features common to all administrative structures. This exercise is preparatory to the development of a set of principles of organization. Indeed, the single most distinguishing feature of the classical theory is its concern with the formulation of principles of organisation. The classical theorists addressed themselves to the task of discovering the true bases on which division of work in an organization could be carried out and devising effective methods of bringing about coordination in it. They, moreover, laid emphasis on precise definition of tasks and their inter relationships, and advocated the use of authority and a system of checks to exercise control over personnel so that the organizational work gets done.

II. The Human Relations Theory of Organization

The single greatest influence which made the classical or the mechanistic theory of organization fall into disfavour, came from the Hawthorn Experiments which were carried out in the U.S.A., in the late 1920s and early 1930s.

The Hawthorne Experiments proved that men are not inert or isolated creature on the contrary, they react in their own way..., responding, for example, to motivational variable other than the lighting. These studies proved that an organization was (also) a social system, a group of people behaving. The Hawthorne Experiments contained startling findings on employee attitude to work and supervision, and disclosed the tendency on the part of employees to for small social groups with their own status system, behavioural patterns, beliefs and goals as which may be different form... Or even opposed to...the stipulations and prescription of the formal organization. So new, indeed, were these that they gave rise to a new theory of organization, called the Human Relations Theory. To contradistinguish it from the formal organization of the classical theorists, the human relations theory focuses on what is called informal organization. In the words of Roethisberger, "Too often we try to solve human problems with non human tools and in terms of non human data. It is my simple thesis that a human problem requires a human solution. First, we have to learn to recognize a human problem when we see one; and second, upon recognizing it, we have to learn to deal with it as such and not as if it were something else, A human problem to be brought to a human solution requires human data and human tools.

The essence of the human relations lies in its dominant emphasis on people, on human motivations and on informal group functioning—in contrast to the classical theorists exclusive concern for principles. The human relations theory of organization rejects formal institutionalization: It considers the informal, day-to-day functioning of the structure more important and revealing than the charts, maps, etc. It assumes that organisational behaviour is quite complex, subject to wide range of influences impinging on human beings from all directions. For analysis and solution of the organizational problem, therefore, it is of the utmost importance to comprehend the multidimensional nature of man. This theory has been termed human relations theory, socio-economic theory, or humanistic theory.

III. The Systems Theory of Organization

The system theory is the modern organizational theory. A system consists of all those elements (or parts) or variables which remain interdependent on each other, a system is characterized by interdependence and interrelatedness, a system does not operate in a vacuum. The importance of Systems theory to organization is that organizations are systems comprising technical, economic, and social subsystems. It, thus, enables us to gain familiarity with both the wood as well as the individual trees. The principal variables affecting organizations can be grouped under five headings: the formal organization or structure, the informal organization, the individual variables, the technical system, and the external environment.

System Theory provides a useful frame work for looking at the whole spectrum of factors and considering them in searching for solutions. The application of Systems Theory to practice is known as Contingency Administration or Management.

CHAPTER—5

Organization and Management

MEANING OF O AND M:

The term O and M is very popular in the science of public administration. It has two meanings: a wider meaning and a narrower meaning. In its wider meaning, the term O and M means Organization and management. In this sense, O and M includes the study of the entire process of management, namely, planning, organising, co-ordinating, motivating, directing and controlling. Thus used in its broader sense. O and M covers all the aspects of administration. But, O and M has its narrower or limited meaning. In its narrower meaning, the term O and M means organization and Methods. In this sense, O and M is concerned with the organization of governmental bodies or departments and the methods to be followed by them for improvement of administration. The second meaning is widely accepted today. So at present, O and M means Organization and Methods.

It is well accepted that the work of the government cannot be carried on without administration. It must be carried on efficiently and successfully, for this, it is necessary to bring in improvements in the nature, organization and methods of administrative machinery. Especially this is necessary in the line agencies of the administration. In order to suggest the methods, ways and means of improving the administrative machinery, there is created a special office or body or division called Organization and methods office, known, popularly, as O and M office. This office is most commonly found in all the advanced states today.

FUNCTIONS OF O AND M

Having understood the meaning of O and M, we shall proceed to consider its functions. The O and M performs the following functions.

1. The first function of O and M is research and development. The new methods and techniques of improving the administrative machinery are invented only by research and development. So the O and M divisions carry on vigorously the research work and suggests the methods of development in matters relating to Organising, staffing, accounting, delegation, co-ordination, supervision etc.,

2. The second function of O and M is to arrange for the training of the personnel of the administration. Whenever the new methods are invented with a view to improve the organization, the officials are to be trained in these methods. So the O and M divisions makes arrangements for training the officials. The officials are taught the technique of using the new methods, problems that confront them. In this way, O and M prepares best personnel to man the administration efficiently.

3. The third function of O and M is to conduct the investigations. Having suggested various methods for the improvement of the administration, It becomes the duty of O and M office to check up whether the different bodies have adopted them. It examines through periodical investigations, the procedures and methods of various administrative agencies. If it finds out any defects in the procedures adopted. O and M gives suggestions to rectify them.

4. The fourth function of O and M is to co-ordinate different programmes, procedure and methods of administration. It avoids overlaping of programmes. It prevents conflict in the adoption of different methods of administrative improvement. The officials of O and M bring harmony between various officials in planning and carrying out their efforts.

5. The fifth function of O and M is the collection of information. The information collected by O and M office is of two kinds. Firstly, it gathers all the information regarding the O and M work done at the state as well as central governments. Secondly, it gathers information regarding the O and M work done at the government of foreign countries. It preserves for future guidance the new methods and techniques, if any, adopted by the foreign O and M offices. Thus in any government the O and M division acts as a store house of vast information.

6. The last function of O and M is to publish, for the guidance of officials, the guides, manuals, research, materials, hand books, bulletins, periodicals and other literature describing the various methods and how to follow them. These will guide especially new entrants into the administration.

It is clear from the above lines that the functions of O and M are mainly advisory. Its principal aim is the improvement of the administration. It is not concerned with fault—finding but helping. It cannot impose its will on the heads of the organizations. However, it may be remembered, that if any official or department consistently avoids taking its advice or neglects in adopting the methods, procedures and techniques suggested by it, the O and M office can recommend suitable action against them.

IMPORTANCE OF O AND M

The importance of O and M in the administration of modern state is very great.

O and M brings about much improvement and efficiency in administration. It secures the improvement by various means such as research and development, training the personnel, conducting the investigations, co-ordinating the different, programmes, collection of information and publication. It reviews the work and methods of various administrative bodies. New methods and changes suggested by O and M bring new light into the administration. The officials of the administration can rely on the wealth of experience put up by O and M as a result of research and development. This experience is useful in two ways: (1) It helps administrative officials to successfully over come the problems of their departments. (2) It helps in planning new organization.

To the extent that past experience is of value in planning the future, O and M units, by pooling past experience, contribute directly to improve efficiency of organization in future. (Avasthi and Maheswari). The officials have neither time nor experience in organizational matters. So there is need to establish a separate O and M division manned by its own staff.

Staff of O and M: The organization of O and M divisions is confronted by certain difficulties. The first problem is the the selection of the staff. There are two views.

1. Some people are of the opinion that the regular officials can take up the work of O and M.

2. Others argue that there should be a separate staff who posses special skill for the purpose of managing the O and M office. The supporters of this view point out that the administrative officers neither find time or possess the knowledge of the special techniques and methods of O and M. This view is generally accepted everywhere. In selecting the candidates for O and M work enough care has to be taken to see that they possess the spirit of co-operation and

accommodation, intelligence, imagination, good temperament, patience and mind for research. The candidate possessing thorough knowledge of organizational problems is an asset of O and M. Thus the recruitment of O and M personnel is a difficult job. In some countries the departmental staff is transferred to O and M divisions.

Another difficulty confronted by O and M is regarding the training of personnel. The government may open separate institutions for imparting special training for the O and M staff on the basis of the prescribed course. The course includes talks, exercises, demonstrations, theory and practice of organization, methods of work etc., Sometimes the candidates chosen for O and M work are placed under the care of a senior official of the division. The latter gives necessary training to the former in handling O & M work. This is called job training.

TECHNIQUES OF O AND M

The O and M agency adopts its own techniques (or methods) in order to secure the efficient working of various administrative bodies. There are two principal techniques employed by the O and M viz, (1) Survey and (2) Inspection. They are explained as below:

1. ***Survey:*** The first technique used by O and M is survey. The O and M undertakes, now and then, the survey of the ministries of departments of the government. The survey is of different kinds: (1) Overall survey (i.e. review of the total work of the department) (2) Organization survey (i.e. review of the problems of the departmental organization), (3) Functional survey (i.e. Review of the departmental functions), and (4) Procedure survey (i.e. the review of the department procedures). At the beginning of the survey, the O and M officials ascertain the reasons

for the survey, the nature of work to be surveyed and the proposals of the departmental head. During the survey the O and M officials collect necessary facts, faults and defects of the organization. At the end of the survey a report is prepared which may consist of recommendations. The survey work may be entrusted to a single person or a team of officials.

2. ***Inspection:*** The second technique used by O and M is inspection. The O & M undertakes, now and then, the inspection of various ministries or departments. It may create a separate inspection branch also. The principal aim of inspection is to find out the extent to which the departments or other bodies are adopting the directives and procedures suggested by the O and M. The inspection may also be conducted in regard to the district administration. At the end of the inspection, the officials prepare a report of their findings and submit it to the head of the inspection division.

O and M in England and U.S.A: The importance of the O and M work has been recognised in England long ago. As a result a special O and M division is created in England. The necessary staff of the O and M is drawn partly from departments and partly from Treasury. Every officials serves on the O and M divisions for a period of five years. The training for the staff is given at the Royal Institute of Public administration. The Central O and M office has its own training branch.

The U.S.A.: O and M units are established. The personnel of O and M is drawn from (1) staff of the regular departments and (2) journeymen possessing technical training. The training for the staff is given by special departmental schools.

O and M in India: The O and M Division in India is located in the Cabinet Secretariat. It undertakes the work relating to the improvement of efficiency in administration. It functions under a Director who is assisted by a Deputy Director, and Assistant Director and other staff. The Deputy Director of O and M Division visits now and then the various ministries and examines as to how far the officials of the ministry are adopting the prescribed procedures and renders advice to them for the improvements of work. Besides O and M there is a special Reorganization units (S.R.U.) located in the cabinet secretariat.

The staff of O and M Division are drawn from the regular civil service. Few I.A.S. persons are also appointed to this unit.

Chapter—6

Structure of Organizations

THE CHIEF EXECUTIVE

The Chief Executive occupies an important position in Public Administration. The chief executive is at the apex of the Administrative Pyramid. The chief executive in India is the President. In Public Administration we consider the chief executive and his functions not as the head of state but as the head of administration. In Public Administration we are concerned with his administrative functions only. His political role is outside the scope of our study. In Public Administration the role of the chief executive has been compared to that of General Manager in a corporate undertaking. Willoughby is strongly of the opinion that the office of the chief executive must be raised to the status of General Manager. He should perform the same functions as are performed by the General Manager.

FEATURES OF GENERAL MANAGERIAL SYSTEM

The system of administration in which the chief executive functions as the General Manager of administration has the following main features:

(i) ***Scalar System.*** It consists of arranging the administrative groups or units steps upon steps in a scale form which the term scalar has been derived.

(ii) ***Chief Executive, the master of civil service.*** All members of civil service are under the direct control of the executive.

(iii) ***Control over Institutional Activities.*** The Executive exercises full control over institutional activities of the administrative services.

(iv) ***Control over administrative Reports.*** All administrative reports are submitted to the legislature through the executive.

ADMINISTRATIVE FUNCTIONS OF THE EXECUTIVE

The chief executive has to perform a number of functions. Luther Gullick coined the word "posdcorb" for the administrative functions of the chief executive. The 'posdcorb' stands for Planing, Organizing, Staffing, Directing, Co-ordinating, Reporting and Budgeting. L.D. White has put these functions under the following main categories:

(i) ***Deciding Administrative Policy.*** The legislature lays down the policy to be followed by the government in general terms. For the implementation of the general policy the executive has to decide a large number of questions pertaining to administrative policy.

(ii) ***To authorize details of organization.*** Legislature usually provides for the establishment of main units of organization, like departments, commissions, corporations. Details are left to be filled in by the executive at his discretion.

(iii) ***To co-ordinate the organization.*** In order to create unity in this huge mass of diversified activities, a very high degree of co-ordination and integration is needed. In spite of the presence of co-ordinating machinery, mutual feuds and rivalries are likely to arise. All these are settled by the executive.

(iv) ***To appoint and remove the personnel.*** The chief executive as said earlier is responsible as general manager for the manner in which the heads of the several departments perform their duties. Since the responsibility ultimately is that of the chief executive it is logical that he should have the power to select and remove the officers.

(v) ***To control the management of finance.*** As general manager he has the duty of making full report regarding past operations and present conditions and to make a statement as to the provision, which, in his opinion, should be made for meeting the revenue and expenditure needs of the government in the future. This recommendation goes in the form called 'Budget'.

(vi) ***To supervise, Control and Investigate the Administrative Operations.*** The function of the executive is not only to carry on the public business itself, but also to see that it is being carried on properly. As such, it has to supervise the work, give necessary instructions, warn when the work is not being done properly, and encourage when it is running smoothly.

(vii) ***To participate in and control Public Relations.*** It is for the executive to maintain relations with the press, interested groups, voters, and the legislature, hear their views and tell them the views of the government. So important is this function that a Department of Public Relations has become almost indispensable for every government.

The above functions of the chief-executive make it clear that he is the administrator-in-chief or the General Manager of public administration. As general manager it is his primary responsibility to see that the administrative affairs of the government are being honestly, efficiently and economically run.

MEANING, ORGANIZATION AND FUNCTIONS OF STAFF AGENCIES

It is known to all of us that all the administrative work is directed and managed by the chief executive of the state. In the words of Willoughby the chief executive is the general managerial manager of the administration of the state. All the powers and responsibilities are vested in him. However, he cannot do all the business of the government single—handed. Mooney observed :Always there are too many things to think about, too many factors to consider, too diversified a knowledge required for solution for the unaided capacity of one leader to encompass. To perform all these satisfactorily, the chief executive needs the assistance and advice of so many officials. In other words, the business of government is transacted by means of an elaborate organization based on the principle of specialization. The principal agencies of any administrative system are of two kinds: (i) Staff Agencies and (ii) Line Agencies: We shall study the meaning, organization and functions of the staff agencies.

MEANING AND ORIGIN OF STAFF

The administrative work is divisible into two branches. The first branch consists of work of advice, planning, preparation etc. The second branch consists of the work of control, co-ordination, supervision etc. The officials who belongs to the first branch are called the Staff. Those who belong to the second branch are called the Line. By staff we mean those officers whose function is to render help., assistance, advice and suggest remedies to the various problems that confront the chief executive. They are concerned with the work of collecting, digesting and summarizing all the relevant information. The staff is an agency which is concerned with preparation but not decision. L.D. white defines, "A staff is an agency advisory to a high ranking Official, but without operating responsibility. The function of civil staff is to plan, to advice, to observe but not direction.

The term Staff is not a civilian but a military word. It is borrowed from military vocabulary and applied to the science of administration. The staff was first organized in the Prussian army which, later on, spread to America and other countries. Today, every military organization consists of these two branches: Viz., staff branch and line branch. The principal duty of the army staff is to plan, to advise, to assist the commanding officer. It means the function of the staff is to observe but not to command. They do not take part in the actual fighting, but make necessary plan to carry on the war successfully.

Organization of Staff Agencies: According to some writers the staff agencies are of three kinds: (1) General staff (2) Technical staff and (3) auxiliary staff. Every branch may need a brief explanation.

1. ***General staff:*** The general staff is also called departmental staff. It consists of those officials who look after general problems of the administration. They are attached to either the chief executive or the head of department. They help him in his work by advising, collecting information, conducting research on the general administrative matters. L.D. White calls this general staff by the name substantive staff. He says that the substantive staff is responsible for advising their principles about the functional field in which they operate, such as agriculture, commerce or finance. An officer of the general staff is a person of

administrative training and experience rather than a specialist in some technical field. The examples of General staff in India are (i) Secretariat of the Prime Minister and the Cabinet. (ii) The Planning commission, (iii) Central Advisory Board of Education, (iv) Finance commission etc,

2. ***The Technical Staff:*** It consists of those officials who look after the technical problems of administration. They may also be attached either to the chief executive or heads of the department. They help him in his work by giving advice, collection of information and conducting research on technical matters. They also supervise the work of subordinate technical staff. The official on the technical staff posses specialised training in the technical branches such as engineering, medicine, finance etc., The examples of technical staff are Engineers, Doctors, Statisticians experts in finance, business, law etc.,

AUXILIARY STAFF

The Auxiliary staff is known by various names given by various writers. (i) Willoughby calls them institutional or 'House keeping' services. (ii) L.D. White names them 'Auxiliary services'. (iii) Some others call them staff services.

But all these writers are of the same opinion regarding the nature of their work. The auxiliary staff consists of those officials who look after the common work of all the departments of the administration. In any administrative system there are certain common needs for all the departments. The examples are purchase, disbursement, printing, recruitment, finance, accounting, auditing etc, The performance of these functions is entrusted to special branches or officers such as central purchasing office, central recruitment agency, central disbursing agency etc, The staff of these branches is called auxilitary staff. There are two advantages of this system, viz., economy and efficiency, (i) It leads to economy because of large scale purchases at the wholesale rates, and disbursement through one agency. There is no much scope for waste (ii) It leads to efficiency because the accounts of the various items can be maintained properly. Some writers refuse to regard auxiliary staff as a part of the regular staff on the ground that they do not satisfy the basic quality, viz., advice, assistance etc, These writers prefer to treat them as apart of line staff because the auxiliary staff, now and then exercises the functions like scrutiny, supervision and checking the accounts of the regular general staff. (iii) They relieve the line of their burden, ensures specialization and increased scope of operation. L.D. White remarks that Auxiliary staff is one of the important means of ensuring unity in the executive branch and the area of administration.

However, the writers have pointed some defects of the Auxiliary agencies. Firstly, there may take place conflicts between the auxiliary services and other departments due to many reasons such as indifference, long dealy and non co-operation on the part of the auxiliary services. Secondly, as W.H. Hogam observes the creation of these services leads to divisions of authority and responsibility hinders and harms the executive. They may even push beyond their limit and try to control and command.

The distinction between staff and auxiliary is regarded by some as unscientific. they say that distinction is one of the origin rather than inherent in the nature of these units.

Functions of the Staff: The staff agencies perform a number of functions. They may be explained under two heads:

1. Informative and 2. Advisory;

1. ***Informative Functions:*** The first function of the staff agencies is that of collecting, co-ordinating, and

codifying the information. The chief or principal executive requires a lot of information, facts and figures in order to formulate the policies. For this purpose he takes the help of the staff working under him. It is the duty of the staff to collect the necessary information and supply it to the executive. The staff collects information by three methods research, study and enquiry. They have the duty to watch the course of events, to forecast trends, to spot emerging problems and to think about future policy (L.D. White). The framing of a sound policy by the chief executive depends on so many other factors, viz., analysis, interpretation, identification and weighing of the problems. All this is the duty of the staff. Further, the staff collects information from various sources such as memorandums, reports, speeches, statements, articles, individuals and other organizations.

2. ***Advisory Functions:*** The second function of the staff is to render advice to the chief or principal executive. The chief executive (generally a politican) may not be in a position to frame the policy without the advice of the staff. Especially, if the policy is concerned to technical matters, the chief executive may not posses necessary knowledge about them. Hence it is essential for him to receive the advice on such matters from his staff. So the important function of the staff is to advice the chief in matters of policy making, organization and management. The chief may or may not accept its recommendation, but the staff has to place it before him. L.D. White summarizes the functions of the staff as follows (1) To ensure that the chief executive is adequately and properly informed: (2) To assist him in foreseeing problems and planning future programmes (3) to ensure that matters for his decision reach his desk promptly and settled intelligently without delay: (4)

to exclude any matter that can be settled else where in the system (5) to protect his time, According to Piffner the staff performs these functions. (1) advising (2) co-ordination (3) fact-finding (4) planning (5) contacting with other organs, (6) assisting the line.

It should be remembered that the functions of the staff are purely advisory. It should not take executive functions in its hands. It stands outside the administrative activity. Its function is not to command, but to advise, not to direct but negotiate, not to order but suggest.

Staff Agencies in India: In India the chief executive is the President of the Union. But in practice, the Union Cabinet which is to aid and advice the President in the exercise of his functions, acts as the real chief executive of the Union. The cabinet is assisted by two principle staff agencies. (1) The cabinet committees. (2) The cabinet secretariat.

1. ***Cabinet Committees:*** There are two types of cabinet committees, viz., permanent and temporary. The former's duty is to give advice on important activities of the government. The latters duty is to deal with the minor or unimportant activities of the government. There are ten cabinet sub-committees at present. They are (1) Economic sub—committee (2) Heavy industries committee. (3) Defence sub—committee (4) Foreign Affairs sub committee. (5) Rehabilitation sub—committee. (6) Man power sub—committee. (7) Scientific sub committee. (8) Information and Broadcasting sub—committee (9) Appointment sub—committee, (10) Parliamentary sub—committee.
2. ***Cabinet Secretariat*:** It is headed by the Prime Minister, It consists of a secretary, a joint secretary, a deputy secretary under secretaries and other staff. The cabinet secretariat is divided into four sections.

(1) Main secretariat, which undertakes the work relating to the meetings, discussions, decisions of the union cabinet. (2) O and M division which undertakes the work relating to the improvement of efficiency in administration. If functions under the Director who is assisted by a Deputy Director and Assistant Director. The function of this division is to visit now and then, the various Ministries and examine how far the officials of the Ministries are adopting the prescribed procedures and to render advice to them for the improvement of the work. Besides these, the cabinet secretariat consists of two other divisions also. Military wing and Economic wing. There is an important office to this viz., central statistical organization. Its main functions are: (1) It prepares and publishes annual, monthly, and weekly statistics; (2) It attends to the work connecting with the U.N. statistics organization. (3) It provides training for the officers of the Union and state Governments in the filed of statistical work (4) It advises various ministries and departments on statistical matters (5) It maintains contact with statistical organization in other countries and (6) It provides necessary statistical information required by the government.

MEANING, ORGANIZATION AND FUNCTIONS OF THE LINE AGENCIES

Introduction. It is known to all of us that all the administrative work is directed and managed by the chief or principal executive of the State. All the powers and responsibilities are vested in him. However, he cannot do all the business of the government single-handed. Mooney observes: "Always there are too many things to think about, too many factors to consider, too diversified a knowledge required for solution for the unaided capacity of one leader to encompass". To perform all these functions satisfactorily, the chief executive needs assistance and advice of so many officials. In other words, the business of the government is transmitted by means of an elaborate organization based on principles of specialization. The principal agencies in any administrative system are two. (1) The staff agencies and (2) The line agency. We will study the meaning., organization and functions of the lines agencies or line staff.

MEANING OF LINE

The administration is divisible into two branches. The first branch consists of the work of advice, planning, preparation etc., The second branch consists of the work of control, direction, co-ordination supervision etc., The officials who belong to the second branch are called the Line. By Line we mean those officials whose function is to control, command, direct and supervise the execution of the work of the government. Their function is to issue orders, and instructions to their subordinates to carry on their work. The line agency is organized on the basis of hierarchical system. The superior officer gives orders, directs, controls and supervises the work of his subordinate staff. Thus, we find that the line agency exists to fulfil the central objective of the government.

The term line is not a civilian but a military word. It is borrowed from military vocabulary and applied to the science of administration. Every military organization consists of two branches viz., staff branch and line branch. The principal function of the line branch is to command. Operate and excute the work or programme. The officers of the line actually take part in the fighting with the aim of achieving victory. Thus the function of the civilian line is command but not to advise.

Organization: The line agency consists of three units: They are :

1. The department
2. The regulatory commission and

3. Government corporations, Each needs a brief explanation.

1. ***The Department***: The first unit of the line agency is the department. The department is also called by other names such as office, agency, council etc., The departments are of two kinds, viz., large and small. In every administrative system the principal departments such as Home, Finance, Foreign, Defence are large. The minor departments are small in size and work. The departments are also organized on the basis of unitary or federal. The departments may also be classified as operating and supervising.

The organization of departments is based on various factors such as purpose or function, process, persons or clientele, area or territory. The headship of the department may be singular or plural. Where a single individual is placed at the head of the whole department (i.e. secretary or director) it is called the single head. On the other hand where a group of persons, i.e. board, commission etc., are placed at the head of the department, it is called plural head. Each system has its own merits and defects. Each department consists of various officials Such as secretary, deputy secretary, assistant secretary and others. Also each department has a number of attached offices. All the departmental work is executed under the control of a Director or Commissioner, as the case may be.

2. ***Independent Regulatory Commissions:*** The second unit of the line agency is independent regulatory commissions. As the very name indicates. These commissions are kept independent of the chief executive. Each commission is an autonomous body, it is neither responsible nor subordinate to the chief executive. The Independent Regulatory Commissions perform mixed functions—administrative, quasi—legislative and quasi—judicial. The independent

Regulatory Commission, first, originated in America. In the U.S.A. we find a large number of such commissions. Though, in theory they are independent of the control of the chief executive (i.e. President), in practice much of their activity is controlled by him. He appoints and removes some members of the commissions. Their powers and functions are defined by the law of the U.S. Congress. There are nine Independent Regulatory Commission in the USA their membership range from 5 to 11 and term of office 5 to 7 years.

3. ***The Government Corporations:*** The third unit of the line agency is the Government Corporations. The Corporations enjoy considerable but not cent per cent autonomy or independence. In certain matters the corporations are subjects to the control of the chief executive. In recent years the legislative and judicial control over the government corporation is also increasing. Their importance is also increasing due to the growth of socialism and welfare states. The regular departments are unfit to undertake all the functions of the welfare state. Hence the government appoints autonomous corporations and entrusts them with certain special functions. There are three types of government corporations:

    1. Those corporations in which the finance and administration are wholly in the hands of the government.

    2. Those corporations in which the finance and administration are jointly controlled by the government and private.

    3. Those corporations in which the finance and administration is wholly in the hand of the private persons though they are established under law. The headship of the corporations may

be singular or plural. In the case of the former, the whole authority is exercised by a single person. In the case of the latter, the authority is vested in a Board of Directors. The accounts of the corporation are subject to the audit of the comptroller and Auditor General.

Functions of the Line Agency

The line agency performs the following functions:

1. ***Direction:*** The first function of the line agency is direction. Direction means giving the order to start the operation for the implementation of a policy or plan: The head of the department always gives directions to his subordinates as to how the work is to be carried on or find out the remedies to a problem or overcome the difficulties or remove doubts in the works. The function of direction is to keep the administrative wheels oiled and moving.

2. ***Supervision:*** The second function of the line agency is supervision, which means watching or observing the methods of work done by the staff. The head of the department or principal administrator supervises the work of the subordinate staff, viz., division heads, section heads and so on. The success of the departmental working depends upon sound supervision; a successful supervision depends upon "order, discipline, skill and team work". For building sound discretion and supervision. L.D. White suggests four methods (1) "greater care in selecting supervisors in the first instance" (2) specific training for the performance of their duties, coupled with periodic 'refresher' 'conferences' (3) to give supervisors more authority and to hold them definitely responsible and (4) incentives for the performance of their duties". However, the success of the supervision depends upon

(i) the nature of work and (ii) nature of the people working in the organization.

3. ***Co-ordination:*** The third function of the line agency is co-ordination. "Co-ordination is the adjustment of the parts to each other, and of the movement and operation of parts in time so that each can make its maximum contribution to the product of the whole". (Terry). The activities of different officials of an organization are to co-ordinate for the purpose of achieving unity in the administration. The head of the department must be in the know of all the activities of his department. He has to settle the confilicts or disagreements between two or more divisions of the department. Co-ordination is achieved by two ways: (i) coercive or compulsory and (ii) voluntary, By the first method, the superior official secures co-ordination by issuing orders or instructions to the conflicting divisions. Second method the officials who are at conflict secure co-ordination by mutual consultation or agreement. This work may be taken up by inter-departmental committees or boards.

4. ***Control:*** The fourth function of the line agency is control. Control is defined as an act of verifying whether every thing occurs in conformity with the plane adopted the instructions issued, and principles established (H. Fayol). The head of the department or principal administrator has to control the activities of the subordinate staff without which administrative units cannot be achieved. Control may be exercised by various methods such as checking, watching, maintenance, scrutiny investigation, Audit etc., Inspection keeps the work of the subordinates upto mark, to detect and punish inefficiency. Investigation brings into light the mal—practices and grave dereliction of duty connected with public property or funds.

Line Agencies in India: In India all the executive power of the Union is vested in the President. He is the chief executive officer of the union. But, in practice it is the union cabinet which executes the law of the land. It looks after the implementation of the policies. For this purpose, the government maintains a vast administrative machinery.

1. Firstly, the work of the whole government is carried on by a number of departments. Each department is headed by a minister who is assisted by Deputy Minister, Next comes the secretary who is the head of the departmental Secretariat. He is assisted by a large staff. There are a number of attached offices to each department. The primary function of the Secretariat is to advice, plan and formulate the policies. It has no business of supervision, control, co-oridnation etc. Each department has a separate executive or line. Machinery headed by a Director General or Commissioner General or Inspector General who exercises the functions of supervision, direction and control.

2. Secondly, there are some examples of Regulatory Commission in India like Medical or Bar Councils, However, it should be remembered, that there, is no good development of these Commissions in India as the USA. The government is not giving serious thought to it.

3. Thirdly there are many government corporations in India. The examples of such corporations are (1) The reserve bank of India. (2) the damodar valley corporation (3) the industrial Finance corporation (4) the industrial employees' states insurance corporation, (5) the Indian air lines corporation. (6) Life insurance corporation etc.,

All the corporations in India are to be established by the law of the parliament. The management of the corporations is vested in a Board of Directors which is assisted by necessary staff. Each corporation posses a chief administrator called managing director or governor or chairman or general manager. He has the responsibility to run the administration of the corporation. The Union Government exercises control over the corporations by means of various methods. (i) it appoints directors, (ii) it issues directions or instructions on matters of general policy, (iii) the accounts of the corporations are audited by the Auditor General (iv) The government calls for necessary information from the corporations. The union parliament also exercises good control over these corporations. The corporations in India are criticised on the grounds of slow progress, lack of planning, waste and inefficiency.

INDEPENDENT REGULATORY COMMISSIONS

It is a feature of the modern state to set up autonomous bodies, free from the control of the executive or legislature to operate essential services required by the people. These bodies are of two types (1) Public corporations and (2) Independent Regulatory Commissions. We are concerned with the latter. An Independent Regulatory Commission is an autonomous body of some members which is neither controlled, nor subordinate nor responsible to the chief executive. They are charged with exercising broad general powers, viz., administrative, quasi-legislative and quasi-judicial. They are set up for the purpose of managing commercial or social or public utility services (eg. Transport, electricity, insurance etc.,) There is no much difference between a public corporation and an independent regulatory Agency except that the latter enjoys more autonomy and more powers.

Origin and growth (the U.S.): The first and the only country where Independent Regulatory Commissions have grown is the United States. Hence our discussion on the organization and working of these commission is based on the system obtained in the US which are given below:

1. The Inter-State Commerce Commission
2. The Board of Governors of the Federal Reserve System
3. The Federal Trade Commission.
4. The Federal Power Commission.
5. The Federal Communications Commission.
6. The Securities and Exchange Commission
7. The National Labour Relations Board
8. The Federal Maritime Board
9. The Civil Aeronautics Board.

Organization of the IRC: The independent regulatory commissions are created by the Congress of the U.S. by statute. It defines the nature of organization membership and functions of the commissions. It also lays down the type of the control to be exercised by the chief executive over the commissions. The law also indicates the nature of responsibility of the commissions to the congress in administrative and other fields.

1. The membership of the independent regulator commissions from 5 to 7, except the inter-state commerce commission which has 11 members. Each commission has a Chairman. The chairman and members are appointed by the President of the US in consultation of the senate. They can be removed by the president on the grounds of inefficiency, neglect of duty and malfeasance in office.
2. The terms of office of the members is determined by the congress. At present, the term ranges from 4 to

7 years, except the Federal Reserve System whose term is 14 years.

3. The administration of the Independent Regulatory Commission is vested in the members. The First Hoover Commission recommended that the president of the US be given the right to designate the chairman of each commission to be in charge of commission's internal administration. The recommendation has been accepted and given effect to by the congress.

Role of the I.R.C: The Independent Regulatory Commissions perform valuable functions. We can classify them into commercial, communicative, power and labour. The commercial and trade functions are performed by the Interstate State commerce commission, the Federal Trade Commission, the Maritime Board. The problems of labour are looked after by the National labour Relations Board. The commissions formulate their own policies and procedures. Take decisions and performs quasilegislative functions. They also hear appeals, thus performing quasi-judicial functions. However, the Second Hoover Commission sent a proposal to the US congress to appoint at Chief Hearing Commissioner with a term of 12 years who will hear all the cases. Thus the functions of the Independent Regularoty Commissions play a Vital role in Public administration.

The Chief merits of the Commissions are as Follows

1. They are autonomous bodies free from the legislative and executive control. Hence they are free to perform their duties impartially and creditably.

2. They are free from political influence as the members are appointed and removed according to statutory provisions.

Legislative and Executive Control over the IRC: Though, the Independent Regulatory Commissions are autonomous bodies, in practice they are controlled by the legislative and executive.

The U.S. Congress controls the Commissions in these ways: (1) Its law determines the nature, organization and functions of the commissions. All the commissions are created and abolished by the Acts of the Congress (2) The required finance of Commissions comes from Congress. It also determines the appropriations of the commissions. (3) The Congress, from time to time, appoints Sub-Committees to examine the work of the Commissions. At times, the Congress appoints commissions to make proposals for reorganization of the bodies. The two Hoover Commissions are the examples of this.

The executive control of the Independent Regulatory commissions is secured in these ways: (1) The members and chairman of the Commissions are appointed by the Chief executive. They are removed by him. However, the control is only limited because the President cannot remove the members or chairman except on the grounds specified in the statutes. In the case of Humphrey Vs. the US (1935), the Supreme Court held the President cannot remove the commissioners except on the statutory grounds. A similar view was expressed by the court in Winner Vs. the U.S.A. (1958) when president Eisenhower removed Winner from the War claims commission. Thus, the executive exercises only a limited control over Independent Regulatory commissions.

BASES OF DEPARTMENTAL ORGANIZATION

Meaning and types of Departments

The government of the states consists of a number of departments. Each department performs one variety of work or business of the government. It means the department is a part or portion of the whole of the administrative hierarchy. Department may be define as a groups of personnel in an administrative unit performing the work entrusted to it and responsible to the chief executive.

Departments are classified into various types on the basis of (i) size (ii) structure (iii) nature of work.

1. ***Size:*** Every government consists of some departments with large number of officials and employees (e.g. Defence, Railways, Posts and Telegraphs). There are two defects in the case of large departments: (i) lack of unity and (ii) complexity of issues. The smaller the size, the greater is the unity and efficiency of the department. There is greater degree of co-ordination as well as comprehensive planing.
2. ***Structure:*** Regarding this the departments may be unitary or federal. A unitary department performs one type of function (e.g. Education) while a federal department performs a variety of functions (e.g. Home).
3. ***Work:*** Regarding this, some departments undertake operational work (P and T Railways) while some undertake supervisory and administrative work (e.g. local self—government and finance). The work of some departments is concentrated at one place (e.g. finance, while some distribute their work throughout the territory of the state (e.g. P & T Defence).

Generally speaking. The departments are organized on the basis of four principles: Purpose, process, persons and Place. Each principal may be explained briefly.

1. ***Purpose:*** This is the first principle of departmental organization. The department is organized with a set purpose in view. It is created with an intention of fulfilling an end or goal in view. All the officials from top to bottom, work towards the, achievement of this

goal. They concentrate on the provision of one service and one particular job. The advantages of this principle are many: (i) It leads to skill, efficiency and specialization, (ii) It avoids overlapping and duplication of work. (iii) It makes administration intelligent and well balanced. The principle suffers from few drawbacks also: (i) It encourages narrow mentality, negligence and ignorance. (ii) It encourages selfishness and non-co-operation among the departments.

2. ***Process:*** This is the second principle of departmental organization. According to this principle, the activities which are specialized in nature. (e.g. engineering, medical) are organized into one department. The merit of this principle is that it leads to specialised skill, economy, uniformity, co-ordination and development of career service. On the other hand, many writers say that it is very difficult to achieve the above advantages.

3. ***Persons:*** This is the third principle of departmental organization. The department organized on this basis deals with only one type of persons, e.g. children, old people, farmers, labour, refuges, tribal—areas etc. The aim of such department is to provide all the services needed by the class of persons with which it deals. For instance, the department of tribal—areas deals only with the needs and services of the tribal people. The advantages of this method are: (i) It establishes close relationship between the department and people. (ii) It helps the staff to understand the problems of their work. The defect is that it serves only one section of society.

4. ***Place:*** This is the fourth principle of departmental organization. The department organized on the basis of this principle consists of various divisions. Each division deals with one part of the territory of the

world or country. The department of foreign affairs in any state is the best example of this principle. In India the department of External Affairs consists of five divisions: American Division, Western Division, Eastern Division, Southern Division and African Division. Each division deals with one section of the world's territory. Formerly, the British government created departments on this basis to govern all her overseas possessions. This principle is useful in serving the people of distant territories. One the other hand, it suffers from certain drawbacks such as lack of uniformity etc.,

It conclusion we may say that it is not desirable to organize the department on the basis of any one principle. If two or three principles are combined in departmental organization, it becomes a good system.

Head of the Department. The next aspect of the departmental organization is the nature of the authority. The headship of the department may be organized into two ways: (1) Single head (2) Plural head.

1. Where the whole authority of the department is vested in the hands of a single person (e.g. Secretary) it is called the single head. All directions, instructions, and control emanate from him only. Here are two heads political head (i.e. Minister), and administrative head (i.e. secretary).

2. On the other hand, where the whole authority of the department is vested in a board or commission or committee, it is called plural head. All directions, instructions and control emanate from him. The examples in India are: Railway Board, Revenue Board etc. Each system enjoys certain benefits, and suffers form certain losses.

Each department may appoint a number of advisory boards. The principal function is to give advice to the head of the department. They consist of technical experts; citizens, officials and politicians. The head of the department, say a Secretary is always assisted by a number of staff subordinate to him, such as personal assistant, policy aides and administrative assistants.

Conclusion: The success or failure of any department depends upon the extent of the unity that prevails in it. The departmental unity can be secured by the following ways.

1. There should be co-operation among all the officials of the department. They should be prepared to operate as a team, to adapt to general directives and to display loyalty to leadership.
2. The authority and responsibility should be concentrated in the hands of a single person. All the subordinate officers should be subject to the control and superintendence of top-most officer of the department.
3. The sense of discipline and equity help men to secure departmental unity.

Nature of Departmental Organization in India. In India the Union Government is divided into a number of departments. In organising the departments all the four principles viz. Purpose, process, persons and place are adopted. The departments of Health and Law may be said to have been organized on the basis of process. The Departments of Labour and Employment, Rehabilitation, and Agriculture, may be said to have been organized on the basis of persons. The Department of Foreign Affairs may be taken as an example of place. Each department is headed by a political head called the Minister and an administrative head called the Secretary. They are assisted by the large number of staff. The primary function of the Secretariat is to advice, plan and formulate. Each department has a separate executive machinery headed by a Director General or Commissioner or Inspector—General. His primary function is to supervise, direct, co-ordinate and control the work of the department. Each department has few attached offices and advisory bodies.

THE CABINET SECRETARIAT

The Cabinet Secretariat was created in August 1947 when the Executive Council of the Viceroy was replaced by a Cabinet headed by the Prime Minister. There are two principal functions of the Cabinet Secretaries.

1. Firstly, the cabinet secretariat is responsible for all the work concerning the meetings and discussions of the Union Cabinet. It preserves all the records relating to the cabinet discussions and decisions.
2. Secondly, the Cabinet Secretariat through Organization and Management Division initiates necessary steps to secure efficiency in administration. It also deals with the matters connecting with the preparation of annual, monthly and weekly statistics.

Organization: The cabinet secretariat is headed by the Prime Minister. It consists of a Secretary, a Joint Secretary, a deputy Secretary, Under Secretaries and other staff. The Cabinet secretariat is divided into four sections (1) Main secretariat which undertakes the work relating to the meetings, discussions and decisions of the Union Cabinet. (2) O and M division (i.e. Organization and Methods Division) which undertakes the work relating to the improvement of efficiency in administration. It functions under a Director who is assisted by a Deputy Director, an Assistant Director and other staff. The Deputy Director of the O and M Division visits now and then the various Ministries and examines how far officials of the Ministry are adopting the prescribed producers and renders advice to them for the improvement of the work. Besides these, the cabinet secretariat consists of two other divisions viz., Military wing and Economic wing. Attached to the Cabinet Secretariat is an important office called the Central Statistical organization. Its main functions are (1) it prepares and publishes annual, monthly and weekly statistics. (2) It attends to the work connecting with the U.N. Statistical organization. (3) It provides training for the officers of the Union and State government in the field of statistical work. (4) It advises various Ministries and departments on statistical matters. (5) It maintains contact with the statistical organization in the other countries. (6) It provides necessary statistical information required by the government.

PUBLIC ENTERPRISES

Meaning of Public Enterprise: The term public enterprise is the most modern. It came into use, perhaps, during closing years of the nineteenth century. The term enterprise means an under-taking—it may be industrial, commercial or banking. These under-takings may be operated or managed by the former, they are called private enterprises where they are operated by the government, they are called public enterprises. Thus public enterprises means the state—ownership and management of economic agencies, viz., industries, lands, commercial institutions.

Growth of Public Enterprises: Until the close of the 19th century, the concept of public enterprise was absent. During the 18th and 19th centuries the doctrine of laissez faire was very popular which pleaded that the state should not interfere with the economic activities of the individual such as trade and industry. During the later part of the 18th century, Adam smith, in his classical book 'Wealth of Nations' advocated for a policy of non—interference by the state in economic matters. But the two famous revolutions viz., The French Revolution and Industrial Revolution brought into vogue a new theory called socialism. It is a theory which aims at securing by the action of the central democratic authority a better distribution and...a better production of wealth than now prevails. The doctrine of socialism aims at bringing under state ownership all the instruments of production (such as land, capital, industries, factories) as well as commercial under takings (such as banks, transport, railways, communications etc.) In other words, socialism, brought into use a new concept called public enterprise. Further, the emergence of welfare concept of the beginning of the 20th century made strong the case for public enterprise. The welfare state idea aims to secure the general welfare of the community. All governmental activities, today, are directed towards the achievement of this goal. This is possible only through planning whose object is the rapid industrialization. Thus the state, today, is entering into the field of industry. In this way private enterprise, which was very popular once upon a time, is slowly yielding place to public enterprise.

Management of Public Enterprises. (1) Management by the Department: The public enterprises becomes a part of the administrative machinery. It is constituted into an independent department of the government. All the activities of the enterprise are managed, directed and controlled by the head of the department, viz., Minister (political head) and Secretary (administrative head). The staff of the department is drawn from the regular civil service and governed by the same rules and regulations as for other departments. The necessary finance is sanctioned by the government at the beginning of every year. the accounts of the enterprise are audited every year by the Comptroller and Auditor General by the government. The examples of public enterprises which are managed by the department in India are: Railways, Transport and Communications, Posts and Telegraphs. This type of management has few advantages. They are:

1. It leads to efficient management of the activities of the enterprises.

2. It establishes parliamentary control over the enterprise.
3. It ensures the financial stability of the enterprise. Yet the department management of the public enterprise is not free from defects. (1) It kills initiative due to governmental interference with the activities of the enterprise. (2) It results in a lot of delay, waste of money and time.

2. ***Management by a Board:*** In this case the public enterprises are managed by a Board or Commission. It consists of a number of directors who operate the enterprise. They are nominated or appointed by the government. Sometimes the Board of Directors simply determines the policy and lays down rules and regulations governing the administration of the enterprise. In this case, the Board appoints a Manager or Chief administration who looks after the administration of the enterprise and holds responsible for it. Sometimes, the Board of Directors formulate policies and execute them as well. They also look after the administration of the enterprise. Each director may handle one aspect of the enterprise. The Board of Directors may consist of officials, non-officials members of the legislature and representatives of the employees as its directors. The Board of Directors elects its own chairman from among its members. He is the chief head of the enterprise. He guides and controls the activities of the enterprise. Sometimes, the chairman of the Board of Directors is nominated by the Government from among the directors or appoint an officer or direct a minister to be the chairman.

3. ***Management by the Public Corporations:*** This type of management has come into vogue very recently. In this case the Public enterprises are managed and operated by an autonomous corporation of the government. A public corporation consists of a

group of persons who act as a single person for the purpose of managing the enterprise. The corporation is created by the law of the legislature. The finance and composition of the corporation differs from country to country. In some countries the finance of the corporation is entirely invested by the government which controls the administration. In some countries the government may invest money and control administration partially. The administration of the corporation may be vested in a Board of Directors or a single individual called Chairman or General Manager. All the corporations enjoy full autonomy from the interference by the executive or the legislature, However, it does not mean that the government and legislature have no control over these corporations. The government exercises control over the corporations by various methods such as appointments, finance, and audit. The legislature also exercises control over the corporations in many ways such as rules and regulations governing their conduct, questions debates examinations of reports represented by the corporation etc. The public corporations are found in all the important countries of the modern world.

Government Control Over Public Enterprise. In all the countries government exercises control over the public enterprises, Firstly, the government has to approve the policies and programmes of the enterprises. It appoints important officials of the enterprise and removes them on the grounds of misconduct, violation of rules and indiscipline. The executive supervises, directs and controls the work of the public enterprises, where the enterprise is managed by a Board, the government appoints and removes the Directors. It may appoint its own official as the chairman. The government controls the public enterprises through the power of purse. They cannot raise loans or incur expenditure without the prior sanction of the government. The accounts of the enterprises are subject to the audit by the Auditor-General.

Secondly, the legislature exercises control over the public enterprises by various methods. It enacts laws within whose frame work the enterprises have to work. The members of the legislature may elicit information regarding the working of the enterprise through ministers by way of questions. The reports of the enterprises may be placed on the table of the legislature and discussed by it. In this way the public enterprises are made responsible and accountable to the government and legislature of the country. However, rigid control is not good because it leads to inefficiency, kills initiative and makes difficult to achieve the object for which the enterprise is established.

Importance of Public Enterprises

1. Public enterprises, generally, function on sound lines and exhibit higher standards of conduct. There is every possibility of selecting the best personnel to operate the enterprises. There is no greater scope for corruption, misappropriation and nepostism. Since the finances of the enterprises are guaranteed by the government, the public funds are safe.
2. Public corporations, generally, work efficiently. There is little or no scope for failure. The reason is that they work under the constant control of the executive and legislature. They are accountable to the legislature. The absence of competition leads to profitable business.

Defects of Public Enterprises. However important they might be, the public enterprises suffer from certain defects.

1. The administrative officials who run the enterprises are not well suited for the task. They have no required knowledge, skill and experience to operate

the business undertakings. The frequent transfers of the officials from one enterprise to the other results in administrative instability.

2. Public enterprises cannot work independently due to the increasing interference from the departments. They are subjected to rigid control by the executive and legislature.

PUBLIC CORPORATIONS

Birth of a Public Corporation

The establishment of Government Corporations has become an important feature of modern state activity. They have come into existence in all the advanced countries during the present century. In England the public corporations were created in 1920's and in the U.S.A. they became important after 1920's. The Government corporations have come into operation as a result of the emergence of socialism and welfare state which compelled the state to undertake industrial and commercial enterprises. The growing needs of society and increasing population are demanding more and more production of essential goods of life. It is not possible for the private individuals to meet these growing demands of the people. Hence the modern state undertakes industrial and commercial enterprises, owns, operates and controls them. For the purpose of operation and management of the public enterprises, the government creates corporations.

Public Corporations

A public corporation is a body of persons appointed by the law of the legislature to operate and manage one or more public enterprises. The whole corporation acts as a 'single person' It is owned and controlled by the government.

1. M.E. Demock defines public corporation as publicly owned enterprise that has been chartered under

federal, state or local law for a particular business or financial purpose.

2. M.C. Shukla defines Corporation as a Corporate body created by legislature, with defined powers and functions, and financially independent, having clear cut jurisdiction over the specified area or over a particular type of commercial activity.

3. Pfiffner: "A corporation is a body framed for the purpose of enabling a number of personas to act as a single person'. He says that it is "an artificial person which is authorised by the law to carry on particular activities and functions". Thus a public corporation has these characteristics. (1) It is a body of persons acting as a single person. (2) It is created by the law of the State. (3) It is owned, and controlled by the state (4) It is created for the purpose of managing one more industrial or commercial enterprises, (5) It has administrative and financial autonomy.

The examples of government corporation in Britain, the U.S.A., and India are given below:

1. ***Britain:*** British Broadcasting Corporations (B.B.C., 1923) British Overseas Airways Corporation (B.O.A.C. 1939) British Corporation (B.A.C. 1946), Overseas Food Corporation (O.F.C. 1947) etc.,

2. ***The U.S.A.:*** Inland Water ways Corporation, Reconstruction Finance Corporation (R.F.C. 1932). It was liquidated on June, 3, 1953. Tennessee Valley Authority (T.A.V. 1933), Defence Supplies Corporation (D.S.C. 1940). The most recent examples are; St. Laurence Seaway Development Corporation (1954), Federal Facilities Corporation (1954).

3. ***India:*** A number of Government corporations came into existence in India since 1948. Some of them are mentioned here: Damodar Velley Corporation (1948),

Industrial Finance Corporation, (1948), Industrial Employees State Insurance Corporation (1948), National Industrial Development Corporation (1954), Industrial Credit and Investment Corporation of India (1955) etc.,

Organization of Public Corporations. The public corporations are established by two methods, viz., (1) by an order of the executive and (2) by an act of the legislature. But the first method is followed very rarely. The establishment of corporation by an act of the legislature is popularly adopted in all the advanced countries of the world. Every public corporation is brought into existence by a separate act of the legislature. The act lays down the nature of the activities, administration, finance etc. of the corporation. The act makes provisions for securing the responsibility and exercising control over the corporation. It defines the spheres of activity in which the corporation can act independently. In the U.S.A. all the government corporations are created by an act of the Congress. In England and India they are established by an act of the parliament.

The public corporations are created for three purposes:

1. Firstly, the corporations are crated for the purpose of extending credit to various public and private enterprises. In the U.S.A. the Reconstruction Finance Corporation, the Commodity Credit Corporation etc. have been created for this purpose. In India, the Industrial Finance Corporation, Industrial and Investment Corporation etc. have been created for this purpose.

2. Secondly, the corporations are created for the purpose of managing the activities of commercial or business enterprises. Some times the corporations are created for the purpose of carrying on commercial activities such as transport, product and distribution. Public

works, housing etc. In the U.S.A., Inland Water ways cooperation, U.S. Housing Cooperation etc. are created for this purpose. In India, Road Transport Corporation, Indian Air Lines Corporation come under this category.

3. Thirdly, the co-operations are created for the purpose of developing a specific area or region. The Damodar Valley Corporation in India is an example of this.

Administration of Public Corporations: Administration of public corporations may be constituted in two ways: (1) Administration by a Board of Directors, (2) Administration by a single individual.

1. In the first case, the administration of the corporation is vested in a Board of Directors. They hold responsible for the proper management of the corporations. Sometimes the Board of Directors may appoint somebody from among them as Managing Director. In India, the Industrial Finance Corporation, Indian Airlines Corporation, Employees State Insurance Corporation, Indian Airlines Corporation, Employees State Insurance Corporation, are managed by a Board of Directors. In the U.S.A. the management of Reconstruction Finance Corporation, Tennessee Valley Authority is vested in the Board of Director. The former consists of six members and the latter three members on the board of Directors. The Directors of the Board are appointed by various methods: (1) The governmental may appoint all the Directors; or (2) Government may a appoint only few directors and the remaining may be elected by various agencies.

In the second case, the administration of the public corporation may be vested in the hands of a single person called General Manager or Chief administrator or Executive Officer. All the authority belongs to him. He alone directs, supervises and controls the administration of the corporation. He holds responsibility for its activities. In the U.S.A. the administration of Inland Waterways Corporation is vested in the Secretary of War. Again the management of the St. Laurence Seaway Development Corporation is vested in an administrator appointed by the President.

The two methods described above have their relative merits and defects:

Control over public corporation. Generaly speaking public corporations enjoy much autonomy in the sphere of administration and finance. However, they are not completely free from the control of the government. The Government control over public corporations is of two kinds (1) Control by the Executive (2) Control by the legislature.

1. ***Executive Control.*** Firstly the executive exercises control over the public corporation by various methods. It directs, supervises and controls the activities of the corporations. It appoints and removes the Board of Directors or the chief administrator of the corporations. The executive may frame rules and regulations. From time to time governing the management of the corporations. In the U.S.A. the President has the power to supervise the work of the corporation. He appoints and removes its a administrative personnel. To transact certain financial activities, the corporations have to obtain the permission of the Bureau of Budget. Some minor transactions are approved by the Secretary of Treasury (Act of 1945). In Britain the executive has the power to appoint the members of the Board, fix salaries and issue directions. Its approval is necessary for the corporations in matters relating to investment, borrowing etc. In India the executive appoints members or chief administrator of the corporations,

nominates their advisory bodies, issues directions or instructions on general policy. The approval of the government is necessary in matters of investment and borrowing by the corporations. It calls for necessary information or reports from the corporations. Thus the executive control over the public corporation is a universal feature in the modern society. The success of a corporation depends on what type of relation it has with the Department. The Minister holds part responsibility in financial and administrative matters. Hence he ought to be consulted by the corporation in very important matters.

2. ***Legislative Control.*** The legislature exercises control over the public corporations in many ways. In fact, the public corporations are created by an act of the legislature. The act defines the structure, functions and purposes of the corporations. The legislature controls the corporation by means of questions put to the ministers in charge of the corporations. The legislature discusses the annual reports of the corporations and finds out commissions or commissions therein. It sanctions finance needed by the corporations.

In the U.S.A. the Congress exercises control over public corporation by three methods: (1) Questions, (2) Voting of annual supplies (3) Discussion and approval of the annual budget. In Britain the parliament controls public corporations in two ways: (1) Questions, to the ministers and (2) discussion of annual reports of the corporation. In 1951, a Select Committee of the House of Commons recommended a Standing Committee of the House to act as a liaison between the nationalized industries and Parliament. In India the union parliament employs the following methods of control: (1) Questions to the ministers (which are limited in nature), (2) discussion of financial estimates, annual reports and accounts. Robsons opposes the Control of Corporations through questions. He observes: If once the Parliamentary questions were given free play over the whole field of activity of a nationalised industry, half the advantage of having a public corporation than an Government department would be lost".

Distinction between Public Corporation and Department. A public corporation differs from a department in two respects, Firstly, they differ in the nature of their relationship with the governance: Secondly they differ in the nature of their administrative procedure. Each may be explained briefly as below:

1. ***Difference based on relationship with the Government:***

   (i) A public corporation is an autonomous body. It enjoys certain degree of independence in the sphere of administration and finance. A department is an inherent part of the general administrative system. It has no any autonomy or independence in matters of finance.

   (ii) A public corporation is free from the rigid control and interference of the executive. No doubt, it is subjected to the control of the executive, but that control is very limited. A department is strictly under the control of the minister. He directs and controls all the work of the department. He can interfere with any aspect of the departmental work.

   (iii) A public corporation is controlled by the legislature only to a limited degree. A department is subjected to the rigid control of the legislature. The minister in charge of the department is responsible to the legislature. Finance is the principle weapons of legislative control over the Department.

2. ***Difference Based on administration procedure.*** (1) A public corporation follows its own procedure in

matters of finance. It can raise its own capital, funds, earn incomes, accumulate savings, build up reserves, borrow, make its own budget. This procedure cannot be adopted by the departments.

3. A public corporation adopts its own procedure for the recruitment, promotion, and removal of personnel. A department has to follow general civil rules in these matters.

Nature of Indian Corporations. Establishment: The government corporations in India are established by the acts of the Union Parliament. The Union Parliament has the right to create corporations in states also.

2. ***Purposes.*** The government corporations in India are created for the purpose of extending credit facilities to various public and private enterprises. The Industrial Finance Corporation and Industrial Credit and Investment Corporation are the examples of this. (2) Secondly, they are created for the purpose of managing the activities of commercial or business or industrial enterprises. The Indian Airlines Corporation, the State Road Transport Corporation (In States) are the examples of this (3) Thirdly, they are created for the purpose of developing a specific area or region. The Damodar Valley Corporation in India is an example of this (4) Lastly, they are created for the purpose of promoting the welfare and providing social security for the people. The Industrial Employees State Insurance Corporation and Life Insurance Corporation hold high objective and laudable purposes.

3. ***Administration.*** (i) In India the administration of the government corporation is vested in the Board of Directors. They hold responsibility for the proper and efficient management of the affairs of the corporation. There are two methods of appointing the Board of

Directors. (1) In the case of some corporations all the Directors are appointed by the Union Government. For example, the Board of Directors of the reserve Bank of India, Rehabilitation Finance Corporation, Damodar Valley Corporation, Indian Air lines Corporations, are appointed by this method (2) In the case of some corporations, the Union Government appoints few directors and the remaining are nominated or elected by the various bodies or organization. For example, the Board of Director of Industrial Finance Corporation and Employee's State Insurance Corporation appointed by this method.

(ii) However, each corporation has a chief executive officer called Managing Director or Chairman or General Manager or Chief Administrator. He executes the policies of the Board of Directors. He conducts the administration of the corporation.

(iii) In the case of some corporations the administration is decentralized. In other words, some corporations have opened branches or local offices in various parts of the country. Each branch or local office is headed by an executive officer. The examples of this type are: Rehabilitation Finance Corporation, Industrial Finance Corporation and Life Insurance Corporation.

(iv) The government may appoint advisory committees to advice the corporation on various matters. The term of office of the directors or executive officers may be fixed by the government.

4. ***Control over Government Corporations.*** Generally speaking government corporations in India enjoy greater degree of autonomy. However, they are

not completely independent of the control of the union government. The government's control over corporations is exercised in two ways:

(i) ***Control by the Executive (i.e. Ministers).*** The executive appoints the Board of Directors, the advisory committees and the executive officers of the corporations. All these officials are liable to be removed by the executive at any time. It issues directions or instructions on the general policy of the corporations. The approval of the executive is necessary for any programme of investment and borrowing by the corporations. A.D. Gorwala is of the opinion that Minister's control should cover all new capital outlay for expansion, he should be consulted and have final voice in matters relating, to investment, borrowing and allocation of profits. The accounts of the corporations are audited by the Auditor-General of India. The ministers who are in charge of various corporations may call for information reports or any other matter from the corporations. The executive has the power of liquidating any of the corporations.

(ii) ***Control by the Parliament.*** The corporation comes into existence only by an act of the Union Parliament. The act defines the structure, administrations, powers and functions of the corporation. The parliament puts questions to the ministers in order to elicit information regarding the activities of the corporations. It discusses the financial and other aspects of the corporations. The financial estimates submitted by the corporation are thoroughly examined by the parliamentary committees (viz. Estimates Committee and Public Accounts Committee).

5. ***Finance of the corporations.*** There are two ways by which the corporations secure their finances. Firstly, the government subscribes the whole capital of some corporations. Secondly, the government subscribes finance only partially to some corporations and the remaining is raised from private people by way of investment or shares.

Government Corporations in India. It is necessary for us to study the constitution, finances and functions of the government corporations in India.

1. ***The Damodar Valley Corporation (D.V.C.).*** It was created in the year 1948. The Union Government, the Government of Bihar and West Bengal are the partners of the corporation. The management is vested in a Board of Directors consisting of three members including the Chairman. They are appointed by the Union Government. The executive officer of the corporation is called the Secretary. It has advisory committees. The entire capital of the corporation is subscribed by the three governments. It can borrow money with the approval of the Union Government. The profits of the corporation are shared by three government. The main purpose of the D.V.C. is to secure the development of the Damodar Valley.

2. ***The Indian Airlines Corporation (I.A.C.).*** It was created in the year 1953. The Management of the Corporation is vested in of Board of Directors consisting of 5 to 9 members including the Chairman. They are appointed by the Union Government. The executive officer of the corporation is called the General Manager. It has an Air Transport Council. The entire capital of the Corporation is subscribed by the Union Government. The corporation can borrow

money. The corporation provides safe, efficient, adequate air transport service. It arranges for the training of the air staff.

3. ***The Life Insurance Corporation of India (L.I.C.).*** It was created in the year 1956. The management of the corporation is vested in a Board of Directors appointed by the Union Government. The executive officer of L.I.C. is called the Chairman. The administration is decentralised. The LIC has its local branches such as zonal officers, branch offices, divisions offices, and sub-branch offices, the administrative heads are called zonal managers, divisional manager, branch managers and assistant branch manager respectively.

4. ***The Employee's State Insurance Corporation.*** It was created in the year 1948. The management of the corporation is vested in a Board of Directors consisting of 32 members. The Union Minister for Labour is the Chairman of the Corporation. Of these. Four directors are appointed by the Union Government. The Director-General is the Chief Executive officer of the Corporation. The administration is decentralsied. The corporation has it regional offices all over the country. It has a number of committees. The finances of the corporation is subscribed by the employees. It receives grants from the Government and donations from others. The main function of the corporation is to provide various benefits to the employees. viz. (1) Medical benefit (2) sickness benefits (3) maternity benefit (4) disablement benefit (5) dependent's benefit.

5. ***Industrial Finance Corporation (I.F.C.).*** It was created in the year 1948. The management of the corporation is vested in a Board of Directors consisting of 12 members. Of these, the Union Government

appoints three directors and the remaining are nominated by various bodies. The executive authority is in the hands of committee.

There is a an advisory committee also. Its administration is decentralised. It has four local offices in the country. The corporation has a share capital of Rs. 5 crores. It performs three functions:

1. It provides credit from medium and long term capital requirements of industries.
2. It makes long term loans to manufacturing concerns.
3. It helps industries to improve their revenues and put themselves on sound economic basis.

6. ***Rehabilitation Finance Corporation.*** It was created in the year 1948. The management of the Corporation is vested in a Board of Director consisting of seven members including the chairman. The Chairman is the chief administrative officer of the Corporation. It has an advisory broad also. The entire finance is subscribed by the Union Government. Its main function is to promote the interests of displaced persons. For this purpose it grants loans to them.

Criticism. The criticism of the working of the government corporations in India can be studied under two heads:

(i) ***Firstly:*** It is maintained; that are certain hindrances in the way of efficient working of the Indian Corporation. There is a lot of Government interference with the affairs of the corporations. The government is imposing serious restrictions in matters of finance. The Estimates Committees of the first Lok Sabha in its 16th report observed that public

undertaking such as corporations are treated by the Ministers in the same manner as departments or offices of the Government. There are difficulties in securing the technical personnel, foreign exchange, and capital goods required. There are no facilities for training the administrative staff. The experience is lacking in the sphere of management.

(ii) ***Secondly:*** The working of the partiality, is criticised on the grounds of partially favouritism, dealy, improper planning, huge loss and inadequate resources.

However, one should not forget the valuable work done by the corporations since independence. During the last seventeen years of their existence. They had made important contributions towards growth of industries, social securities, labour welfare, and transport. They are playing highly creditable role in establishing the socialist democratic welfare state in India. In this connections, it may be necessary to mention the suggestions made by M.C. Chagla for the efficient work of public Corporation (1) There should be no governmental interference with the working of autonomous corporations. If the government wish to interfere, directions should be in writing (2) The Chairman of a public corporation should be chosen form person having business and financial experience, specially where the activities involve investment. (3) The officials of the corporations who are drawn from Civil services should be told to be loyal and duty bound to the corporations. They should be asked to resist the influence by the officers of the Government.

The implementation of the suggestions will bring about efficiency in the working of corporations.

FIELD SERVICE

The needed for Field Service: Every state has administration. If the State is very small in size and limited in population, the whole administration can be conducted from a single central office or head quarters. For example, the ancient great city-states were very small in size as each city was an independent state. So the administration of each city was conducted from one central office only. But there is no justification in applying the same principle to the modern state. The present day state is very wide in territory and huge in population. It possesses an administration which is vast in size and complex in structure. It serves the whole state. Hence it is neither desirable nor practicable to conduct the whole administration from a single centre. It is obviously impossible for all the people of the state to travel to the capital each time they want to meet the officials and get their things done. Therefore, the administration of the modern state is carried on by different centres or offices at different places in the state. Each centre serves the needs or looks after the administration of the area under its jurisdiction. These administrative centres are called field agencies or field establishment or field organizations or field offices. All the field offices are ultimately subordinate or attached to or governed by one central administrative office called Head quarters. L.D. White observes. A field service is a physical necessity: the government has to send its agents to the people and indeed has always done so.

Meaning of Field Services

The meaning of field service is clear from the above few lines. It is an administrative office situated at a far away distance from the central office consisting of required personnel to carry on the administration of the area under its jurisdiction as directed by the head quarters. It is part or branch of the central office and subordinate to it. Dr. M.P. Sharma defines: 'By field services or field organization of an administrative agency we mean the personnel stationed away from its head quarters into the country, to carry on its work from the numerous sub-centres within the easy reach of the people. The first field services in the USA were set up in 1789, viz., customs and post offices. In India each department of the Union Government has a number of field offices. The examples are; post offices, railway stations, police, customs offices and others.

Organization of Field Service. Different writers of Public Administration suggested different methods of organising field agencies. There are four such methods: (1) Unitary method, (2) Multiple method, (3) Short Arms and Long Fingers method, (4) Long Fingers method. A brief explanation of each method is necessary for its proper understanding.

1. ***Unitary method.*** Under this system all the field agencies are placed under the common and control of a single administrator or officer. All the field officers are subordinate to him and deal directly with him. The central office or head quarters has no direct contact with the field offices. All its directions or instructions are passed on to the chief officer under his control. It means the line of authority runs from central office to the officer in change of the field offices and from the field offices is passed on to the officer from whom it passes on to the central office at the seat of government. In France the field service is organized on this model. The Officer in charge of the field service is called the perfect. In pre-independent India the service was organized on this model. The District Collector was in charge of all the field services.

2. ***Multiple Method.*** The multiple method is quite opposite to the unitary method. Under multiple system all the field offices are placed under the direct control and command of the head quarters offices. It has direct dealing with the various offices in the field. All its directions or instructions pass on directly to the field offices. It means the line of authority runs from central office to the field agencies. So also all the

information from field agencies is passed on direct to the central office at the seat of the government.

Thus the differences between the unitary type and multiple type is that in the case of the former there is a middle officer between the head quarters and field offices, whereas in the case of the later there is no such middle officer.

3. ***Short Arms and Long Fingers Method.*** Under this system all the divisional offices are located in the central office or headquarters only. They control the field under their jurisdiction from that office only.

4. ***Long Arms and Short Fingers Method.*** Under this system all the divisional offices are located far away from the head quarters office. It means they are located in the actual field itself. They are nearer to the field offices under their jurisdiction.

Administration of Field Services

The administrative power of the field service may be examined under two heads: (1) Centralization and (2) Decentralization. Each aspect needs a brief explanation.

1. ***Centralization.*** Under this system all matters are decided by the central authority. It defines every policy and directs field services to execute that policy. It means, under centralized system, all policy-making and decision making authority rests with the head quarter office only. The field offices have no power to take decisions even in small matters. They are mere executing agencies. "They have no power to act on their own initiative; the action is the action They of the central office, and even as regards matters of internal administration such as promotion of employees, the purchase of supplies etc., authority for action from head quarters must be received". (Willoughby). This system of centralisation has certain advantages:

1. It secures maximum control of head quarters over field offices.
2. It locates administrative responsibility in one central office.
3. It ensures uniformity in the execution of policy.
4. It prevents administrative abuses.

However, this system has certain defects: (i) It results in undue delay. (ii) It makes administration costly and rigid.

2. ***Decentralization.*** Under this system all matters except very important are decided by the field officers themselves. It means the decision-making authority rests with the field services. The central authority delegates its authority to the field agencies. They act under general grants of power, and their action is final except when special provision may be made for an appeal to central office (Willoughby). Under this system the power of initiative rests with the field services. They system of decentralization has two advantages: (i) It results in quick decisions and prevents red—tape (ii) It makes administration cheap, economical and flexible. However, this system has few defects also; (i) It does not give adequate control to the central office over field offices. (ii) It is not possible to locate responsibility for any administrative error or mischief. (iii) It leads to diversity in the execution of policy and brings in many administrative errors.

It is not so easy to decide as to which of the two system is quite satisfactory. Every thing depends upon the character of the work to be performed and the special conditions to be met (Willoughby).

Methods of Control (or Relation Between Field and Head quarters)

Whatever may be the name of organization and authority of the field agencies, it is universally accepted that headquarters office should have control over the agencies in field. There are various methods or techniques employed by the had quarters to control the field officers. These methods may be briefly considered.

1. The first method by which the head quarters controls field office is the right of information. Every central authority calls for necessary information regarding the activities and the work done by field agencies. It also calls for information regarding the needs of personnel and equipment of the field offices. On the basis of the information the head quarters comes to know the ommissions and commissions committed by the field agencies and takes appropriate action to check them in future.

2. The second method by which head quarters controls field offices is the right to make rules and regulations governing the activities of the field officers. All the field services are required to act within the frame work of the rules and regulations. They cannot exercise their authority in excess of what rules authorise them. In case these rules and regulations are violated, the head quarters can take appropriate action against them.

3. The third method by which head quarters controls field offices is the right to sanction expenditure. The field offices cannot spend any amount without the prior sanction of the central office. Sometimes the field offices may be authorised to spend upto a prescribed amount; in that case they cannot incur expenditure in excess of that figure.

4. The fourth method by which head quarters controls field offices is the right to inspection. The head quarters has the power to inspect the records, accounts and work of the field office. For this purpose it maintains an inspection service. By means of inspection the central office comes to know whether

the powers delegated to the filed have been properly and correctly used and rules and instructions followed or not. Inspection helps headquarters to detect the irregularities and shortcomings of the field establishments. These faults may be corrected at the meetings between head quarters officials and field officials.

5. The fifth method by which head quarters, controls field establishments is the right to investigation. The head quarters, now and then, conducts investigation into allegations against the field officers. The complaints of malpractices and corruption made by the public are enquired into by the head quarters. In order to secure efficient investigation central office may appoint committees. Thus, by means of investigation, the head quarters is able to enforce the responsibility of the field officers.

6. The last method by which head quarters controls field establishments is the right to give instructions or directions. Specific instructions flow in an endless stream from head quarters to field officers, periodically combined into an operation manual which itself is steadily supplemented by new directives. Further, the head quarters gives suggestions to the field office regarding the conduct of their activities. So also, the field officer himself may ask for advice of the head quarters on difficult matters. "The government long distance telephone bill is a heavy one". (L.D. White).

We may conclude by saying that the success of administration depends upon the extent of co-operation and co-ordination between the field agencies and headquarters.

ADVISORY COUNCILS

The present century in which we live is well-known for its two basic features, viz., democracy and welfare state based on planning. Today, the world is rapidly proceeding into the lap of democracy. Democracy, as defined by Abraham Lincoln, is a government of the people by the people and for the people. Its aim is to provide social welfare. It should act constantly in accordance with public opinion. Hence it is suggested that government in democracy should keep in touch with the voluntary, advisory and private bodies while making policy decisions. In other words, according to this idea, the government should consult and take advice, before formulating major policy decisions, from the private bodies effected by its decisions. The whole argument can be explained by means of few explanations. Whenever the government wants to formulate major policies in the field of education, it must consult and obtain advice from the associations consisting of those who are effected by the decisions. It may also consult those bodies consisting of master minds of education. So also, whenever, the government proposes changes in the sphere of economic, industrial or agricultural or scientific spheres, it must consult and take advice from the associations consisting of those who are effected by such changes. It can also associate itself with the bodies consisting of the experts in the concerned field.

In this way, the government must proceed on democratic lines and obtain the co-operation of those effected by its policy for this purpose, the government in democracy should do two things.

1. To encourage the public to create a number of voluntary bodies representing different interests or activities.
2. It can create some advisory bodies consisting of experts in different fields (such as educational, industrial, scientific etc.) and associate them with administration. The government may consult these bodies to know their views before formulating policies.

Growth of Advisory Bodies

1. ***The US.*** The present century witnessed a rapid growth in the establishment of advisory and consultative bodies in several advanced countries. The United States is well—known for this. In this country, every private organization has its Head Quarters at Washington to make known its views to the Congress as well as the President whenever a major law or policy is under discussion. The steps to create advisory bodies were taken in the U.S. as early as 1902, when, for the first time; the Public Health Service Department consulted effected interests. It was followed by the War Department which has sought the assistance of the leading nationals, industrial and other associations in working out plans for the mobilization of the industrial means in case of war. About 1200 conferences have been held and 343 permanent committees created. In 1918, Advisory Statistical Council was created which advised the President on matters relating to the collection, compilation and publication of the census data. The Bureau of Census has created two special advisory committees to aid it in the collection and publication of statistics of the Municipal and State finances. By the end of World War II the Department of Agriculture had 115 national and 14 regional advisory committees concerned with the food industry. They held 400 meetings during the War period.

The following are the prominent private organizations available for consultation and advice to the government of the U.S.

1. The Chamber of Commerce of the US
2. The American Farm Bureau Federation
3. The American Council of Education
4. The Federation of American Engineering Societies.

5. The National Health Council.

India: The need for creating voluntary associations and advisory bodies is being felt in India. In recent years, there have been several attempts to create voluntary organizations whom the government may consult. The examples are:

1. The Indian Chamber of Commerce and Industry
2. The Bar Council of India
3. The All—India Medical Council
4. The All—India Railway men's Federation

In recent years, the Union Government have set up many advisory bodies to advise them on important policy matters. These bodies consist of master minds in different fields of activity. We may mention some examples of such bodies.

1. The Planning Commission which advises the Union and state government in the formulation of five year plans and the execution.
2. The National Development Council which advises the Government in developmental activities and planning.
3. The National Defence Committee which advises the Government on defence matters.
4. The Central citizens Committee
5. The Tariff Board
6. The Export Promotion Council
7. The Industrial Development Committee
8. The Industrial Licensing Committee
9. The Company Law Advisory Board
10. The National Sample Survey

The above bodies are composed of experts in the concerned field and tender advice to the Government on matters relating to exports, tariffs, industries and company administration.

Of all the departments of the Union government, the Ministry of Railways is noted for advisory bodies. It has associated itself with several private bodies whom it consults on such matters like operation, commercial goods, fares, amenities to the passengers etc. The General Managers of the Railways consult these bodies before deciding on the major issues. It may be suggested in this connection that the Government should set up more and more advisory bodies at all the Ministries.

Composition of the Advisory Bodies

The next question which attracts our attention is the mode of the composition of the bodies. Writers like K.C. Where, H.J. Laski, and Willoughby have given their views:

1. ***K.C. Wheare expresses the following views:***

    (i) The size of the advisory bodies should be small so that they can discuss matters effectively. The small size help to achieve the desired objects. He suggested that 15 or near about is an effective number.

    (ii) The committees should consists of less eminent people than people of national distinction. The latter will be busy and find no time to attend the meetings.

    (iii) The members should be chosen by interests concerned and the Department concerned; with the former in majority.

2. H.J. Laski is of the view that the members of the advisory bodies must be elected by the various bodies and paid sufficiently. He suggested a term of three years with eligibility for re-election.

3. ***Willoughby offers the following suggestions:***

   (i) The advisory councils should have on them the representative of the officials and interested groups. The term should be fixed without salary. But payment of expenses for attending the meetings.

   (ii) The Committees should meet regularly. The executive officer of the Council should be from the staff. The deliberations of the bodies should be published.

The Need for Advisory Bodies: The Value of associating advisory bodies with public services is great in modern times. The following arguments will bring into light the real need for creating such committees.

(i) Firstly, the association of consulative and advisory bodies in public service is a mark of democracy. Democracy is a government by popular consent. A government must do things according to public opinion. It has to ascertain, from time to time, the wishes of the people and act upon it. The public in democracy are interested in knowledge about major policies of the government. They must be assured of the competence and efficiency with which the work of the administration is performed. The ideal of democracy can be secured through the advisory bodies consisting of the representatives of the interest. Sir Aruthur Salter remarked: "The proper use of advisory bodies is the right answer of representative democracy to the challenging of corporate states. It is thus essential that the committees composed of fully equipped persons with necessary talent should be associated with administration. Millet observes: Consultation with interest groups achieve epitome of democratic participation when administrative action depends on actual

referendum among the effected group. Between 1938 and 1941, 26 referendums were conducted by the US Department of Agriculture.

2. Secondly, association of consultative and advisory bodies with the public service helps to secure welfare state. Modern state is a welfare state. Its aim is to secure the general welfare of all through planned economic development. A welfare state should always keep in mind two considerations.

   (i) It should act in conformity with the interests of the public. And (ii) It should work in harmony and co-operation with private bodies whose interest are effected by its policies. Planning requires exercise of wide discretion and judgment. So administration will do better if it keeps in touch with the advisory bodies composed of experts. Such a step not only secures best policies possible but also easy enforcement.

3. Thirdly, the association of consultative and advisory bodies with administration provides a sort of citizenship training to the public. The private interests who participate in discussions on policy matters will receive sound training and adequate opportunity to play a Vital role in policy making. H.J. Laski remarks that discussion between the officials and representative bodies is the life and blood of democratic governance. The only way todo things for people is to make them todo things for themselves. Millet is of the view that association of popular bodies with service avoids violent and revolutionary acts in society.

4. Fourthly, advisory councils render a valuable service by acting as an aid to the executive and legislature. Ministers who are laymen may require expert

knowledge to deal with the technical issues. This expert knowledge and advice is provided by the advisory bodies. The preparation of budget also receives aid from the advisory councils.

The above discussion leads us to a conclusion that association of advisory bodies is an asset to public administration. At the same time we must point out that the functions of the councils must be wholly advisory. The committees should be composed of men of sincerity, integrity and honesty.

CHAPTER—7

Personnel Administration

NEED FOR SOUND PERSONNEL POLICY

The work of the government is very vast. The head of the state alone cannot do all the work the government single-handed. So the government of the modern state maintains a vast administrative machinery consisting of a number of officials of different grades. They are called civil servants or public personnel or public servants. They constitute an essential and integral part of the present day public administration.

It is the duty of the government to devise various ways and means of securing the efficient functioning of the civil servants. For this purpose, the government lays down statutory policy governing the personnel administration. This policy is called the personnel policy. A sound personnel policy is an essential requisite of a sound public administration.

ESSENTIALS OF SOUND PERSONNEL POLICY OR PERSONNEL ADMINISTRATION

The success of any personnel administration depends upon certain factors. Theses factors. are: (1) good recruitment system (2) fair conditions of service, (3) sound training (4) good conduct of the public servants, (5) good discipline of the employees (6) good system of promotions and retirement and (7) the nature of the rights of the servants. A critical discussion of each factor is essential.

1. ***Good Recruitment System.*** The first essential factor of a sound personnel policy is good recruitment system. Recruitment is a big problem of personnel administration, which has to be solved satisfactory. There are two methods of requirement, viz, recruitment by promotion and direct recruitment. Under the second system the candidates are chosen by direct selection and appointed to the posts. In the interest of a sound personnel management it is not desirable to adopt any single method. A good system of recruitment should combine the two principles. In U.S.A., UK, and India certain percentage of officials are appointed by direct recruitment and others by promotion. Then comes the question of selection. In the interest of a sound personnel administration the selection of the candidates should be on the basis of merit. In other words the selection of the candidates for employment in the public service should be made taking into consideration their qualifications, ability suitability, character and conduct. In order to test the merit various methods are adopted such as examination, interview, performance test, physical test etc. However no one of these methods is exclusively good and sufficient. Hence depending upon the nature of the job to be filled in, different methods will have to be adopted. Many reasonable and thoughtful persons are of the view that the selection of the candidates for the public service should be made by independent and impartial civil service commissions.

2. ***Fair Conditions of Service.*** The second essential factor of a sound personnel policy is fair conditions of service. The civil servants cannot function efficiently in the absence of reasonable and fair condition of service. Hence every modern government

lays down certain conditions or rules or regulations governing the service of its personnel (I) The first conditions relates to pay scales. While fixing the pay scales the government should take into account the cost of living prevailing in the state. In India there are two systems of pay scales of the civil servants. (ii) The second condition of service relates to the allowances. In addition to pay the civil servants should be paid allowances such as dearness allowance, house rent allowances, education allowance, medical and travelling allowances, (iii) The third condition of service relates to leave. The civil servants require rest, now and then and so provision must be made to grant leave to them. The leave is of various kinds viz., earned or privilege leave, sick or medical leave, study leave and casual leave. In every state all the public servants are eligible to utilise the leave for taking mental and physical rest. Besides these the government should declare certain days holidays. (iv) The fourth condition of service relates to the hours of work. The total number of hours of work that an employee has to work should be moderate. (v) The fifth condition of service relates to office accommodation. The office should be well-furnished and fully equipped so as to enable the employees to work happily. (vi) The sixth and the most important condition of service is that there should be proper and adequate machinery for redressing the grievances of the employees. If, at any time, the public employees are dissatisfied with the conditions of service, they should be able to bring it to the notice of the government and obtain redress. For this purpose the government should set up necessary machinery of negotiations. The examples are Whiteely Councils in England and staff Councils in India. (vii) The last condition of service is that there should be security of job.

3. ***Sound Training.*** The third essential factor of a sound personnel policy is sound training. A civil servant cannot perform the work of his job efficiently without prior training. A sound training helps the administration to function efficiently. It promotest skill, power, intelligence and aptitudes of the employees. So in the interest of strong personnel administration, the government of the state should make necessary arrangement for training its personnel. A good personnel policy should define the object of training. The objects of training should be to (1) improve skill, (2) inculcate the sense of responsibility and duty and (3) broaden the mental horizon of the public servants. Next arises the question of the type the training. There are two types of training, informal and formal. The former is training by experience and the latter is training by guidance, direction, advice and assistance. The formal training is again is two kinds, viz, pre-entry and post-entry. The former is a training given to the candidates long before he joins the service at school, colleges and universities. The latter is training given to the candidates after he is selected to the post. A good personnel policy should combine both informal and formal training instead of different methods such as instruction, communications, discussions, seminars etc., In England, U.S.A. and India the system of training is built up on sound lines.

4. ***Good Conduct of Public Servants.*** The fourth essential factor or a sound personnel management is the conduct of the public employees. Where the conduct of the civil servants is not high, there the standard of the administration would suffer. So a good personnel Policy is one which defines the rules and regulations governing the conduct of the public employees. The rules should require them to be

obedient, respectful, sincere, not to hold any trade or business, to maintain high moral and ethical standards in life, maintain good professional standards, and refrain from participating in political activities. In India the Central Government formulated a number of rules defining the conduct of its servants.

5. ***Good Discipline of Public Servants.*** The fifth essential factor of a sound personnel management is the discipline of the civil servants. In the absence of discipline, it is not possible to build high conduct on the part of the employees. Hence a sound personnel policy should find out the causes of indiscipline. All indisciplinary actions should be dealt with reasonably. In India the Central Government has formulated necessary rules of the disciplinary action.

6. ***Good System of promotion and Retirement.*** The *sixth* essential factor of a sound personnel management is the good system for promotion and retirement.

CIVIL SERVICE

Meaning, Definition and Characteristics of Civil Service

The work of the modern government is very vast. It can not be performed by the chief of State and Ministers alone. Every department has a lot of administrative and other work to do. All this work cannot be done by the heads of the departments alone. The head of the state, the Ministers and heads of departments are fit to do certain type of work, but not all type of work of the government. F.A. Ogg observes: "These people cannot be expected to collect taxes, audit accounts, inspect factories take census, to say nothing of keeping accounts, delivering mail, and carrying messages". Therefore, in order to perform all these functions the government appoints a large number of officials or servants. They are called civil servants or civil service. It means civil service is a vast body of administrative personnel or government officials, It includes heads of various departments, heads of sub-departments, executive assistants, minor officers, clerks and professional, technical and scientific personnel. The civil service constitutes the most important body of the government of the modern state. While the parliament, the cabinet and president may reign, it is civil service which really govern.

Definition and Characteristics: The true character of civil service is well brought out by Dr. Finer in the book *"The Theory and Practice of Modern Governments"*. He defines: "The Civil service is a professional body of officials, permanent, paid and skilled". From this definition, we can make out the principle characteristics of the civil service.

Firstly, the civil service is a *body of officials* who are employed in the service of the government. All these officials do not fall in one and the same category. There are different grades in the service. At the top of service, there are permanent secretaries, deputy secretaries, under secretaries and assistant secretaries. All these officials occupy the positions of authority and responsibility. Below them, there are divisional and sectional officers. Below them are the assistants and clerks who constitute the bulk of the civil service.

Secondly, the modern civil service is a body of *professional officers.* The officials who join the civil service adopt it as profession or career and carry on that profession till retirement. In other words, the civil service is to-day considered a profession. Baveridge says: "the civil services is a profession". Just as in society one may take the profession of a business-man or a lawyer or a journalist or teacher, so also one may take the profession of a civil servant. "Ancient Athens did not possess a professional civil service on account of its extreme democratic theory that A was as good as B for public services".

Thirdly, the modern civil service is a body of permanent officials. When once they join the service, the officials continue in that service till the age of retirement, provided their behaviour and conduct are good. The cabinets may come and go, but the permanent officials of the civil service don't come and go, with the rise and fall of political parties. They are uneffected by party intrigues. They would serve every government with the same zeal and loyalty, honesty, and faith irrespective of its party level. It means they are non-partisan. Ancient Athens did not possess permanent civil service. Recruitment was made only for one year. Officers were form most part elective.

Fourthly, the modern civil service is a body of paid officials. The officials receive salaries for the services rendered by them to the government. Not only they are paid during the tenure of their office, but also they receive pension after retirement from the service.

Fifthly, the modern civil service is a body of skilled officials. Government in a democracy is ultimately run by the representatives of the people, viz., the ministers. These ministers are amateurs. They are not experts in the administrative work. They have no special qualifications, skill and training. Administration is today a highly technical job which they are not expected to master. The holding of a ministerial appointment is but an accident in the life of a politician. Hence it is necessary under such a set up that the officials of the government should be highly trained body of men. Therefore, the officials of the modern civil service are highly trained and skilled. They specially qualify themselves for the post they hold. They possess special training both in the science and education. They are in touch with the educational problems, experimentation, and administration. The political executive provides the popular element and the civil service supplies the expert content of the art of government. In the words of Jennings: It is the function of the civil service to administer and of the ministers and the cabinet to control administration.

Thus the chief characteristics of the civil service are: (a) a body of officials, (2) professional service, (3) permanent service, (4) paid service and (5) specialized and skilled service.

Recruitment to the Civil Service

1. The next thing that we have to discuss is the question of recruitment and training of the civil servants. In the early stages of its growth, the recruitment to the civil service was based on the patronage. It was on this basis, that the officers of the East India Company were mostly recruited, But in 1853, Macaulay abolished patronage system and introduced the system of recruitment by a competitive examination. He laid particular emphasis on mental alertness and capacity to do work.

2. Today, in many states, the recruitment to the civil service is made by a competitive examination conducted by an independent body known as the 'public service commission'. The body enjoy, security of the office, perfect independence and freedom from fear or favour of the political executive. In some countries the public service commission is appointed by the law of the parliament and in some the constitution itself provides for its creation. The method of recruitment by a competitive examination conducted by an independent body is acclaimed as the most satisfactory method in all corners of the world. It is considered the only means of attracting young men and women into the service.

3. In England, the servants of the Crown are recruited by open competition conducted by an independent body known as the civil service commission. It consists of three members directly appointed by the Crown by an order -in-council. The British system lays special emphasis on the general ability of the candidates to do their work. The test consists of a written examination and a viva voice. Britain has established honest tradition in the system of recruitment to the public service.

4. In India, the recruitment of the civil services under the union is made by the competitive examination conducted by the Union Public Service Commission. The Chairman and the Members of the U.P.S.C. are appointed by the President of India and can be removed by him only on the grounds of proved misbehaviour after the supreme court on enquiry has recommend for their removal for such reason. The rules of recruitment are made by the president in consultation with the U.P.S.C. The Indian system lays emphasis on the general fitness of the candidate for the post.

5. In the USA till the year 1883 the recruitment to the civil service was based on the basis of nomination system. According to this system, the political parties filled the public office with their supporters whenever they come into power. Whenever a new President came into office, he used to cancel all the appointments made by his predecessor belonging to the rival party. This system was introduced by President Jackson in 1828 and it came to an end with the assassination of President Garfield in 1881. This system is popularly known as 'The Spoils System', The Pendleton Act of 1883 abolished this system and introduced a new method of recruitment by the competitive examination. At present, in the USA the

recruitment to the American Civil Service is made by a Federal Service Commission consisting of three members appointed by the President and the Senate. The commission prepares the rules of recruitment. The American system lays special emphasis on the technical fitness of the candidate for the job.

Age and Training: Generally, civil servants are recruited at an early age because of the receptiveness of youth to new ideas. In every country the age limit is prescribed for the recruitment of civil servants. After the selection, the successful candidates are required to undergo necessary training in order to equip themselves to the administrative task. Generally, in every state all the selected candidates are appointed on probation for one or two years. In India candidate selected for Indian Administrative Service is given intensive training before he is appointed to the post. In England during the period of training, the candidates are required to study general subjects, social sciences and law.

Conditions of Service. If the state is to secure the best possible services from it servants, it should maintain adequate conditions of service. The conditions are: Security of service, adequate salary, promotions etc.,

1. The first condition of civil service is that there must be security of tenure. Every servant of the state must be free from the insecurity of the job. At present many states have laid down statutory rules regarding the security of office of the civil servants. For example, the constitution guarantees two important rights on all civil servants in India. They are (1) No member of the civil services can be dismissed or removed by an authority subordinate to that by which he was appointed. (2) No member of the civil services can be dismissed or removed or reduced in rank until he has been given a reasonable opportunity of

showing the cause against the action proposed except in certain cases.

2. The second condition of the civil service is that the members of the civil service should be paid adequate and reasonable salaries. It means that the salaries paid to them should be neither abnormally high nor abnormally low. Before independence, the civil servants in India were paid very high salaries. It may be desirable to revise the salaries of the civil servants from time to time. Recently the Government of India enhanced the salaries of the civil servants on the lines suggested by the pay commission.
3. The third condition of the civil service is that the civil servants should be given reasonable chance of promotion. Now it is every where recognised that the promotion must be on the basis of seniority tempered by factors of efficiency.
4. There are other conditions of service. They are adequate leave facilities, provision for pension, health and insurance facilities, right of association etc., allowances, leave, hours of work, good office accommodation etc.,

Functions of the Civil Services

1. The first function of the civil servants is to carry out the execution of the law of the land entrusted to their care and to implement the policies laid down by the government.
2. The second function of the civil services is to assist the political executive in drawing up the policy of the government. It gives necessary advice and suggestion, puts forward the proposals to the consideration of the political chief.
3. The third function of the civil services is to act as semilegislative and semi-judicial authority. The

officials of the department are empowered to make rules and regulations binding upon their subordinates and the general public. The members of the civil service determine the details of the manner in which the parliamentary statues are to be given effect. There are some departments whose officials perform some judicials functions also. For example the income tax department in India, Inter-State Commerce Commission in the U.S.A. perform such functions.

Duties of Civil Servants: According to Finer the duties of the civil servants are:

1. Conscious discharge of public duties;
2. Sincerity and priority without regard to private advantage;
3. Punctuality;
4. Readiness on the part of civil servants to do additional work;
5. Truthfulness;
6. Respect for superiors,
7. Courtesty to the public;
8. Sensitiveness;
9. Avoidance of any other job except that which is given to him;
10. Observance of official secrecy.

Problems of Civil Service: In recent times certain problems have arisen in regard to the organization and functions of civil service. These problems are mainly three:

1. Growth in number;
2. Growth in powers;
3. Neutrality.

Each problem needs a brief explanation.

1. ***Growth in Number:*** The first problem of modern civil service is its numerical growth. A careful look into the statistics of any country shows the rapid growth of civil service. The rapid growth of civil service presents the problems of control, supervision co-orientation and finance.

2. ***Growth in Power:*** The second problem of modern civil service is its growing powers. The present day state is a welfare state. It has assumed manifold functions. As a result, civil service expanded and its role became increasingly big. To play this increasing role it is becoming necessary to give more and more powers to the civil service. The power of the civil service is to be found not only in administration but also in legislation and finance. The similar development has taken place in India, too, since we have decided to build up a welfare state. "Our civil servant is no longer a mere police and revenue official; he is engaged in a large variety of developmental activities and is involved in implementing thousands of projects in different parts of the country" (Avasthi and Maheswari).

3. ***Neutrality of Civil Service:*** The third problem of modern civil services is its neutrality. The civil servants are expected to be free from political parties and serve loyally whatever party is in power. Public interest demands that they should be neutral in so far as the politics are concerned (1) In England, the civil servants enjoy considerable freedom to participate in political activities. (2) In the USA civil servants are strictly prohibited from participating in political activities. Any violation of the law is punishable with heavy penalty (Viz, suspension and removal). (3) In India the civil service rules prohibit civil servants from

active participation in political activities. He cannot take part in any election or campaign.

RECRUITMENT

Introduction: The business of government cannot be carried on without enough personnel, viz., civil servants. The management of civil service is an extraordinarily difficult task. There are many problems to be solved in regard to the civil service such as, recruitment, training, promotion, salary, discipline, etc., The efficient functioning of the civil service depends upon the extent to which these problems are overcome. L.D. White remarks: "To find and to hold capable men and women and to help create and maintain working conditions under which they can do their best are the great tasks of personnel management". A student of public administration should understand the problems of public personnel, We shall examine the problem of recruitment.

Recruitment is the big problem of personnel administration. It is an important problem also. It is "cornerstone of the whole public personnel structure". (Stahl). The U.S. Commission of Inquiry on Public Service Personnel observes: "No element of career service is more important than the recruitment policy". So it is necessary to learn the different methods of recruitment, merits and defects of each.

Method of Recruitment: There are two methods of recruitment of public personnel. They are: (1) Recruitment by Promotion and (2) Direct Recruitment it is essential to examine each method.

1. **Recruitment by Promotion.** The first method of recruiting the public personnel is by promotion. W.F. Willoughby calls this method "recruitment from within". This method is applied in recruiting the personnel to higher jobs in the government such as

Secretaries, Directors, heads of district administration etc., It is neither possible nor desirable to appoint candidates to these posts by direct recruitment. Hence whenever vacancies arise in the higher jobs, they are filled by promotion. It means that the officials already in service are promoted and appointed to the posts. In other words, recruitment is made from among the personnel already in public service.

(i) **Merits.** The recruitment by prcmotion has few merits and defects. The merits of this method are: (1) It brings into service the men of rich experience, training, ability and responsibility: The success of any administration depends upon these quantities. Promotion secures the best possible incumbents for the higher positions, while maintaining the morale of the whole organization.

2. **It is an incentive to efficient working.** The officials in service work actively and loyally when they come to know that there are chances of their promotion to higher jobs.
3. **This method reduces the cost of training**. Since the officials have enough training already, there is no need to give them any fresh training.
4. It improve the quality of the administration.

(ii) **Defects:** However, the method of promotion has few defects. They are:

1. It is undemocratic. Democracy is based on the principle of equal opportunity. So it is necessary to give opportunity to all the persons within and without.
2. It fails to secure fresh talent, vigour, ability and competency,
3. It makes public service unattractive.

4. It does not seek the administration attuned to the changing socio economic conditions of country.

2. Direct Recruitment: The second method of recruitment of the public personnel is by direct selection. W.F. Willoughby calls this method 'recruitment from without'. This method is, usually, applied to recruit the personnel to lower jobs in the government such as superintendents, deputy collectors, section heads etc. Whenever vacancies arise in lower positions, candidates are directly recruited to fill the posts. It means that recruitment is made from among the persons outside the public service.

   (i) ***Merits:*** Direct recruitment has few merits and defects. The merits of this system are:

1. It is democratic. Democracy is based on the principle of equal opportunity. So this method gives equal opportunity to all persons to serve the government.
2. It secures fresh talent, vigour, ability and competence.
3. It makes public service attractive,
4. It keeps the administration attuned to changing ideas and outlook of society and prevents it from the exclusive preserve of old and conservative people. Due to all direct recruitment is considered good.

   (ii) **Defects:** However, direct recruitment has few defects too. They are: (1) It brings into service the men who lack rich experience, training ability and responsibility. It leads to the administrative inefficiency. It may harm the morale of the whole of the administration.

2. It kills incentive on the part of the officials already in service. They do not work actively and loyally when they come to know that there are no chances of their promotion to the higher jobs.

3. The direct recruitment involves much expenditure on training of the personnel. The fresh recruits require a lot of training in administrative work.
4. The quality of the administration may suffer due to the fact it is difficult to assess the abilities and personal traits of the applicants. Due to all these, direct recruitment is considered not good.

A good system of recruitment should combine the two principles. For example in countries like Britain, the USA and India recruitment of public personnel is based on two principles. Certain percentage of officials are appointed by direct recruitment (e.g. Britain 80%) and others by promotion.

Methods of selections: The direct recruitment of Public personnel is made through selection. Different systems of selection have been adopted in different countries at different times. They are (1) Sale of office, (2) patronage system (3) spoils system and (4) merit system. The first two system are discarded at present. The spoils system was in existence in the USA till recently, but is given up at present. The merit is a recent one and adopted in many countries today.

1. ***Spoils systems:*** In the USA till 1883 the recruitment to the civil service was based on nomination. The political parties filled up the public offices with their supporters whenever they came into power. Whenever a new President came into office, he used to cancel all the appointments made by his predecessor belonging to the rival party. This system was introduced by President Jockson in 1828 and it is came to an end with the assassination of President Garfiled in 1881. This system was popularly known as the spoils system. The Pendleton Act of 1883 abolished this system and introduced a new method of recruitment by competitive examination.

2. ***Selection by Merit (or Merit system):*** The selection of the candidates for public service on the basis of merit is universally acclaimed as the best system. It is adopted in almost all the advanced countries of the world. In the USA the merit system was launched by George Washington. But it fell on evil days from 1828 to 1881 during which the appointment were governed by spoils system only to about 14000 posts. By 1954, 90% of the posts were filled up by the merit system. In England and India the merit system was introduced in 1854 and 1855 respectively.

Method of Testing Merit: The merit system gives rise to another question, viz., what are the methods of testing the merits? The answer for this question is that different methods are adopted for testing real merit of the candidates. They are (1) Examination, (2) interview, (3) Performance test (4) experience and physical test. Therefore it is necessary for us to understand each of them.

1. ***Examination:*** The first method of testing the merit of a candidate is examination. Any qualified person may come forward and appear for the examination. The examination is conducted in various subjects forming the part of University curricula. Macaulay was the strong supporter of holding examination in the above manner. This method is followed in India. In some countries examination is conducted in those subjects which are closely related to the job to the filled up. The examples are France and USA. The answer written at the examination may be long or short. The duration of the examination may be long or short. In the USA for the great mass of examinations, short answer questions are the standard practice. The written examination has intrinsic merits of its own. It is democratic, fair and equitable. It is flexible.

2. ***Interview:*** The second method of testing merit of candidate is interview. If the written examination tests the knowledge, the interview tests the presence of mind of the candidate. Some times selection to the public service is made simply by oral test conducted by a selection committee. Sometimes interview is conducted as a part of the written examination. Sometimes interview is conducted prior to the written examination. The critics argue that the interview does not reveal the real worth and true personality of the candidate. "It has been said the God takes a whole life time to judge a man's worth while interviews have to do it in a quarter of an hour". Gorwala observes: "A fifteen minutes conversation with laymen, although possessing wide experience of public service commissioners, can be no substitute for an expert psychological examination....". However, the interview test cannot be totally discarded as it has its own inherent merits.

3. ***Performance Test:*** The third method of testing the merit of candidate is performance test. The test is mainly conducted for selecting the candidates for skilled jobs like electricians, typists etc., The candidates will be selected on the basis of the performance shown at the examination.

4. ***Physical Test:*** A candidate chosen for the job must be physically fit. Hence a candidate will have to undergo a medical test before joining the service.

No one method described above is exclusively good and sufficient. The suitability of particular method depends upon the nature of job. For higher administrative jobs, the written examination combined with an interview is well suited. This should be supplemented by a certificate of character and conduct given by responsible person.

Selection by service Commission: The selection of candidates for public services by an independent and impartial service commission is of most modern. Today, in many states, the competitive examination are conducted by public service commissions. This body enjoy security of office, perfect independence and frees dome from fear or favour of political executive. In some countries the public service commission is appointed by the law of the parliament and in some the constitution itself provides for its creation. This system is acclaimed the most satisfactory in all corners of the world.

In England, servants of the crown are recruited by open competition conducted by civil service commission established in 1835. It consists of 3 members called commissioners directly appointed by the crown by an order in council. The British system lays special emphasis on the general ability of the candidates to do their work. The test consists of a written examination and a viva voice. Britain has established honest traditions in the system of recruitment to the public service.

In India, the recruitment to the civil services under the union is made by the competitive examination conducted by the Union Public Service Commission (UPSC). The Chairman and Members of the UPSC are appointed by the President of India and cannot be removed except by procedure. The commission is assisted by a Secretary. The Indian system emphasises on the general fitness of the candidates.

In the USA the recruitment to the American Civil Service is made by the Federal Service Commission consisting of three members appointed by the President and the Senate. The Commission prepares the rules of recruitment. The commission is assisted by an Executive Director. The American system lays special emphasis on the technical fitness of the candidate for the job.

Similar commissions prevail in other countries also.

Qualifications: The candidates for recruitment to the public service should possess certain qualifications. They are two kinds of qualification. (1) General and (2) Special. Under general qualifications may be included citizenship, domicile or residence and age. Under special qualifications may be included educational qualifications, experience and other personal qualifications such as executive ability, tact, resourcefulness, integrity, energy, faithfulness, and capacity to get along with others.

PUBLIC SERVICE COMMISSION IN INDIA

Original and Growth PSC in India

There was no public service commission in India until 1919. The first civil service commission was up in India by Montague-Chelmsford Reforms of 1919. It performed only limited functions. The act of 1935 set up separate provincial Service Commissions for each province. After Independence the constitution of India created public service Commission both for the union and the states. The public service commission for the union is called the union Public service commission.

The Union Public Service Commission (UPSC): The provisions relating to the UPSC are mentioned in Chapter II of chapter XIV of the constitution.

1. Art. 315 provides for the establishment of the Union public service commission. It serves the needs of the Union Government. It may also serve the needs of any state if requested so to do by the Governor.

2. The UPSC has a chairman and other members. They are appointed by the President. At least one-half of the members must have held office for at least ten years either under the Union or state Government. The term of office of a member is six or until he attains age of 65 year whichever is earlier. No member is eligible for re-appointment to that office on the expiration of the term(316).

3. The chairman and members of the UPSC enjoy security of office. They cannot be removed except as provided for in the constitution. The procedure for removal is governed by Art 317. According to this, the chairman or member of the UPSC can be removed in one of the two ways:

   (i) Firstly, they can be removed on the ground of misbehaviour by the President after the Supreme Court on inquiry reported that they ought to be removed on such ground. The Supreme Court makes inquiry only on reference being made to it by the President. Any concern or interest on the part of the Chairman or members in any contract or agreement made by the Government or participate in any profit or benefit or emoluments arising from such contracts amounts to guilty of misbehaviour. The member in respect of whom a reference is made to the Supreme Court may be suspended from office by the President until he has passed orders on receipt of the report of the Supreme Court.

   (ii) Secondly, the chairman or member of the UPSC can be removed by the President if he,

1. is adjudged an insolvent or
2. engages in any paid employment ;or
3. is infirm of mind or body.

In this case no reference need to made to Supreme Court.

4. The number of members of the UPSC ans their conditions of service are determined by the President.

The condition of service shall not be varied to member's disadvantage after appointment (Art 318).

5. The Chairman of the UPSC is not eligible for further employment either under central or State Government after he ceases to hold office. A member of the UPSC is not eligible for employment either under the Union or State after he ceases office except as the Chairman of the UPSC or the Chairman of a State PSC (Art 319).
6. All the expenses of the UPSC including salaries, allowances and pensions payable to the members or staff are charged from the consolidated Fund of India. (Art. 322).

Functions of the UPSC: The functions of UPSC are as follows (Art 320,321 and 323).

1. The UPSC conducts the examinations for appointments to the services of the Union Government. It assists the states on their request, in recruitment for services where special qualifications for candidates are required.
2. The UPSC advises the Union Government on these: (i) on matters relating to recruitment (ii) principles relating to appointments, promotions, transfers from one service to another, (iii) disability matters and (iv) matters relating to claims, suits etc.,
3. The UPSC present annual reports to the President. Report contains a brief sketch of the work done by the commission and recommendation if any for introducing reforms. A copy the report shall be laid before each House of the Parliament. In case were an advice of the commission is not accepted by the President, the reasons for not accepting the advice should be enclosed to the report.
4. The functions of the UPSC can be enlarged by an act of the Parliament (Art. 321).

Role of the UPSC. The UPSC has been playing a commenable role ever since its inception. It has been performing its functions in an able manner. Every year it is conducting competitive, examinations for several categories of services. It has been rendering valuable advises to the Union on all matters pertaining to appointments, promotions, transfers and discipline. Its annual reports have been acclaimed as valuable. It was fortunate to have a galaxy of eminent men as chairman and members.

State Public Service Commission

1. The constitution provides for a Public Service Commission for each state in India. It is known after the name of the State. The State of Andhra Pradesh also has Public Service Commission (APPSC). The constitution makes provision for setting up a Joint Public Service Commission for two or more states provided a resolution for creating such a commission is passed by the Legislatures of those States (Art. 315).

2. A state Public—Service Commission has a Chairman and other members. They are appointed by the Governor of the State. At least ½ of the members must have held office for atleast ten year either under the Union or State Government. The terms of office, of the member is six years or until he attains the age of 62 years which ever is earlier. A member of a State Public Service Commission can resign his office by writing under his hand and addressed to the Governor of the state. No member is eligible for reappointment to that office on the expiration of the term (Art 316). The Andhra Pradesh State Public Service Commission has a Chairman and other members. They are appointed by the Governor of Andhra Pradesh for a term of years or until they

attain the age of 62 years whichever is earlier. The other provisions mentioned above are the same.

3. The members of a State Public Service Commission enjoy security of office. They cannot be removed except as provided in the constitution. The procedure for removal is governed by Art. 317. According, to this, the Chairman or a member of a State P. can be removed in one of the two ways.

   (i) Firstly, they can be removed on the ground of misbehaviour by the President after the Supreme Court on inquiry that they ought to be removed on such ground. The Supreme court makes inquiry only on reference being made to it by the President. Any concern or interest on the part of the Chairman or member any contract or agreement made by the government or participated in any profit or benefit or emolument's arising from such contracts amounts to guilty of misbehaviour. The member in respect of whom a reference is made to the Supreme court may be suspended from office by the State Government until the president passed orders on receipt of the report of the Supreme court.

   (ii) Secondly, the chairman or member of a State PSC can be removed by the president if he.

1. is adjudged an insolvent; or
2. engages in any paid employment; or
3. is infirm of mind or body.

In this case no reference need be made to the Supreme Court.

4. The number of members of State PSC and their conditions of service are determined by the State

Governor. The conditions of service shall not be varied to a member's disadvantage after his appointment (Art. 318).

5. The chairman of a State PSC is not eligible for any other employment under the union or State after he ceases to hold office except as the Chairman or member of the UPSC or as the chairman of any other State PSC. A member of a state PSC is not eligible for any other except as the chairman or a member of the UPSC or as the Chairman of that or any other State PSC (Art. 319).
6. All the expenses of a State PSC including the salaries. Allowances and pensions payable to the members or staff charged from the consolidated Fund of the State (Art. 322).

Functions of a State PSC (Art 320, 321, 323)

1. A State PSC conducts the examinations for appointments to the services of the State Government. In all the States, the PSC conducts examinations every year for appointments to different services of the State.
2. A state PSC advises the State government on these (1) matters relating to recruitment, (ii) principles relating to appointments, transfers from one service to another, (iii) disciplinary and (iv) other matters.
3. A State PSC presents annual reports to the State governor. The report contains a brief sketch of the work done by commission and recommendations if any for introducing reforms. Copy of the report shall be laid before each House of the State legislature. In case where on advice of the Commission is not accepted by the Governor, the reasons for not accepting the advice should be enclosed to the report.

4. The functions of State PSC can be enlarged by the Act of State Legislature (Art. 321).

Significance of the PSC in India Administration

The Public Service Commissions have great significance in the administration of the Country.

1. They help in selecting highly qualified and best fitted candidates for appointment to the public services. The candidates are selected purely on the basis of merit and fitness. There is no scope for any influence to creep into the selections as the commissions are independent bodies. The Public Service Commissions in India are created and governed by the constitution. They enjoy full security of office. They are free from control or influence of any authority. Hence they are in a position to conduct competitive examinations and make selections.

2. The Public Service Commissions promote efficiency in administration of the country. It is possible because they supply to the government the best stuff available in the country. They advise the Union and State Governments in matters of promotions, transfers and discipline of the public servants. In usual course, the recommendations of the PSC are accepted by the Government. As the recommendation of the commission are free from influences, they promote administrative efficiency. The officials also perform their duties effectively since their interest are taken care of by the commissions.

3. As the public Service Commissions are meant for the job of recruitment, the members can concentrate their attention, conduct research, find out new ways of testing merit etc. The annual reports of the commissions have been very valuable.

TRAINING

Meaning and Importance: A person who wants to do a thing or things, cannot do successfully unless he is very well aware of the methods of doing that thing or things. If he has no knowledge about them, he goes to some one who knows about them and requests him to explain the ways and means of doing that thing or things. So also, a person, before taking upon him a job in government service, requires some guidance or instruction as it how he should do the work attached to the job. This guidance or instruction is called training in the vocabulary of Public Administration. So training may be defined as "conscious effort made to improve or increase an employee's skill, powers, or intelligence and to develop his attitudes and scheme of values in the desired direction". (Dr. M.P. Sharma). M.M. Mandell defines: "Training is the conscious effort on the part of management to give assistance and direction to the employees in learning their jobs and their actual development". With the help of this definition, we can formulate the following characteristics of training:

1. Training is an effort on the part of a public servant to acquaint himself with methods, procedure and rules governing the work he is expected to do.

2. The object of the training is to promote the skill and intelligence of the public employee to tackle any administrative problem which may arise in course of his job.

3. Training helps him to develop the attitude and understand the value of the job in which he is placed.

The importance of training in public service is very great. It helps the administration to function efficiently. It prepares the civil servants to handle the task entrusted to him. It promotes skill, power, intelligence and aptitudes of the employees. These qualities are necessary for the over—all efficient operation of the public services. A century ago, no great value was attached to the training of public servants. It was confined entirely to the military, naval and educational services. But since the beginning of the present century, the importance of training has come to be realised every where. In the year 1944 the Assheton Committee (England) said that "the Civil service need to be more consciously directed towards still higher ideals and standards of service and this can only be done by planned and purposeful training". In the year 1948 the General Assembly of the UN recognising the need for training to the public servants resolved "that an international centre for training in Public Administration shall be established under the direction of the United Nations. The present day administration is complex and ever growing. Hence to man such administration, it is necessary to give enough training to the employees. "The historical belief that the duties of public officers are simple and may be readily understood by any man of good intelligence is long out of date" (L.D. White).

Object of Training

Training is an essential requirement of good administration. Having understood the meaning and importance of training, next arises the question, viz, what are the objects (or ideals) with which public servants are trained? In order to answer this question, it is necessary for us to enumerate the various objects of public training in the following lines:

1. The first object of training is to improve the skill of the public employees so as to enable them to perform their duties satisfactorily and efficiently. An employee who has no training cannot acquire this skill and understand clearly the nature of the work entrusted to him. So a good training is one which is directed towards the improvement of the skill and intelligence

of the individuals who are actually at work. "Such training is a recognizable investment in longtime service. The specific object in view is performance" (L.D. White). Training helps the civil servant to acquire precision and clarity in the transaction of business'. Hence training is an essential requisite of good public administration.

2. The second object of training is to inculcate the sense of responsibility in the public employee. Without the feeling of responsibility, a public employee is not fit to undertake the job in public service. Every job is attached with certain duties the performance of which demands responsibility of some kind on the part of the employee. Responsibility not only leads to the administrative efficiency but also inculcates in the public employee "the right attitude towards the public and towards the business". L.D. White observes: "Training to improve performance may be special or general, but the immediate objective is definable in terms of present and future responsibility". The Assheton Committee (Britain, 1944) observed: "Training must be directed not only to enabling an individual to perform his current work more efficiently, but also to fitting him for other duties and, where appropriate developing his capacity for higher work and greater responsibility" Hence training is an essential requisite of good public administration.

3. The third objective of the training is to improve the morale of the public employees. It builds the right attitude on their part towards his duties. The prestige of the administration is largely dependent on the moral of its personnel. It builds integrity and sincerity in him without which he cannot perform his duties honestly. These high qualities can be secured only by means of good training. "Training, of course, is only one factor in the building up of the morale but it is

a very important factor' (Dr. M.P. Sharma). Hence "training plans, to be successful, must pay substantial regard to staff morale" (The Assheton Committee). Training stimulates right mental attitudes to questions of personnel and public conduct (Avasthi and Maheswari). Hence it is an essential requisite.

4. The fourth object of training is to help the public employee to adjust himself to the changing goals and techniques of administration. A civil servant should always be ready to handle the tasks in a changing world. He must be community conscious. He must be, in other words, flexible. "The civil service must continuously and boldly adjust its outlook and its methods to the new needs of new times (The Asshetom Committee). This is possible only by means of good training. Hence training is an essential requisite of good administration.

5. The last object of training is to broaden the mental horizon of the public servant. A public employee should have broader out look and respect to the general public. He should think that he is an integral part of the general public. He has necessarily to understand the basic principle that he is a public servant and not a master. The Assheton committee reported: "The inculcation of the right attitude towards the public and towards business should, therefore, be one of the principal aims of civil service training". As Avasthi and Maheswari put it: "Training fosters homogeneity of outlook and espirit de crops in the employees". Hence training is an essential requisite of good administration.

It can be concluded by means of the above discussion that in the interests of the general efficiency of the public service, a good and prospective training for civil servants is an essential minimum necessity. So all the modern states provide enough training to their employee either before or after joining the service. This practice is to be found in India also.

Types of Training: Having understood the meaning, importance and objects of training, next comes the question, viz., how many types of training are there? Broadly speaking, training is of two kinds: (i) informal training and (ii) formal training. Formal training is again divisible into pre-entry training and post entry training. A proper understanding of each type is necessary.

(i) ***Informal Training:*** It is otherwise called training by experience. This is, when a civil servant learns the work of his job by gradual experience without being guided by anybody, it is called informal training. It is training by trail and error. Under this system, a candidate is directly put into the job with minimum advice and is required to carry on the work of job. And he gradually acquires skill by doing the work and learning from mistakes. The various means by which an employee acquires informal training are: contacts with the superior officers, conferences, meetings, news papers, publications etc., These help the public servant "to imbibe the art of administration by actually practicing it as well by seeing how it is practiced". The informal training "has been the traditional method of training in public administration and still holds the field to a large extent" (Dr. M.P. Sharma). As Avasthi and Maheswari observes: "The ultimate success of informal training, however, depends upon the experience and seniority of the superior officer, and his interest in the new entrant".

(ii) ***Formal Training:*** It is other wise called training by guidance, direction, advice and

assistance. That is, when a civil servant learns the work of his job with the help and under, the guidance of some one, it is called formal training. Under this system a candidate is given some training, first, and then put into the job. This training may be given to the candidate either prior to his appointment or after. Where the training is given prior to the appointment, it is known by the name "pre-entry training". On the other hand where the training is given after the appointment, it is called post-entry training." Thus formal training is further divisible into two categories. Each is explained in the following lines:

Pre-entry Training: L.D. White describes it "pre-entry education". Pre-entry training is a training given to the individual long before he joins the government service. This training is provided to him even while he is a student studying at the High School, the College and the University. It is given to him along with or as a part of his regular course of education. The U.S.A. is famous for pre-entry training scheme. In this country, pre-entry training is provided into two ways: Internship and apprenticeship (1) under the system of Internship intensive training for public service is given to few selected men (chosen from all the varsities in the country) at the National Institute of Public Affairs, Washington. This method not only had acquired a wide-popularity but also had 'thrown quite a good number of outstanding young persons into the public service' in the U.S.A. This system is in practice in countries like India, Britain, Palestine, Philippines etc., (2) Under the system of apprenticeship, the candidate is placed under the guidance of an experienced officer. The former learns the work with the help of the latter. This type of training is provided in the USA at the Newyork Bureau of Municipal Research (1906).

In imparting the pre-entry training, the professional schools, the graduate schools, and arts colleges play an outstanding role. The professional schools like law, medicine, engineering etc., offer instructions which are useful for the students to undertake public service. The graduate schools offer training and provide adequate knowledge about the techniques of public administration. The arts colleges provide instruction in humanities such as political science, public administration, economics, statistics etc., which give the students insight into political frame work within which public work is conducted. The pre-entry training is, however, surrounded by few problems.

(ii) Post- entry Training: Post-entry training is a training given to the individual after he joins the service. After entering into the service, the department gives him necessary training in the methods, procedure etc., of the work of his job. Necessary arrangement for giving training will be made within the department itself. Sometimes, the government may conduct training centres or schools or institutions in which new recruits are given necessary training. Such training institutions are being run in all the advanced countries of today. The examples are the Administrative Staff College at Henley in England, the Administrative staffcollege at Hyderabad (India). These institutions which are equipped with experienced staff give training to the new entrants in different administrative practices. They also cultivate administrative skills and talents in the trainees so as to enable them to do full justice to their jobs.

The post-entry training may be long or short. Under the former the period of training of the recruits is larger.

Under the latter the period of training of the recruits is comparatively shorter. The short term training is usually given in times of emergency. The post-entry training may be provided in the specialised branches like teaching, legal, criminal etc., It is called the skill training. At times the instruction may be provided to explain the historical background of social, administrative, and political problems and remedies adopted to solve them. It is called back ground training. Now and then the officials who have been in service are deputed for fresh training in order to provide them further training. It is called orientation (or vestible) training. There are two major objectives of this training:

1. to enable them to secure the better performance of present work
2. To equip them for higher positions. The Government selects the officers and sends them to training institutes to undergo refresher courses at his expenses. In India all these training's are being provided.

Methods of Training

The training for the public personnel is provided by different methods. Each method requires a brief explanation.

1. ***Training by Experience:*** The first method by which training is given to the public servants is experience. According to this the new recruits are required to get training by gradual experience. They are put in such a job which will give them at glance the nature of the whole departmental work. Having worked in that for some time, they will be transferred at frequent intervals to various branches so as to enable them to learn the work of these branches. The department may arrange for visits and tours to semi-government bodies and corporations.

2. ***Training by Instruction:*** The second method by which training is given to the public servants is instruction. The senior officers in the department will deliver series of lectures, and arrange group discussions by which the new entrants are provided with the knowledge about the work they have to do. This method corresponds to the tutorial system. It is widely followed in England. "This is helpful although it may convey only a superficial impression" (L.D. White).

3. ***Training by Communication:*** By this method, the information regarding the nature of work is printed in the book or pamphlets which are circulated among the new recruits. On going through them, the candidates will be able to acquire a birds's eye view of the departmental organization. The rules and regulations governing the service, salary, promotions and retirement are printed in separate booklets and distributed among the new recruits by which they come to know the true picture of their job. Sometimes, the departments (in England and USA) provide well equiped libraries to impart education in the employees.

4. ***Training by Conference:*** According to this, periodical meetings of the whole departmental staff are convened by the head of the department. At these meetings, he will address them on the general problems of the department and their remedies. He may invite the opinions of the participants. This method is highly popular in the USA.

Illustrations. Before we close the whole discussion it is essential to understand the nature and methods of training of the public servants in Britain, USA and India.

1. ***Britain.*** In Britain the public servants are given informal training. They believe in acquiring training by actual deeds to 'trail and error'. Until 1944

informal training was the only type of training prevalent in the country. In this year the government appointed Assheton Committee under the Chairmanship of Ralph Assheton to examine and make necessary suggestions for the improvement of the training of civil servants. The Committee submitted its report to the Government in which it had recommended the creation of a separate division for the training the public personnel. Accordingly, a Division of Training and Education' was opened in the Treasury. Its function is to conduct training courses for the fresh recruits. Each department has a training courses for the fresh recruits. The Government has started the Administrative Staff College at Henley for the purpose of providing instruction in the course of public administration. Besides all these, in Britain, training is imparted by various methods such as lectures, seminars, conferences etc.,

2. ***The USA.*** Until 1906, in the USA the training for the public service was entirely confined to the military services. In the year the Newyork Bureau of Municipal Research was established with a view to provide training for public servants. By 1954 the training opportunities were provided throughout the country. In the USA facilities are available for imparting pre-entry as well post-entry training. In providing pre-entry schools, the graduate schools and the liberal arts colleges play an outstanding role. At these institutions regular training courses are taught along with the education. The post-entry training is provided by means of tutorial system, inspection trips etc., The federal government has opened various institutions to train the public personal. The important of them is the Graduate School of the US Department of Agriculture. The US Civil Service Commission operates a junior executive training

course for the departmental service. The duration of the training is two weeks. The training of field agencies is undertaken by the Newyork branch of the U.S. C.S.C. The course runs for six months. In some states the departments of civil service have their own training divisions. Separate training institutions are being run to train the police, industrial and other personnel.

3. ***India.*** Prior to independence, the public servants were given only informal training. However, special training was given to the recruits for Indian Civil Service. Since independence emphasis has been laid upon the training of public servants. In India there is hardly any pre-entry training scheme in existence. The schools, colleges, or universities do not provide instruction in public service. However, the Indian Institute of Public Administration and some Universities are doing good service in the field of pre-entry training. Hence the only method available is post-entry training. However, informal training is the system followed in case of lower categories. Systematic training is being imparted to the candidates selected for Indian Administrative Service. For this purpose the central government is running a National Academy of Administration at Mussorie. Inservice training is also given to them after training. Separate training institutes are functioning throughout the country to train the personnel of different service. The examples are: Central Secretariat Training School, New Delhi, Railway Staff College, Barod; Administrative Staff College, Hyderabad; National Academy of Administration at Mussorie etc. All these are doing notable service in training our public personnel.

The whole discussion will help to understand the importance as well as the hardships involved in the problem of training.

Nature and Methods of Training of Public Personnel in India

Training in Pre-Independent India: The importance of training in public administration is very great. The training of public personnel helps the administration to function efficiently. It prepares the civil servants to handle the tasks entrusted to them with ability. It promotes skill, power, intelligence and aptitudes of the employees. Prior to independence, the public servants in India were given only informal training. The British rulers simply appointed the young men to the job and left them free to learn the work by experience. In fact, there was no much necessity for higher training of the public personnel because the functions of the government were very limited. However, systematic training was given to all candidate recruited for the All India Services. For example an young man recruited for Indian Civil Service (ICS), was required to undergo an intensive training for a period ranging 1 to 2 years. After that he was required to take two departmental examinations on passing which he was appointed to the job. Separate arrangements were made for training the police officials at central training schools.

Training in Post-independent India. It is only after independence that the better and greater emphasis came to be laid on the training of the public employees in India. All the agencies of the government came to realise the great need to improve the training methods in the country. In fact the importance of providing training to the public personnel has become great since 1950 due to the "adoption of the policy of planned development of the country to realise the ideal of a welfare state". The Planning Commission, too, observed: "Next to recruitment, the training of personnel has considerable bearing on administrative efficiency. Each type of work in the government requires a programme of training suited to it".

The training given to the public servants in India, to-day, is both informal and formal. Informal training is given mostly for the class III and Class IV employees. They are directly put in the job and left free to pick up the necessary training in the course of their work. On the other hand, the employees of higher services and All India Services are given formal training. Fornal training is of two varieties, viz, pre-entry training and post-entry training. The former is the training given to the public servants before they join the service. The latter is the training given to the public servants after they are chosen to the service. In India there is hardly any pre-entry training scheme. The schools, colleges and universities have no provision for offering instruction in public service. However, an experiment was made in this regard in the Universities of Allahabad and Nagpur under the guidance of Dr. M.P. Sharma. The Indian Institute of Public Administration is doing good service in providing liberal education and promoting research in public administration. It is providing instruction in the course which help the students to understand the process of making public policy as well as techniques of its implementation.

It, therefore, follows from the above that most of the training given to the public employees in India is post-entry training. This is more so in the case of All India Services. Hence it is necessary for us to understand the nature of training given to the recruits for All India Services.

Training for All India Service: A well-organized training is being provided to all the candidates selected for recruitment to the All India Service. However, the training provided for all the categories of All India services is no uniform. Hence, it is necessary for us to understand the nature of training provided to each service.

1. ***Training for the I.A.S:*** The candidates selected for recruitment to the Indian Administrative Service are given one year's training at the National Academy of administration at Mussorie. The Academy offers

instruction in such subjects like law, constitution, etc., The I.A.S. probationers take part in short courses, seminars, conferences etc., The also undergo military and police training for about two weeks. They visit a number of places of historical and cultural interest with a view to broaden their mind. At the end of the year the recruits will have to pass an examination conducted by the UPSC. After wards, they are given practical training for a period ranging 10 to 20 months in different branches of the administration. Having successfully undergone all this training, the IAS recruit is appointed to the job. After putting in service of six years, he is placed in charge of a district.

2. ***Training for Other All India Service:*** (i) Firstly, the candidates recruited for the Indian Police Service, are given first five months intensive training at the National Academy of Administration of Mussorie and then at Central Police Training College, Mount Abu. The study and training include "criminal law and procedure, criminology physical training, riding, shooting etc. (2) Secondly, the candidates recruited for Indian Foreign Service are given first, five months training at the National Academy of Administration and then some practical training (3) Thirdly, the candidates recruited for Indian Audit and Accounts are given training at the Departmental Training School at Simla in subjects such as according, audit, financial regulations and codes etc., At the end, they write a department Examination and receive practical or job training. (4) Fourthly, the candidates recruited for Income-tax Service are provided with a training at Training School, Nagpur, (5) Fifthly, the railway staff has its training college at Baroda which provides -3 months training for the new recruits and refresher courses for the serving officers. (6) Sixthly, the candidates recruited for Central Secretariat Service, undergo five months training at the National

Academy of Administration. The recruits for lower grade receive training at the Central Secretariat School, New Delhi. They are trained in O and M, procedure, rules and regulations. At the end they are put on job training.

3. **Orientation Training:** Training is necessary not only the new entrants into the various services,·but also for those who have been already in service. The officers in charge of responsible positions require some kind of orientation or refresher training at brief intervals. As they undergo more and more training, they prepare themselves for still higher responsibilities. It is with this view that the central government has started two staff colleges. One at Hyderabad and the other at Mussorie.

    1. The Administrative staff College, Hyderabad provides training for the "experienced executives of proved administrative capacity" with a view to equip them to take up still higher responsibilities".

    2. The Central Institute of Study and Research in Community Development, Mussoire provides training and orientation training to the high ranking officials such as Secretaries, Deputy Secretaries, Commissioners, District Collectors, Planning and Development officials etc. With a view to stimulate thinking and exchange thought and experiences.

Training Institution in India: In order to provide system atic and purposeful training, it is essential to establish training centres or institutions. Therefore, the Government of India, soon after independence, brought into existence a number of institutions and training schools to provide training to its employees. We shall study briefly the organization and purpose of these institutions:

1. ***The national Academy of Administration, Mussorie:*** The Academy came into existence in 1959,

as a result of the amalgamation of the IAS Training School at Delhi (1947) and IAS Staff College at Simla (1957). It provides training for all the recruits to the All India Services and Central Services. The period of training is five months. The training includes various courses such as constitutional, economic, social and administrative problems, as well as the ethics of profession. The methods of training include seminars, conferences etc. The Academy also provides refresher courses of senior officers.

2. ***The central Police Training College, Mount Abu:*** It came into existence in 1948. It consists of a Commandant and other staff. The college provides training for the recruits to the Indian Police Service. The training course includes criminal law and procedure, criminology, drill, handling of weapons, riding, shooting etc.

3. ***The Railway Staff College, Baroda*:** The school provides training for the recruits to the railway service. The period of training is 3¼ months. It also provides refresher courses of the officers of the railway service.

4. ***The Central Secretariat Training School, New Delhi:*** It came into existence in 1948. The school is incharge of a Director. The staff includes a number of instructions. The school provides training for the officials of the lower grades such as section officers, assistance and lower division clerks etc. The course includes O and M, office procedure, financial rules, regulations. etc.

5. ***Administrative Staff College, Hyderabad:*** It came into existence in 1957. It provides orientation training to the experience officers of the government. The special feature of the college is that it provides training to the officers serving in private industries: and commerce. The training includes these course of study (i) Planning (ii) Labour problems (iii)

Constitution and its workings (iv) Management (v) Accounts (vi) Information. The large part of training is given in the form of group discussions for which purpose the trainees are grouped into a number of syndicates. At these discussions they discuss the problems, duties, relations, objective etc., of the administration.

6. ***The Central institute of Study and Research in Community Development:*** The CISRCD came into existence in 1958. It provides orientation training in the fields of research, and community development to the high ranking public officers such as Secretaries, Directors, Commissioners, Collectors etc.,

7. ***The Indian Institution of Public Administration (IIPA):*** It is the institution in India which provides pre-entry training to men and women. It offers instruction in various subjects of public administration. It also conducts short term course leading to the Diploma in Public Administration. The staff of the school is drawn from high officers of the government such as Deputy Secretaries, Under Secretaries and senior officials. The students pay visits to Central Government Offices frequently.

Thus with the help of the above discussion, we may conclude by saying that training of public personnel in India is making rapid strides. However, the present system of training excludes a vast body of clerical employees and state officials. Hence the Central Government should take necessary steps to overcome these short comings.

PROMOTION

After an employee is selected and placed, adequate training has undoubtedly to be provided so that he is ready for future higher position. In fact, an employee seeks to build his career within the organization, and at the same time, a personnel system cannot remain efficient without providing ample opportunities and career openings within the establishment, accompanied by the assurance that experience, merit and devotion to duty will bring them the necessary reward in due course. All this necessitates to develop a system of promotion. A well developed promotion policy is very essential for a sound personnel system and for the efficiency in an organization.

Meaning

The word promotion means 'the act of rising further' or rising to upper grade. For an employee it means a rise in level with change in his duties and responsibilities. It can be defined as an upward advancement of an employee in an organization to another job, which commands better pay/wages, better status/prestige and higher opportunities/ challenges, responsibilities and authority, facilities and a higher rank." According to Scott and Clothier, "A promotion is the transfer of a employee to a job which pays more money or one that carries some preferred status. However, as we will see later, this definition is incomplete and does not explain a number of aspects of promotion.

Prof. L.D. White has given an elaborated definition. He defines promotion as "an appointment from a given position to a position of higher grade, involving change of duties to a more difficult type of work and greater responsibility, accompanied by change of title and usually an increase in pay." Promotion should not be confused with the annul increase of salary. Every employee starts on a basic salary and gets an annual increment, till he reaches maximum of his pay scale. This increment or advancement is different from promotion and it is generally automatic. Similarly, the promotion differs from transfer. Although transfer also brings about a change in the conditions of service and it may also lead to a change in duties and responsibilities. Transfer simply means a change of service from one place to another without any change in rank or emoluments. But promotion brings about a basic change in position and status of an employee.

Thus, promotion means progress from a lower to a higher class leading to a change in duties and responsibilities, with or without transfer from one agency to another and with or without a rise in immediate salary. Promotion generally leads to enhancement of grade but may not lead to any immediate monetary benefit.

Promotion may be looked at from two points of view. From the point of view of employee, it is an advancement from a lower grade or class of the service to a higher one carrying a larger salary and higher duties and responsibilities, while from the point of view of the employing authority it means filling up the higher posts by the selection of the most suitable persons within the service.

Importance of Promotions

The system of promotion is of great significance to the sound personnel system. A well developed promotion policy is very essential for the efficiency of the employees. Promotion is a continuous incentive to efficient working on the part of the employees. The hope of promotion is sufficient to keep the man interested in the job. Willoughby regards the promotion system as of a vital significance from two stand points, the securing of the most competent employees to fill several positions and the provision of that continuing incentive to good work for the personnel without which no system can be efficient.

To pin-point the merits of promotion system the following points can be raised:

1. Promotion serves as the most important incentive for the employees. In the words of Arthur W. Proctor, "Promotion is of direct significance to the management,

in as much as the regards given to employees and the incentive held out to them react in important way on practically all of the phases of employment administration. The actual promotion given to employees tends to create a contended, stable and efficient personnel."

2. It keeps the personnel efficient and thus leads to overall efficiency in the administration.

3. Promotion system ensures rewards for efficient employees. The expectation of the promotion as a reward for honest and intelligent employees heightens their morale.

4. The experience gained by the employees in the lower jobs helps them in undertaking jobs entailing higher responsibilities.

5. It provides, ample opportunities for advancement to the employees and thus attracts qualified and capable persons to join the service.

6. From the point of view of the employer, a promotion policy is very advantageous. He fills the higher and responsible posts from the experienced and capable persons who are already in service. Thus the employer makes full use of the experience of his employees. Watkins and others mention that purposes of promotion are:

   (i) To furnish an effective incentive for initiative, enterprise and ambition.

   (ii) To conserve proved skill, training and ability.

   (iii) To reduce discontent and unrest;

   (iv) To attract suitable competent workers; and

   (v) To suggest logical training for advancement.

However, a promotion system is advantageous only if it is properly planned system. L.D. White says that a badly planned promotion system harms an organization not merely by pushing ahead unqualified persons but also by undermining the morale of the whole group. In the absence of proper promotion, ambitious, intelligent and capable persons do not stick to the job. There are great many resignations of the competent persons leading to inefficiency and demoralization in the organization. In such circumstances the high standard of individual and group efficiency is difficult to maintain.

Essentials of Proper Promotion System: If a promotion system should be proper or a planned one, then what are the features of a proper promotion system. Prof. Willoughby has pointed out certain essential features of proper promotion system, which are:

1. The adoption of standard specifications setting for the duties and the qualifications required of incumbents of all positions embraced with the government service.
2. The classification of these positions into distinct services corresponding to their several character, and the arrangement of the position in each of such service into a hierarchy of position corresponding to their relative importance.
3. The inclusion within this classification of all the higher administrative positions except those having a political character.
4. The adoption of the principle that, as circumstances will permit superior positions will be filled by promotion from lower positions in the service to by transfer from other services; that is, of the principles which has been designated by the term recruitment from within.
5. The adoption of the principal that merit alone shall determine the selection of employees for promotion.
6. The provision of adequate means for determining the relative merits of employees eligible for advancement.

7. Eligibility for promotion should be based on (i) personnel qualifications, and (ii) Service status.
8. Factors that go to determine selection among those eligible for promotion are (i) Seniority or length of service (ii) Service rating or efficiency records (iii) Competitive examinations and (iv) Personal judgement of the appointing officer.
9. There is a difference between promotion and an increase in compensation when an increase in compensation is made without making any change in the position occupied by an employee or the nature of his work, the increase in salary or the increment, but promotion means that an employee is transferred from a lower to a higher position.

A sound personnel policy is very essential in order to achieve the objectives of promotion. The policy must contain all the essential of a sound promotion system as noted above. A well developed promotion policy, therefore needs to fulfil the following requirements.

First requirement of a sound promotion policy is that it must provide for a uniform distribution of promotional opportunities throughout the organization. This means that the ratio of internal promotions to external recruitment must be the same at various levels in all departments. If this ratio differs greatly from one department to another, morale of employees may be seriously imparted in the department notorious for its low ratio of promotions.

Second requirement of a sound promotion policy is that it must ensure consideration of all eligible in service candidates and not of the few highly visible ones only. This means that the promotion system should be open and not closed so that the candidacy for a job remains open for all individuals with in the company.

Third requirement of a sound promotion policy is that there should be some definite system for the selection of employees who are to be promoted from within the promotion zone. This of course, calls for the choice of promotion criteria. In the absence of a contract to the contrary the employer has the right to establish any criteria for evaluating promotability if they are reasonable, pertinent to the job and are not applied in a discriminatory manner. The two criteria often used for making promotion decisions are merit and seniority, which are discussed later on. In any case, the demonstrated ability to perform a given job provides no assurance of the potential to perform at a higher level or in a different type of a job. The "Peter principle" certainly is relevant in this context. This principle enunciated by L. J. Pater in his light-hearted book, characterizes the common practice of promotion people of their level of incompetence". The confirmation of the principle is demonstrated by many examples of individuals who have been promoted from time to time because of their satisfactory performance in their past positions and who then are promoted to position exceeding their level of ability-in other words, to positions matching their level of incompetence". The moral of this is that in considering individuals for promotion one needs to assess future potential, although this assessment may take into account demonstrated past performance in areas relevant to the positions for which they are being considered.

Fourth, requirement of a sound promotion policy is that all promotions should be finally sanctioned by the concerned line heads. The personnel department may propose the names of potential candidates and send their history records to the department making the requisition to fill vacancies. In this way, the staff position of the personnel department does not intrude upon the authority of the department served. In addition, subordinates are impressed favourably by their line superior's concern for their progress.

Finally, a sound promotion policy must provide for a suitable system of follow up, counselling and review. Say, a month or two after the change the personnel department should hold a brief interview with the promoted employee and his new superior to determine whether all is going on well. All promotions should be made for a trial period so that if the promoted employee is not found capable of handling the job he can be reverted to his former post and his former pay scale.

Factors affecting a Promotion Policy: The above discussed points are essential for a sound promotion policy but there are always some limiting factors affecting the implementation of such a policy. In fact a promotional policy depends upon the nature of the organization and is conditioned by its internal as well as external environment. Such factors may be playing different role in the public and private organizations. These may be Trade Unionism, job openings within the organization, job opportunities in open market, legal framework, social and economic conditions, political factors, fairness in administration, nature of higher responsibilities and so on. In the organizations, requiring more dynamism and change, the promotion is generally discouraged and hiring from outside is preferred. In government organizations most of the higher posts are filled from within.

Principles of Promotion: A number of principles of promotion have been suggested by various authorities, for instance, the broad principles laid down in 1921 by the Whitely committee on Promotion in Britain are: the first principle enunciated by the committee was the head of the department must have responsibility for making promotions in his department whatever machinery may be adopted for this purpose. Secondly, the consideration ruling all promotions should be the advancement of the efficiency of the public service which can best be secured by determining promotions on the ground of fitness. This principle, the committee said, should be invariably adopted in case of promotions where greater responsibilities and initiative are required; where the work is of a routine, character seniority should be given greater weight. In most of countries today, the two basic principles followed are; principle of seniority and principle of merit. Both these principles have their advantages as well as disadvantages. In government as well in private organization the problem as to what should be the basis of promotion seniority or merit. The policy makers or the management tries to adopt the criteria which helps to keeping the morale and efficiency in the organization. Griffith says, "While the paramount consideration must be the interests of the service, no staff it likely to be efficient unless, it has a measure of confidence in the general fairness of the methods of promotion".

1. ***Seniority Basis:*** Seniority or the length of service of the employee is the first and the most common basis of promotion. It is the traditional and generally accepted criterion for promotion of the employees. According to this the employee who has the longest service to his credit is entitled to the promotion. Determination of seniority is not always an easy task. More than one employees may claim their seniority on different basis. Conflict may arise when different employees working on different positions but of the equal rank claim their seniority. Or when a person getting more salary than the person having more total experience. To avoid such conflicts or confusions rules are prevalent in every public service.

Merits of Seniority Principle: According to Dr. Finer, "It is automatic, and avoids the needs for making invidious distinctions between one person and another of placing the young, over the old, of measuring the responsibility for the result of the promotion, In particular the following merits can be pointed out:

1. It is a fair system and generally acceptable one.
2. It is also acceptable because it provides everybody an opportunity for promotion in turn.

3. Senior man is more experienced. Hence more experience ordinarily should be enough qualification for promotion.
4. Outside pressures and the impartiality can be avoided if this system of promotion is adopted.
5. It keeps the morale of the employees boosted and they are sure of promotion at their turn.
6. Better people may be attracted to the jobs when there is certainty of promotion.
7. It is an automatic system of promotion and saves the time and energy of the authorities to chose the persons for promotion.
8. Finally the old employees stand for this system in particular as they have not to be lorded over by the youngers.

This system is considered to be fool—proof and provides against favouritism and intervention of politicians in the career of the employees. Every body knows whose turn it is and, therefore all are reconciled to it.

Demerits of Seniority Principle: The seniority principle of promotion also suffers from certain defects. First and foremost defect of this system is that there is no guarantee of the fact that a senior man will be more competent. Another major defect of this system is that if seniority alone is the basis of promotion, employees do not make any effort for self-improvement.

E.N. Gladden says that the principle of seniority is based on the following wrong assumptions:

(a) It assumes that all members of the grade are fit for promotion.

(b) It assumes that seniority list is arranged in an order more or less confident with the age of staff,

so that all in due turn shall obtain an opportunity to serve in a higher post (Seniority list shall give opportunity to all. It does not happen).

(c) It assumes that the percentage of higher posts of lower ones is high, so every one shall get a chance.

(d) It assumes that vacancies are arising in a reasonable flow.

In practice, the occurrence of such ideal conditions is extremely improbable. All members of a grade are not for promotion; promotions are usually few and far between and abnormal rather than a normal process; while changes in personnel are most likely to be subject to irregular fluctuations.

Arguing against the seniority principle, Statil writes: Too often the highly touted twenty years of experience, before which all those within hearing are expected to bow down, is merely one year of experience multiplied twenty times staying power is not by itself a virture unless it has been accompanied by progress and growth. Similarly, Pfiffner is of the opinion that "A system of promotion by seniority will frequently result in raising to supervisory and directing positions the persons who have crank complexes. Frequently advancing years, mellowed by the give the take of competitive life, acquire an intolerance in nonessential which dampers the initiatives of subordinates. Seniority alone will tend to fill the higher places with incompetent persons. It will discourage the ambitious and remove those incentives which develop personality, courage, self-reliance and progressive outlook. It will foster self—satisfaction, a dead level of mediocre performance, and that general let down which goes with security.

It is generally observed that less competent persons who cannot compete with the young and the meritorious, are the greatest supporters of the seniority system. For the old and the senior, this system is equitable and undisturbing but for the organization as a whole it is dangerous, because the senior may not be efficient and intelligent. If one has the fortune of coming to the world earlier than the others, it does not mean that he has brought merit and intellect also. As the promotion mean more duties and responsibilities and these cannot be entrusted to a man who is merely a senior and nothing else.

Merit Basis: As against the principle of seniority there is principle of merit which stresses the system of making promotions on the basis of merit or capabilities of the employees. It is self-evident that the most meritorious or best qualified persons should be selected for promotion otherwise they will feel frustrated and will not be motivated for excelling in work. In particular the principle of merit has the following advantages for the organization:

(i) It recognizes and rewards the meritorious work, extra competence, achievement and initiative.

(ii) It generates greater motivation and encourages the employees to work hard so that they may get an opportunity for advancement in the organization and do not have to wait merely for their turn for promotion.

(iii) Competent employees are likely to be retained instead of being lost to the organization.

(iv) It leads to increased productivity, for individuals are satisfied that their merit and competence will be properly appreciated and rewarded.

A number of commissions and committees appointed by the government of a number of progressive countries have emphasized the adoption of merit principle as the basis of promotion in the public service. For instance, the Northcote- Trevelyan in their report of 1853 emphasised the same in the following words..... The public service should be carried on by the admission into its lower ranks of a carefully selected body of young men, who should be employed from the first upon work suited to their capacities and their education, and should be made constantly to feel that their promotion and future prospects depend entirely on the industry and ability with which they discharge their duties, that with average abilities and reasonable application they may look forward confidently to a certain provision for their lives, that with superior powers they may rationally hope to attain to the highest prizes in the service, while if they prove decided incompetent, or incurably indolent, they must expect to be removed from it. "Similarly, the Ridley Commission (1886-90) in its report dealing with lower division clerks stated: We think that routine promotion by seniority is the great evil of the service, and that it is indispensable to proceed through every branch of a strictly on the principle of promotion by merit, that is to say, by selecting always the fittest man, instead of considering claims in order of seniority, and rejecting only the unit.

It is since the Northcote-Trevelyan Report that merit principle is being followed in U.K. in the United States too, on the basis of certain Commission in civil service that the merit system is followed. There, the system of efficiency rating is followed doing with other techniques to determine the merit of the individuals.

Although the principle of merit is advocated widely for making promotions, it poses a number of problems. Making promotions on the basis of merit may create a feeling of jealously among the employees who have more experience. Moreover, determining the merit of an employee is much more complex than of his seniority.

The present day government organization are too large and complex that no officer can be supposed to remember about the efficiency of individual employees working under him. This is not possible also on account of the fact that the officers are frequently transferred. Therefore, it is desirable to keep some written record of the performance of the individual employees. These records are called personal records. These are supposed to give a complete picture of the conduct and efficiency of the employee.

Apart from service records or efficiency records other methods of testing the merit are examinations and personal judgement of appointing officer or of a special promotion board. In the examination system it may an open competition for all categories of employees or for restricted persons. An examination may also take the form of qualifying examination followed by an interview. On the other hand, promotion may also be made on the basis of relying upon the one who is in closest contact with employees and having the best position to learn their administrative and personal capacities and who also best knows the needs of the post or posts to be filled. The importance of the personal judgement of an officer depends upon the following factors:

(a) the capacity to make good judgement;

(b) the freedom of action employed by him; and

(c) his good intentions.

The above three methods, i.e., service records, examinations and judgement of appointing authority have their respective advantages and disadvantages. As mentioned earlier, in the large organizations of today, it is not possible for the head of the department to be in direct contact with all the employees in his department. Secondly, the subjective elements may creep in. The head of the department may favour or disfavour an employee on personal and other extraneous considerations. So to check these defects it is suggested that the system of personal judgement should be discouraged and the merit rating should be done by an independent board.

The examination method may eliminate favouritism, corruption and arbitary promotions. It is argued that this method is quite objective and relieves the promotion making authorities of the troublesome responsibility of making selections. However, it also suffers from certain defects. Firstly, it is considered to be an interference with the ordinary official work of the candidates and is thus detrimental to public interest. Secondly, examination is not a sure test of the personality of an employee. An intellectually superior person may not be a man of initiative, tact and judgement which cannot be judged by written examination. Moreover, memorizing the details or learning new things is generally not possible for older employees. Thus due to these defects, examination method is generally avoided to determine the merit of the employees.

Efficiency Rating: As state earlier, in the United states, promotions are made on the basis of well designed efficiency rating system. Americans have made efficiency rating a very detailed affair. The major categories of efficiency rating are: (i) Production records; (ii) graphic rating scale; (iii) substantiating-evidence reports; (iv) personality inventory or analytical check lists.

On the basis of production records rating of the individual efficiency is made. The system is simple but its application is limited to the repetitive and mechanical work like typing, stenography, machine operating, etc., that is where the work can be quantitatively measured. Sometimes, it is applied to some other measurements also such as punctuality or attendance of the employees. Under the graphic rating scale system (also called trait-rating) sixteen qualities are judged under five grades such as:

excellent, very good, fair, poor and very poor. The elements of graphic rating are: (1) knowledge of the branch and the department, (2) power of taking responsibility (3) judgement, (4) personality and force of character, (5) initiative (6) execution of work, (7) organizing ability (8) leadership qualities (9) neatness and orderliness of work (10) accuracy (11) co-operativeness readiness to give new ideas, (12) official conduct (13) success in improving and developing employees, (14) speed, (15) zeel, and (16) dependability. The third category, i.e. substantiating evidence reports, proceeds on the assumption that all the employees are satisfactory, and only a small percentage fall into very poorly rated or excellent classes. If such very poor or very good is awarded to any employee, a description of the reasons for such a grade is required to be recorded.

Finally, there is a system of personality inventory or analytical check lists. It seeks a comparative record of service by different means, or at least with a markedly different emphasis on some common means. It was devised by J.B. Probst in 1927. The main features of the system are: (a) It is very comprehensive list of human qualities relevant to employment, (b) The rating officers are able to pick up ten to twenty five items from the list about a particular employee, (c) In spite of the fact that the list is very descriptive or comprehensive special forms have also been devised for different types of employees. The Probst forms lists about a hundred positive and negative traits or qualities such as, quick, active, lazy, slow, indifferent, industrious outspokesn, good team worker, cooperative, pleasant, crank, offers good judgement, etc., The rating officers merely check the presence or absence of these traits in an employee, and finally, the lists of rating officers is compared and compiled.

The Hoover Commission of America found that the efficiency rating system was too complicated and recommended to stop its use for determining merit of the employees. The commission recommended the use of ability and service record in place of efficiency rating, but it again is subjective. The US Civil Service Commission in 1938 issued orders to the individual departments to hold competitive promotion tests and procedures. The commission fixes only general standards, leaving to the departments the problem of working out the details within the broad limits prescribed.

In England, on the other hand 'annual reports' play important role in determining the merit of the individuals. Annual reports are examined carefully by the Promotion Boards which exist in each department. The Board may also interview the candidates recommended for promotion. Along with merit, seniority is also given some weightage. Consultation is also made with the staff representatives to the Whitley Councils.

Promotion System in India

In India no criteria of promotion is adopted uniformly and not all the posts are filled by promoting officials from lower posts. But almost all the highest costs are filled up through promotion. In certain cases a percentage is fixed for the posts to be filled up through promotion while other posts are filled up by direct recruitment. Promotions are made by the departmental heads but our constitution provides for the Public Service Commission to be consulted "on the principles to be followed... in making promotions from one service to another and on the suitability of candidates for such....promotions." As far as the principle is concerned by and large, seniority—cum—merit is the governing principle of promotion in India.

The promotion between direct recruitment and promotion differs from service to service. With regard to highest administrative posts, like Secretary, Joint Secretary, Deputy Secretary and members of the Central

Board of revenues, the pool system is followed. under this system a Selection Committee, appointed by the Government in consultation with the Public Service Commission, interviews eligible employees from all over the country. It also examines their officials records and then draws up a list of eligible official for the posts.

In Government of India, the criteria followed, for the promotion to All India Services as under:

(i) All eligible officers in the consideration Zone (a minimum number of years of service in the feeder cadre is to be fixed as a condition precedent for eligibility and consideration zone is to be determined by multiplying the number of vacancies by three) are Categorised on the basis of their overall service record into the following categories:

(a) Outstanding, *(b)* Very Good

(c) Good *(d)* Satisfactory, *(e)* Unfit.

In each category the candidate will be arranged in order of seniority in the feeder service.

(ii) First the officers from the first category seniority-wise are taken to fill up existing vacancies. If there are more vacancies to be filled after exhausting all the officers from the first category, then candidates will be promoted from the second category and so on upto fourth category.

(iii) The seniority of the officers selected for promotion will also be fixed in the order given in (ii) above.

In the Union Government, each ministry set up a departmental promotion committee for considering promotions to superior posts in the Ministry. The departmental promotion committee consists of a Member of the Union Public Service Commission as Chairman and senior officers of the Ministry or Department who generally have personal knowledge of the work of the officers out of whom the selection is to be made. The committees arrive at their decisions on the basis of the confidential annual reports (ACRs) and other service records of the officers concerned; they are rarely, if ever interviewed. The officers considered for promotion include not only the officers who are recommended by the head of the department but also those who are likely to be superseded. The recommendations of the departmental promotion committees accompanied by the confidential annual reports and service records of the officers concerned, are then forwarded to the UPSC for its approval.

As regards the UPSCs approval of the recommendations of the committee, there are two types of cases: those which have to be compulsorily referred to the commission; and those which may or may not be referred to it. In all cases which are to be compulsorily referred to it, the mere fact that a Member of the Commission presided over the departmental promotion committee, does not carry the commissions sanction to those cases. So they have to be officially referred to the commission. In other cases, i.e. second category, recommendations made by the departmental committee on which the commission is represented are treated as recommendations of the committee. Generally, the commission's advice is accepted, other wise the commission is requested to further elaborate its stand point and review its decision. If it is ultimately rejected, the commission records it in its Annual Report and the Government is under a constitutional obligation to submit the Commission's Report to Parliament with a Memorandum thereon, justifying its action in the matter.

The posts which are to be filled through promotion, may broadly be divided into two categories: (i) selection posts promotions to which are made on the basis of merit-cum-seniority; and (ii) non selection posts promotions to which are made on the basis of seniority subject to the rejection of the unfit. In the second category, each individual officer has to attain a minimum standard of efficiency in order to be promoted to the higher grade. Before 1959 such promotions were not necessarily decided by the D.P.C. but only by the head of the office department. In case of the first category., i.e., the selection posts, promotions are made not merely on the basis of his service record but also on the basis the future responsibility—attached with the job, taking into consideration the capabilities of the individual, Normally, no sharp line of demarcation exists as far as the qualifications of the candidates are concerned.

The percentage of posts filled through promotion in Class II is over sixty percent which are filled through Class III posts. However, promotion from Class IV to Class III is not usual except in the Department of Railways and Post and Telegraphs. For promotion in the middle level posts, the Ministry concerned sends the commission a list of officers proposed for promotion with their confidential reports.

At the state level, the pattern of promotion making is similar to that of Union Government in most of the states. At the state level too a majority of states follow the seniority-cum-merit principle. Promotion to gazetted posts are made in consulation with the Public Service Commission; In the rest of the posts promotions are made by the head of the concerned department. In most of the states there are departmental promotion committees constituted on the central government pattern. However, in some states such committees are not presided over by a member of the state public service commission. It is a common practice to prepare waiting lists of the candidates selected for promotion in order of preference or merit. Public Service Commissions advise is then sought on the list, but the commissions act only on the basis of confidential reports and other information provided by the government. The waiting lists are prepared for future vacancies too instead of taking decision every time a vacancy arises. It has advantage of avoiding any ground for the imputation that the person who was head of the department at the moment of the vacancy assisting endeavoured to show favour to any particular individual."

In Punjab, the service rules provide that all the promotions should be made on the basis of merit principle and "no person shall be entitled to claim as of right to promotion to such post on the basis of seniority". However, the seniority principle is followed in most of the cases and the government instructions also reveal that seniority principle is preferred more than the merit principle. For instance, as per a notification of 2.7.1989, the Punjab Government has decided to promote PCS officers as Deputy Secretaries after eight years of service and as Joint Secretaries after 18 years of service. This has been done with a view to raise their morale and meet the long-standing demand of the PCS officers, and because, as an official spokesman expressed. "Punjab today requires unstinted co-operation and dedicated service of all Civil Services."

The Indian Promotion System is criticised on the grounds of unfairness, partiality, imporper maintenance of personal records, lack of wide publicity about the occurrence of vacancies, arbitrations and absence of sound system of appeals. However, in certain respects, the Indian system of Promotion is good.

DISCIPLINE

(A) General

1. The principal task of any good government is to maintain an efficient administration. The success or

failure in this regard, to a greater extent depends upon the conduct of the employees of the government. In order to secure the high standards of conduct, the government of the modern state lays down rules of conduct. Every public servant is required to follow these rules and act accordingly. Any official or officials-who violate these rules should be punished: so also any official who neglects his duties, cultivates undesirable practices etc. is liable for punishment. This action, viz., "punishment meted out to government employees for lapse of duty or violation of the rules of conduct" is called discipline. Discipline provides the starting point for constructive moral action (S. Sayara).

2. L.D. White in his notable book "Public Administration" discusses the problem of discipline in a remarkable way. In his opinion the causes for disciplinary action are six: (i) inattention of duty' (ii) inefficiency (iii) insubordination, (iv) intoxication, (v) immorality and (vi) lack of integration.

3. The learned author says, further, that the discipline is of two types (i) informal discipline and (ii) Formal discipline under the former (i.e. informal discipline). the punishment given to the employees is very mild or light. The examples are: (1) reassignment to less desirable work; (ii) loss of privileges (iii) curtailment of authority; (iv) diminishing his responsibility etc. Under the latter (i.e. formal discipline), the punishment given to the employees is very severe. The examples are: (i) warning, reprimand, delay in salary, increment, or loss of seniority rights; (ii) suspension, demotion, removal and criminal prosecution. The difference between the informal and formal types of discipline is that in the case of the latter, the employee is given the right of appeal. These appeals can lie either with the administrative tribunal or judicial court.

4. The disciplinary action can be taken by the Head of the Department. In certain cases, the disciplinary action is taken by the government on the advice of the Public Service Commission. However, this system is opposed by some.

5. All the disciplinary actions are taken in accordance with the prescribed proceduce. The usual procedure includes: (1) explanation by the employee; (2) framing of charges, (3) suspension, (4) giving opportunity to the accused to defend himself, (5) report, (6) punishment and (7) appeal.

Reference to India. Having agreed on the necessity of taking suitable disciplinary action against the erring officials, it is necessary to find out the position in India in this regard. The procedure governing the dismissal, removal or reduction in rank of persons employed in the civil services of the Union or a State is laid down by Art. 311 of the constitution. It is as follows:

Art. 311 (1) No person who is a member of a civil service, of the Union or an All-India service or a civil service of a State shall be dismissed or removal by an authority subordinate to that by which he was appointed.

2. No such person as aforesaid shall be dismissed or removed or reduced in rank until be has been given a reasonable opportunity of showing cause against the action proposed to be taken in regard to him.

1. The Central Government has formulated necessary rules governing the disciplinary action. The Indian civil service rules prescribe seven forms of formal disciplinary action. They are: (i) Censure, (ii) With holding of increments or promotion, (iii) reduction in rank or grade or scale, (iv) Recovery of loss (if any), (v) suspension, (vi) removal and (vii) disqualifying from future employment.

2. Regarding the authority to take disciplinary action there are two methods. (i) In the case of All India Services, the informal or mild action can be taken by the President of India. (ii) In the case of other services the informal and formal disciplinary actions can be taken by the government (or Head of the Department).

3. The Indian Civil Service Rules prescribed the following procedure for taking disciplinary action against the employees (i) An explanation as to why the proposed action should not be taken against an official should be called for (ii) If the explanation is not satisfactory, charges should be framed on an official. (iii) He should be suspended forthwith if his remaining in the service is prejudicial to secure evidence. (iv) He should, then, be given opportunity to defend his case either in person or writing. (v) There should be conducted an inquiry into the charges and a report with the findings of inquiry should be made (vi) Another opportunity should be given to an official to defend his case (vii) The punishment is to be decided and communicated to an official if the Government satisfy that the charges are true. (viii) The permission to appeal should be given to an employee.

4. The Indian Civil Service Rules give the right of appeal to a public employee. The procedure regarding the appeals is as follows: (i) All appeals must be permitted by the authority deciding the disciplinary action. (ii) An appeal should not be defective in form. (iii) An appeal should be preferred within six months after the order is communicated (iv) An appeal should be made to the proper authority.

MORALE

Meaning of Morale. It is essential that public administration should be efficient. In order that it should be efficient, several conditions should be present. One of the conditions is Morale. Morale means "self confidence" or "strong will power to do something or desire to do one's duty. In other words, morale in public administration means that atmosphere where public servants are enabled to perform their duties whole heartedly and with self-confidence. It is a sort of mental quality that the employees possess. That administration is efficient, where the employees are fully confident of performing their duties effectively with self-discipline. L.D. While defines: It is a state of mind in which men and women voluntarily seek to develop and apply their full powers to the task upon which they are engaged. This definition brings out the qualities of morale.

1. It is a state of mind. It is a mental quality. It is self-confidence, a strong belief, a will-power that is necessary for all the employees. It is not a quality to be seen but only understood and felt. It is something felt by an employee that he is confident of doing or performing or carrying on the duties entrusted to him.
2. It is developed voluntarily both by men and women. The employees should build up morale so that they can apply their full powers to the task upon which they are engaged.

Factors of Morale. Morale in public administration is possible only under certain conditions. The following are the factors which are essential for building up sound morale.

1. Sound conditions of service
2. Good promotion system
3. Incentives to employees
4. Team work and fairness of treatment
5. Personal knowledge and unity of purpose on the part of the employees.

A brief explanation of each factor may be given below:

1. ***Sound Conditions of Service.*** In order to build up morale in the public employees, there should be present sound conditions of service. Where the conditions of service are unsatisfactory or bad, the employees do not like to work well. They cannot develop in themselves the qualities of mind which are necessary for efficient working. Firstly, the public service should carry good emoluments. The pay scales should be high carrying decent allowances. After all, a public servant or an employee of public or private service is a human being who works to his best ability when he is fed well and materially happy. The other conditions of service necessary for building strong morale are provision for leave (casual; privilege, medical and study); holidays, convenient hours of working, healthy office accommodation and adequate machinery for redressing the grievances of the employees. Above all these factors; one factor that is essential for building morale is security of office. An employee can be expected to build self-confidence only when he is free from insecurity of job. If he is afraid of the future security of job, he cannot have mental peace a condition essential for morale. Hence, the government of modern state should lay down rules governing the service of the public personnel.

2. ***Good Promotion System:*** In order to build morale in the public employees, there should be a good system of promotions. After all, every human being desires to get an elevation in life, so also an employee. If an employee feels that his long experience, ability to work, and merit would be rewarded in the form of promotion, he does his duties satisfactorily. A good system of promotion instills self confidence in the employees and make them apply their full powers to the task upon which they are

engaged". Mere seniority or mere merit is considered not good. A system of promotion which combines these two is desirable. Promotion based on favouritism, nepotism, partnership, and suspicion not only brings down morale and also kills efficiency in public services. A justifiable and rapid promotion builds morale.

3. ***Incentives to Employees:*** Some writers suggested that there should be strong incentives to employees in order to build morale. S. Sayare divides incentives into economic incentives and non-economic incentives. The former (ie., economic) includes rise in the pay and other monetary awards. The latter (i.e. Non-economic) includes security of job, prestige, provision of comforts (eg. housing schemes) etc. It is true that incentives help to put in hard work. Additional work done by or entrusted to the employees awards. Cash payments for extra work done would certainly produce good results. It makes them work more and shoulder new burdens willingly and voluntarily. Good incentives force the employees to apply fully their mind to the task upon which they are engaged.

4. ***Team work and Fairness of treatment:*** Among the employees of an office or organization, there should be spirit of team work in order to build morale. They must have unity and co-operation among themselves. The whole organisation should work as a unit. Another important factor that is necessary to morale is fairness of treatment. The higher officials should treat their subordinates fairly, affectionately and humanly. They should take their employees, into confidence encourage them. The higher officials by their hard work and sincerity should set an example to their lower officials. They should give lead and necessary protection to the employees.

It is then that the employees have confidence in the integrity of their superiors. III-treatment, teasing, discouragement, comments but no appreciation on the part of the superiors would bring down morale, self-confidence and mental peace of the employees. The result is inefficiency in administration.

5. Personal knowledge and unity of purpose on the part of the employees is required to build morale. An employee can perform his job eminently only when he possesses the full knowledge of his job. This condition is necessary in all services. A teacher who has no knowledge of his subject cannot teach with self-confidence. A doctor, an engineer or a mechanic cannot perform duties with confidence if they lack the knowledge of the work which they have to do. So also, a public employee, higher or lower, cannot carry on the job confidently if he has no complete knowledge of the task upon which he engages. He has to understand the purpose behind the job he holds. It is this factor that is lacking in the present day administration.

Conclusion: There may be other factors necessary for building morale, but the above are principal. Morale is an essential condition of public administration. It makes administration efficient. It helps to achieve the purpose of administration S. Sayare observes: Morale is both an index of a sound employment situation and a positive means of building an efficient organization. Morale is the very essence of successful administration.

SERVICE CONDITIONS WITH A SPECIAL REFERENCE TO INDIA

Every government lays down certain conditions (or rules and regulations) governing the service of its personnel. So it is necessary to examine the various conditions of public service.

1. ***Allowances:*** The modern public servant not only gets salary but also allowances permissible in the pay scale. These allowances are of various types.

(i) Firstly, there is dearness allowance paid to the employees to meet the rising cost of living. In India every pay scale carries fixed percentage of D.A.

(ii) Secondly there is housing or house rent allowance (HRA). The government may provide free residence or pay certain amount to meet the house rent. In India this allowance is paid to the employees serving usually in big cities like Hyderabad, Madras, Bombay etc. where the house rents are enormously high.

(iii) Thirdly, there is children's education allowance. It is granted only to select and low-paid employees. In India the sons and daughters of class III and IV employees are exempted from tuition fees in educational institutions.

(iv) Fourthly, there is medical allowance paid to the public employees to meet the increasing medical expenses. In India the government servants are entitled to free medical treatment or medical allowances.

(v) Lastly, there is travelling allowance (TA) paid to the government servants who travel to other places to attend to official work. In India TA is permissible for the public servants. The employees of certain services like railways are provided with free passes.

2. ***Leave:*** The second condition governing the modern public service is leave. There is a question, viz., whether leave can be demanded as a matter of right or enjoyed as a matter of privilege by the employees. W.F. Willoughby is of the opinion that the annual leave should be deemed to be a right. Leave is an essential necessity for all the employees. They 'require leave for rest and health, during sickness, or to attend

their private business'. Hence modern states formulate liberal rules governing leave. It is of many kinds.

(i) Firstly, there is earned or privilege or annual leave. Every public servant is eligible to enjoy this leave on full pay. Normally privilege leave should be taken during the year in which it occurs. In India different services have different rules governing the earned leave. In some cases, the accumulation of the leaves is permitted.

(ii) Secondly, there is sick or medical leave for which the public employees are eligible. W.F. Willoughby is of the view that sick leave 'should normally be subject to accrual up to a fixed number of days' because it acts as 'a strong incentive against: the abuse of the privilege for minor illness'. In India the leave rules permit the employees to enjoy medical leave on half—pay. A limited accumulation of this is also permissible for the employees of certain categories of services.

(iii) Thirdly, there is study leave which is granted to the public servants who are willing to prosecute higher studies. It provides an opportunity for those who are in lower classes of service to equip themselves with additional qualifications for further promotion. In India study leave is granted for some categories of officers. A gazetted officer who has put in 5 years of service is eligible for 2 years of study abroad on half-pay (4) Lastly, there is casual leave granted to all the classes of employees for 14 to 15 days a year. Where an employee is not eligible for any of the leave mentioned above, he can be granted leave on loss of pay. In India there is provision for casual and leave on loss of pay.

3. ***Holidays:*** The third condition governing the modern public service is holidays. The government in every country declares certain days holiday for its employees. For example holidays are declared on Sundays, festivals, days of national importance such as independence, Republic, New-year, etc. In India all these days are declared holidays.

4. ***Hours of work:*** The fourth condition governing the modern public service is hours of work. The government in every state fixes the number of working hours per day for all the employees. In England the total number of working hours per week is 45. In India there is no uniform rule regarding the number of working hours. The central pay commission recommended 38½ hours per week. It discouraged over time work.

5. The fifth condition governing the modern public service is good office accommodation. It is the duty of the government to provide all the amenities in the office so as to enable the employees to work happily. With the help of ever growing sciences the offices can be equipped with good furniture, ventilation, light and facilities for taking rest. It is necessary to provide for a canteen inside the campus of the office. The provision for 'a library, a garden, play grounds or a convenient transport' will add to the welfare of the office staff. In India these amenities are being provided by the government slowly.

6. The sixth condition is that there should be an adequate machinery for redressing the grievances of the employees. For this purpose in Britain the government established Whitley Councils consisting of the representatives of the staff and government. The functions of the Whitley Councils is to act as a ventilation of staff grievances. The central pay commission recommended the creation of Whitley Councils in India on the British model. Accordingly,

in 1957, the staff councils have been set up in each ministry. Each ministry has two staff councils, viz., a senior staff council for class II and III employees, and junior staff council for Class IV employees. The councils consider the condition of service and other grievances of the public employees.

7. The seventh condition is the security of tenure. Every public employee must be free from insecurity of job. If he is afraid of the future security of the job, he cannot be expected to work efficiently. At present many states are laying down rules governing the conditions of service of the public personnel. The best example is India. The constitution lays down: (1) No member of the civil services can be dismissed or removed by an authority subordinate to that by which he was appointed. (2) No member can be removed or reduced in rank until he has been given a reasonable opportunity of showing the cause against the action proposed except in certain cases.

8. The eight condition is reasonable and adequate changes of promotion. If there are no genuine chances of promotion, the incumbent cannot work with interest. The administrative efficiency suffers a lot. So all the employees must have equal opportunity for promotion. The basis of promotion must be seniority combined with the factors of efficiency.

9. Other conditions are pension, health, insurance etc. The Study Team of the Administrative Reforms Commission in its report submitted to the Government in December 1967 recommended a statutory enactment regarding all conditions of service of civil servants.

RETIREMENT

1. A person finds it difficult to do any work when he becomes old. As the age advances, he becomes old,

weak and becomes unable to do any hard work. Hence he needs rest during the old age. So also, an employee in the government can do useful service only so long as his age permits him. He cannot be hoped to perform his duties satisfactorily as he becomes old. Sometimes, on account of physical disabilities an employee may be rendered incapable of doing any service to the government. In those circumstances he wants to leave the service and take rest. It is known as retirement. In every modern state provision is being made for the retirement of the public personnel. It is an important development in the field of public administration. Retirement is necessary for another reason, viz., that it enables young men to get promotion and unemployed to secure employment in the government.

2. Modern states prescribe the age of retirement. In the USA it is 65 to 70 years. In Britain 60 to 65 and in India 55 to 60. Recently the Central Government has raised retirement age of the employees to 58. What should be the age of retirement higher or lower? There are two views. There are some people who argue that the age of the retirement should be higher. According to them the higher age leads to efficiency in administration on account of the accumulated training and experience of the employees. On the other hand there are some who argue that the age of retirement should be lower. According to them the lower age of retirement provides greater opportunities to the young officials to get promotions to the higher position. As a compromise between the two views, it may be said that the age of retirement should be neither too high (as in the case of USA) nor to low (as in India) but moderate. Retirement at the age of 60 may be good.

Reference to India: Regarding the age of retirement in India, the Central Pay commission recommended to raise retirement age from 55 to 58. The Government of India accepted the recommendation. So under the existing rules, every government servant, other than a workman, is to retire on the day he attains the age of 58. Requests for extension can be made, but they are granted only rarely and under really exceptional circumstances. In November, 1965, the Home Ministry, in a circular, has asked all the central ministers not to grant extension of services and send quarterly returns of extensions and employments beyond the age of 58. The Home Ministry observed that extension of service hinders the promotional prospects of the younger employees to the top positions.

3. ***Retirement takes place in two ways:*** (1) An employee may retire from service in his own accord earlier than the maximum age prescribed. For example in England a public servant is free to retire at the age of 60. This is called voluntary retirement. Voluntary retirement may take place either on the ground of health or other grounds (2) At times the government may issue an order compulsorily retiring an employee from the service if his continuance in the service is not in the public interest and prejudicial to the interest of the state. Generally speaking, Compulsory retirement takes place on the grounds of corruption, negligence of duties, gross indiscipline and insubordination and subversive activities. However, an employee may be given an opportunity to present his explanation for the charges framed against him and defend his case. All India Services (Discipline and Appeals) Rules 1955 have added compulsory retirement as a punishment for the employees of the above services.

Reference to India: In India there is provision for both compulsory and voluntary retirement. At present a government servant continues until 58 and normally retires after 30 years of service. A government employee can voluntarily retire after attaining the age of 50 or on completion of 25 years of service provided he gives three months notice intimating his intention to retire.

Compulsory retirement is used as a means of discipline action. In October, 1966, the Government of India have prepared a scheme under which officers provided wanting of integrity will be retired compulsorily at 50 or after 25 years of service which even is earlier. Advisory committees were proposed to be formed in each Ministry to prepare a list of officers considered to be of doubtful integrity.

4. ***Retirement has certain advantages:*** After certain age (say 60) the people cannot keep good health physical and mental. They cannot sit for a long time in the office and work hard at the desk. They cannot think deeply the ways and means of solving the day to day problems of the administration. So their continuance in the government leads to inefficiency of the administration. Another point is that in the absence of the retirement system, the employees continue in the public service life long. In that case there cannot be any possibility for young and educated men to joint the service. Opportunities for employment are denied to them. The young people serving in the lower posts are denied the opportunities for promotions. Hence the government service becomes unattractive. "The retention of these employees, moreover, clogs the paths of promotion and by so doing lessens the incentive to do good work by the younger employees and materially impairs the general morale of the service". So the great advantage of the retirement system is that it helps the people in service to get promotions and unemployed to secure employment in the government. Another advantage of the retirement system is that it gives rest and leisure to the people.

PENSION

The problem of pension is closely related to the problem of retirement. If one agrees that there is need for retirement, one has to agree that there is need for some kind of provision for the old an employee cannot do any hard work to earn his living. Hence it is the fundamental duty of the government to take the care of an old employee who had retired after having spent all his energies in the service of it. For this purpose the government of the modern state makes financial grant to all the retired employees. This grant is called the pension (or annuity). Thus, it is clear that the provision for pension is an important feature and latest development in the field of personnel Administration Dr. M.P. Sharma observes: "if there is no provision for retirement benefits, one of the two consequences would follow. Either the employees would have to be retained in service for life in which case the service would be over burdened with old and inefficient men, or if retirement is insisted on, many of the ex-employees would have to live in want and destitution".

There are four views regarding the pension system.

(i) Firstly, there are some people who argue that the provision is a fundamental duty of the government. The considerations of humanity demand that it should maintain the old employees retired from service. They say that the proper performance of this duty makes the state benevolent towards its old employees. It enhances the dignity of the state as an employer.

(ii) Secondly there are some people who argue that it is the duty of the government of a welfare state to make provision for social security of its employees. The retired employees should be free from want and ill health. For this purpose

the government should provide them life pension. It means that pension is a part of social security scheme.

(iii) Thirdly, there are some people who express the view that a good service needs reward. An employee who served the government for a number of years honestly and sincerely should be honoured with proper reward. The best reward for past good service is pension.

(iv) Lastly, there are some who argue that pension is a matter of right, while some do not agree with this view. In India the employees cannot claim pension as a matter of right.

The financial grant sanctioned to the retired employees is of two types. There are: (i) Pension and (ii) provident fund. The former is called the monthly pension, while the latter is called the annual pension or annuity. In both the cases the pension is provided for life. In some countries the pension continues even after the death of a retired employee. For example, in India, the Central Government introduced a life pension for widows of the Central Government Employees. (ii) Provident fund is an amount paid to the employee after retirement in lump sum. The employees of non-pensionable service contribute certain amount of their salary every month, to the provident fund, to which the government adds its own share at the time of the disbursement of the money. So the difference between pension and provident fund is that in the case of the former the employee does not contribute any share. While in the case of the latter, the employee contributes his share.

Of the two, viz. Pension and provided fund, the question arises as to which is more beneficial. The answer is that each has got its own advantages and disadvantages. The advantages of pension are:

(i) Pension is beneficial during the period when the interest rate is low. (ii) Pension enables the government to have control over the employees even after retirement. (iii) Pension does not give rise to such problems as investment, safety loss or squandering away. The disadvantages of the pension scheme are: (i) It is not beneficial during the period when the interest rate is very high, because a retired employee cannot invest it (ii) Pension fails to give freedom to the employee even after retirement because they depend on government for regular payment of it. (iii) Pension fails to safe guard family in case an employee dies either before or soon after retirement.

The Advantages of Provident Fund are: (i) It is beneficial during the period when the market rate of interest is higher because a retired employee can invest the lump sum amount received from the governmental (ii) It is also beneficial to an employee who, on account of failing health or other, desires to retire from the service before hand, (iii) Provident Fund safeguards the family and children in case the employee dies either before or on the verge of or soon after retirement. Because the family can utilise the lump sum amount payable or paid to the employee. The disadvantages of provident fund are: (i) it is of no great benefit during the period when the interest rate is very low, (ii) It gives rise to such problems as safety, investment, care, loss etc.

Thus it is clear that both have their own draw backs. "The thoughtful employees, therefore, press for mixed scheme which will partake of the character of a pension and lump sum payment both". (Dr. M.P. Sharma).

6. ***Pensions are of three kinds:*** (i) The non-contributory (ii) the partly contributory and (iii) the wholly contributory. In the case of the first. (i.e. non-contributory) the government undertakes to contribute the entire cost of making the retirement allowances.

In the case of the second (i.e., partly contributory), the cost is met partly by the government and partly by the employees. The share of the employees is compulsorily deducted from the salaries. In the case of the third (i.e., wholly contributory). The entire cost is met by the employees through the deductions made from their salaries, though the cost of aministering the system is met by the government.

7. ***Pension in India:*** Prior to independence, there were two systems of pensions, viz., contributory (till 1919) and non-contributory (Since 1919). The provident fund scheme prevailed in the Limited way. In order to be eligible for drawing the pension, an employee of the Central Government must possess certain qualifications, prescribed by the Civil Service Regulations as modified in 1950. These qualifications are (i) An employee to be eligible to draw the pension must have put in atleast ten years' of qualifying service under the Union Government, (ii) An employee is free to retire voluntarily after having put in 25 years of service. A person who retires or leaves government service without satisfying the above conditions is not entitled to pension, (iii) An employee must have worked in substantive and permanent post.

At present, in India there are two varieties of pensions, viz., ordinary and extra-ordinary. The following are the ordinary pension.

(i) Pensions given to the employees who retire at superannuating age (superannuating pension); (ii) pension given to the employees who retire after having put in qualified service (retiring pension); (iii) pension given to the employees who are rendered physically or mentally disabled (invalid pension). (iv) pension given

to an official who leaves the government service, as a result of the abolition of the post (compensatory pension).

The extra-ordinary pension is payable to the family or children of the employee after his death. The Central Government introduced Life pension for Windows of Central Government servants' which had come into force from January 1964. According to this scheme the Government would provide for the grant of pension for life to an employee's widow. The scheme provides for a pension ranging from Rs. 150 per month according to the pay scale of the employees. The new scheme covers about 20 lakhs employees.

The cost of the pension is met out of the current governmental expenditure. In the U.S. the pensions are paid out of the special funds provided for the purpose.

PUBLIC EMPLOYEES ASSOCIATIONS

Meaning of Association: Since the State alone does not embrace the whole life of man, he crates other associations to develop and express his personality. It means the associations have spontaneously emerged to fulfil the needs of human beings. Thus within the territory of the states we find a large number of associations. An association may be defined "as a group of persons or members who are associated and organized into a unity of will and common end." R.M. Maclver defines an association as a group organized for the pursuit of an interest or a group interest in common. In a more simple language an association is a group of persons who are associated for a promotion of common object in accordance with the prescribed rules and method. Hence an association has three essential characteristics. (i) a group of people, (ii) common purpose; and (iii) prescribed rules.

Right to Association: Having understood the meaning of association, it is not difficult to understand the meaning of right to association. It means that every citizen should be free to form associations in order to express, propagate and exchange his views with those of others. Many constitutions, today, both recognise and guarantee the right to association of the citizens. Where this right prevails, it becomes the duty of the State not only to protect the associations, but also to give them necessary independence.

The Need for Employees' Association: (Or Organizations or Unions): Now the question is whether the public employees have the right to form their own associations or not. In other words, should government employees be permitted to form organizations or not? Two answers are usually, found to these questions. Some argue that employees should be permitted to form their associations or unions, while some do not support this view. It is necessary to examine the both.

The public servants should be permitted to form associations (or unions) for the following reasons. (Or trade unionism among the public employees secures the following advantages).

1. The first argument is based on the principle of equality. According to this, democracy is based on the principle of equality. It guarantees equality of right and equal opportunities for all the citizens without any discrimination. All people are equal in the eyes of law. The term people includes both private persons and public employees. Therefore according to this argument just as private citizens are free to form associations, so also public employees should have the liberty to create their own unions. In the matter of the right to associations there should be no any discrimination between the citizens and civil servants.
2. The second argument is based on the promotion of personality. The associations or unions promote the

personality of the public employees. They provide best opportunities for them to exchange their views with those of the fellow-employees. The associations help the employees to develop friendly contacts among them selves. Dr. M.P. Sharma observes: "The employees organizations foster the growth of esprit the corps and group consciousness among their members. By belonging to one of these, the employee feels an expansion of his personality, and a heightening of his morale.

3. The third argument is based on moral principle. The public employees have certain grievances relating to the conditions of service viz., pay allowances, leave, working hours, pension etc., In that case the employees must have the opportunity to bring to the notice of the Government their grievances and secure redress for them. Not only they should secure the redress, but they should also exercise a voice in determining the conditions under which they are to labour. These two objects—viz., (i) redress of the grievances and (ii) a share in the determination of service conditions—can be best secured if there are well organized associations. The employees associations carry the grievances to the government. They bring pressure to bear on the government for improvement of pay and conditions of service. In the absence of these associations it is not possible for the individual employee to contact the government and represent their difficulties.

4. The fourth argument is based on the educative value. The efficiency in the administration depends upon the conduct of the public servants. The necessary education to build up sound conduct of the employees is provided by the employees organizations or unions. They provide leadership for the employees. They stimulate the interest of employees in their work. They

prevent abuses and cultivate responsibility on the part of the employees. The associations are the source of strength and unity among the employees.

From the point of view of the above argument trade unionism is considered essential among the public servants.

Arguments against: Those who argue against the right of public employees to associations point out the following disadvantages of employees associations (trade unionism among the employees).

1. The first argument is based on the distinct position of the employees. The public servants occupy a position in society which is distinct from that of the private citizens. As the servants of the government, the employees have special responsibilities and distinct duties to perform. They are responsible for keeping on the machinery of administration. They are responsible for maintaining the essential services in society. The public servants enjoy certain special privileges which are ordinarily denied to the private citizens,. So also, it is but natural, that the private citizens possess some extra rights (such as rights to associations) which are denied to the public employees. In the interests of the public welfare and administrative efficiency, some time the government of the state does not permit the formation of employees unions.

2. The second argument is that in order to secure redress for their grievances, the employees have other means such as the Whitley councils in Britain and staff councils in India. Further, there is no guarantee that the employees unions would give education, training and leadership to their members. At times they many encourage their members to organize strikes and exert unreasonable pressure on the government to secure unreasonable demands. This

factor becomes more serious, especially, when employees associations are affiliated to outside organizations. Further, public service is statutory, i.e., the conditions of service of the public employees are determined by law in changing which associations have no part to play.

Having noted the arguments for and against the trade unionism among the public employees, we may conclude as follows:

1. The government may permit the employees to form associations under well—defined conditions.
2. All the associations of employees have to be approved and recognised by the government.
3. The activities of the employees organization should be non-political. The government should have the right to ban any association of its employees whose activities are detrimental to the interest of public welfare and the security of the state.
4. The object of the Employees Unions should be the promotion of economic welfare and education of employees and foster harmonious relations between the employees and the government. Such associations of the employees are always liable to be encouraged.

Reference: The practice with regard to the right of the public servants to form associations differs from country to country to country. In this context we shall study the practice as obtained in Britain, the U.S.A. and India.

1. ***Britain:*** The trade unionism among the public employees came into existence in England during the last quarter of the 19th century. By the end of the century there were only two employees organizations. By 1919 the government recognised the right of the

employees to constitute associations. In the beginning the associations have been constituted in industrial establishments, and later on in the sphere of civil service. The position at present is that the civil servants are at liberty to form service association and affiliate them to any political party after satisfying the prescribed procedure. There are a number of employees associations or trade unions through out Britain.

2. ***The U.S.A:*** The trade unionism among the civil servants come into existence during the second half of the 19th century. By 1912, the government recognised the right of the employees to constitute associations. There are two types of public service organizations and unions in the U.S.A. viz. (i) organizations of scientific and professional personnel and (ii) Civil service unions.

   (i) ***Scientific and Professional Associations:*** These are the associations meant for the employees of scientific and professional service such as scientists, physicians, engineers, lawyers, teachers etc., Among the associations the important are these: (1) The National Teachers Associations (1857) whose name has subsequently been changed as National Education Association, (2) International Association of Chiefs of Police (1871), (3) National Association of Insurance Commissioners (1878), (4) Association of Food and Drug officials (1899). The number of such associations is very large.

   (ii) ***Civil Service Unions:*** These are the associations meant for the employees of regular civil service. Among these associations the important are these: (1) The National Association of Letter carries (1889). (2) National Federation of Post Office Clerks (1906), and so many other

associations. The most prominent civil service union of the USA is the National Federation of Federal employees (1917) consisting of more than a lakh employees as its members. This federation aims at promoting economic welfare, education, training and co-operation among the employees of the federal services. Its membership is open to a wide variety of occupational groups in the federal service.

Besides the above, there is an important outside organization called American Federation of Labour (A.F.L.) to which many employees associations are affiliated. For example the first two associations mentioned in the above paragraph are affiliated to the AFL. The aims of the Federations are to secure conditions in matters of salary, wages, retirement benefits and hours of work for labourers.

(ii) ***Working:*** The position at present is that the attitude of government towards the employees association is very friendly. They do not participate in the political parties. L.D. White observes: "They do not take part in campaigns; they have no candidates for public office their task is to aid all officials, not to cultivate the personal interests of some. Every association observe some taboos.

3. ***India:*** Trade unionism in India came into existence only at the end of the World War I. The first associations were formed by the employees of railway and postal services. The establishment of the trade unions was legally recognised in the year 1926. By 1946 there came into being a number of employees organizations of all kinds-national, state, local and departmental. The First Central Pay Commission (1946) expressed the view in favour of giving proper encouragement to the growth of the service associations and unions. After independence, the

constitution conferred on all the citizens the right to form associations and unions [Article 19(c)].

The position at present is that public servants enjoy only limited right to form associations and unions. They can join as members only those associations or unions which are recognised by the central government. The government recognises only those associations which fulfil certain conditions. Those conditions are (1) The members of the associations should be government servants only. (2) The executive committee should consist of only the members not outsiders. (3) They should not have any political affiliation or take part in political activities. The violation of these conditions results in the withdrawal of recognition by the government.

Since associations play an important role in building the personality of the public servants, it is the duty of the government to encourage the growth of the unions in strength or organization. On the other hand, the service associations should recognise their fundamental duties and undertake only those activities which promote the national welfare. The service associations which act as instruments against the government have no right to be encouraged and recognised.

RIGHTS OF THE CIVIL SERVANTS

The civil servants occupy a special position in the society which is distinct from that of the private citizens. They enjoy certain privileges such as pay, power, promotion and pension for life which are denied to the ordinary citizens. Besides these, it is said, the public servants have certain special rights which are either unnecessary or not granted to the private citizens. Generally speaking these rights are: (1) Right to Associations; (2) Right to Affiliation; (3) Right to Strike; (4) Right to Lobby; (5) Right to Political Activity; (6) Right to Collective Bargaining. Each right needs a brief critical examination.

The Right to Association: According to this the question is whether the civil servants should have the right to form their own associations. Regarding this there are two views. According to some the employees should have the right to form associations. According to these people, associations promote personality of the employees by giving them opportunities to exchange their view with those of other employees. The associations bring to the notice of the government the grievances relating to the conditions of service of the employees and secure necessary redress of them. The associations also build an efficient administrative machinery by educating and training the employees. However, there are some who argue that the public employees have special responsibilities towards the public and so cannot demand all the rights which a private citizen enjoys. At times the associations of the employees encourage undesirable activities such as organising strikes etc. They bring fourth unreasonable demands to be granted by the government.

The practice with regard to the right of the employees to form organizations differ from country to country. While in England and the USA the governments are liberal in granting this right, in India the rules are stringent. In the USA there are two types of employees organization viz. (1) Scientific and professional associations and (2) civil service unions. There are out side organizations also. In India the government laid down clear rules governing the formation of employees associations. Every staff association has to be recognized by the government. In conclusion, it may be said that the civil servants should be encouraged to form such associations whose activities are liable to promote the public welfare.

The Right to Affiliation: According to this the question is whether the employees organizations can affiliate themselves with any outside or private trade unions. In every country there are some private unions such as Labour Union Working hard for the promotion of the welfare of their members. In some countries the employees organizations are permitted to affiliate themselves to such union. For example in the USA the National Association of Letter carries and the National Federation of Post Office Clerks are affiliated to the American Federation of Labour. However, the US Congress prohibits certain organizations of the employees from affiliating themselves to the A.F.L. In England the employees associations are permitted to affiliate themselves even to a political party. In India all such affiliations are prohibited. There are certain advantages of affiliation (1) The employees maintain close contacts with organized unions. (2) The unions assist government employees in securing their demands approved by the government. However there are certain disadvantages too. The unions, sometimes, may encourage the employees to organize strikes etc. against the government.

The Right to Strike

According to this the question is whether the civil servants should have the right to strike. Regarding this there are three views among the reasonable and thoughtful persons. (1) The first view is that the public servants should not be given the right to strike because it paralyses the administration and results in social catastrophy. The strikes by the employees bring the life of the community to a standstill. Hence any strike by the civil servants should be strictly forbidden. (ii) The second view is that were the government is arrogant or conditions of service are intolerable, and all constitutional means to change such conditions fail them the employees should have the right to go on strike. (iii) The third view is a midway view which holds that any strikes which would involve direct, certain and serious danger to the community should be prohibited by law, whether they occur in the public service or in privately owned institutions. Otherwise the law should remain silent.

The practice with regard to this right differs from country to country. The example from England, the USA and India may be noted here.

1. In England, the public employees are free to go on strike. The British parliament has not enacted any law prohibiting the strikes by the civil servants. However an employee who goes on strike is able for disciplinary action.

2. In the USA the government thought about this matter only in 1919 when the famous Baston Police strike occurred. But the matter was given a serious consideration only at the end of the World War II when the teachers of the public School in Buffalo went on strike. The Taft-Hartely Labour—Management Relations act of 1947 prohibited the strikes by the employees. The Act declared that an employee who participated in the strike was liable to be discharged from the service. Again the Act of 1955 prescribed greater punishment in this regard.

3. In India the problem did not arise until 1960. In this year the strike of the Central Government employees had forced the government to give serious thought to it. The position at present is that the civil servants of certain categories are prohibited from participating in the strike. The violation of this rule constitutes a breach of discipline. There are many people in India who are in favour of total ban of the strike by the civil servants. Shri B. Sivarao observed. A general strike of government employees; however it might be described by its leaders, is a political weapon. Its successes must mean the collapse of administration and that no government can permit.

The Right to Lobby

According to this, the question is whether the civil servants should have the right to influence the legislation before the legislature of the state enacts it. This question applies, peculiarly, to only the USA. Until 1895 the civil servants used to come to Washington with a view to influence the acts of the Congress. But in this year the postal employees were prohibited from using the right to lobby. The Lloyd La Follette Act, 1912 prohibited all the employees of the U.S. from influencing any legislation pending before the Congress or its committees.

The Right of Political Activity

According to this the question is whether the civil servants should posses the right to take part in political activities. Regarding this there are three views. (1) The first view is that the civil servants should be strictly prohibited from taking part in the political activities as it is not conducive to administrative efficiency. (2) The second view is that the civil servants like the private citizens, should be free to take part in the political activities and support any party they like. (3) The third view is a midway view which holds that the public employees may be permitted to take up political activity, but they should sincerely serve whatever party comes to power after elections. In other words. Whatever may be their political affiliation, the employees in their official life should be strictly neutral.

The practice with regard to this differs from country to country:

1. In England, the government is very liberal in granting the right of participation in the political activities. For the purpose of granting this right, the civil servants are divided into 3 categories, viz., free, intermediate and restrict. The free, employees are free

to take part in all kinds of political activity. The intermediate, employees are allowed to participate in all the political activities except contesting election to parliament. The restricted employees are prohibited from taking part in all the political activities but are permitted to vote in the elections.

2. In the U.S.A. the federal civil servants are prohibited from participation in all the political activities. The Hactch Act of 1939 prescribed both mild and severe punishments for the violation of the rules. The former includes 90 days suspension and the latter includes dismissal from the service. The intention of the U.S. Government in imposing a strict ban on the political activities of its servants is to maintain clean and neutral administration. L.D. White remarks. The limitations on political activity by public service employees grew out of a desire to protect them against political pressure and to maintain the politically neutral character of the public service rather than to curtail their bargaining strength.

3. In India, like the USA the civil servants are for bidden from taking active part in any kind of political activity except that he can vote at an election. Any employee of the government who participates in political activities is liable for disciplinary action.

Right to Collective Bargaining

According to this the question is whether the government should consult the employees before taking a decision on the matters relating to service conditions of the employees. This practice is found in the industrial field but not in public service in all the states. However, in the USA the practice of collective bargaining prevails.

CHAPTER—8

The Bureaucratic System of Personnel

MEANING OF BUREAUCRACY

Originally, bureaucracy was meant "desk government". In other words, bureaucracy was understood to mean a government by the officials who did work at their desks. It was also defined as a government or management by bureaus. But to-day, the meaning of bureaucracy has undergone a change. In fact, there is no universally accepted definition of bureaucracy and it is differently interpreted in different ways. Hence, it is necessary to mention some of the views given by Writers before we draw the features of bureaucracy.

Willoughby: Bureaucracy is a body of public servants organized in a hierarchical system which stands outside the sphere of effective public controls.

Laski: Bureaucracy is a system of government the control of which is so completely in the hands of the officials that their power jeopardises the liberties of ordinary citizens.

J.A. Vieg: If thus denotes the sum total of the personnel, apparatus and procedures by which an organization manages its work and accomplishes its purposes.

We can draw the following features of bureaucracy with the help of the above definitions.

1. It is a body of officials organized in a hierarchical system. It consists of different ranks of officials the lower working on the directions of the higher.
2. They are outside the control of the public or the representatives of the public. Even if there is any public control, it is not exercised effectively.
3. The officials enjoy more powers and control government completely even to the extent of restricting the liberties of citizens.
4. They are too conscious of the rules, regulations and procedures governing their official work. They rely on written documents, files and records. They stick to the rules to accomplish their ends.
5. The officials in a bureaucratic Government consider them selves the servants of the head of the state, but not the public. They lack human considerations. They maintain political neutrality.

According to J.A. Vieg, bureaucracy is prevalent wherever the above features are noticeable whether it is a public organization or private, governmental, commercial, educational, ecclesiastical.

MERITS OF BUREAUCRACY

We shall, first, mention the good points of bureaucracy as given by some writers and then have a discussion of the dangers inherent in it.

1. J.S. Mill considers bureaucracy an efficient government. He defines bureaucracy as a government, by public functionaries. It is a government of sustained mental ability and vigour. The officials who are trained for the work can conduct

the affairs of government in a better way. They possess experience, well—tried and well considered maxims, practical knowledge and technical qualifications.

2. Bureaucracy secures uniformity of treatment as it is governed by rules and regulations. It is free from out side interference and political influence. Thus it is free from defects which are usually found in democracy. This freedom from out side elements is necessary to enable government to do its business effectually or permanently.

3. The long experience or years of competent and faithful service, high professional qualifications and continuity in service of the professional officials are an asset to the amateur political head in formlation of policies and enacting good laws. It is why J.S. Mill was full of praise for government of professional officials. He points out two positive evils of representative governments: (1) general ignorance and incapacity of the controlling body and (2) influence of interests not identical with the general welfare of the community. He observes that these two evils are not found in aristocracies of public functionaries.

DANGERS OF BUREAUCRACY

The writers have concentrated their attention in listing charges against bureaucracy. Among them, the important names are W.A. Robson, J.S. Mill, Begehot. Russel and Lord Hewart. We shall summarize their views here under.

1. ***Red—tapism:*** The first and the foremost charge levelled against bureaucracy is redtapism. This is a major charge too. The officials in bureaucratic government are too conscious of rules and procedure. The one is their food and the other water. Even a minor decision is taken only on the basis of lengthy

procedure. They are fond of lengthy and round about way of doing work. Where a thing can be done in an hour, the officials take weeks to do it. They cut the cloth but do not find the body. J.S. Mill remarks: The disease which afflicts bureaucratic governments, and which they usually die of is routine. They perish by the immutability of their maxims. He further, says, a bureaucracy always tends to become a pedantocracy. On account of this red-tapism, citizens do not get quick justice. Justice which is delayed is justice denied.

2. ***Formalism and unresponsiveness:*** While Mill praised bureaucracy for its sustained mental ability and vigour. Bagehot charged it with excessive adherence to formation. He noticed loose sense of judgement and initiative in the officials.

He says that the officials enter office at an young age take years to learn work and retire before they being doing work. Another defect of bureaucracy is its unresponsiveness to the popular feelings. W.A. Robson points out four bad qualities which are often found in this government: (1) excessive sense of self-importance (2) undue importance of their office (3) inflexibility of decisions and (4) absence of any feeling towards individuals. This is what Russel calls, "negative psychology."

3. ***New Despotism:*** The most expensive and sweeping charge against bureaucracy comes from Lord Hewart. "Britains doughty defender of the Rule of Law." He, in his book 'New Depostism', points out that the officials, to-day, possess vast authority which is beyond the reach of ordinary law. He says that the expert officials take the advantage of amateur political heads and slowly, step by step usurp the legislative, executive and judicial functions of government. Thus they clothe themselves with despotic power and then start defying the laws. This, Lord Hewart calls, a New

Despotism. The argument of Hewart is that the officials get the law enacted in skeleton form, fill it with their rules, interpret them to justify their actions and become all—powerful.

Conclusion. Before we conclude, it may be necessary to quote the views of J.A. Vieg. He tries to refute the charges made against bureaucracy. Regarding the charge of red-tapism, he says that it is so because the officials are expected to proceed according to objective rules rather than subjective intuition. He considers red-tapism the best insurance the public has that all citizens receive equal treatment in the hands of government. The officials act according to rules because they are accountable to the public.

4. ***Regarding the charge of desporism:*** J.A. Vieg says that everything depends on how one understands the activities of the services. He says that there should be good understanding between the citizen and civil servant. The citizen has to understand the years of competent and faithful service of the officials who do not expect any comment or commendation. He expects that a good co-operation and mutual understanding will help to make things clarified. Our conclusion is that we may agree with the views of the learned writer.

CHAPTER—9

Financial Administration

MEANING AND IMPORTANCE

Finance is an important factor of administration. In the words of L.D. white: Every administrative act has its financial implications....nothing can be done without the expenditure of money....management of finance is the first responsibility of administrators" The management of finance is called financial administration. It includes: (1) Budget making (2) Legislative sanction, (3) Execution of budget, (4) payment and custody of funds (5) Accounting and Auditing.

MEANING OF BUDGET

Budget is a term which is very familiar to all the people. Every individual, family, association etc. prepare their own budgets at the beginning of every month or year. So also every business concern or commercial firm or industrial estate prepares budget at the beginning or end of the year. But, here we are not concerned with the budgets of the individuals, associations or business concerns. The term budget 'as used in public administration refers to the budget of the state or public authority. Every state, to day prepares its budget at the beginning of every year. The term Budget was first used in 1773 in Walpole's time in England. The chancellor of Exchequer used to carry financial papers in a bag for presentation to the House. Since then budget came to denote papers relating to annual financial statement. The term budget has two meanings (i) narrow meaning and (ii) wider meaning. There are some writers who explain the meaning of budget in its restricted sense. According to them budget means a statement showing the estimates of revenue and expenditure of the government. The writers who hold this view are: Beaulieu, Rense stourm, G. Jeze and others.

(i) L. Beaulieu says: "A budget is a statement of the estimated receipts and expenses during a fixed period; it is a comparative table giving the amounts of the receipts to be realised and of the expenses to be incurred..."

(ii) According Rense Stourm it is a document containing a preliminarily approved plan of public revenues and expenditure."

(iii) Tò G. Jeze a budget is an "estimate of all public receipts and expenses... an authorization to incur them and to collect them".

Thus these writers define budget as a statement showing all the estimate of government revenue and expenditure only. It is in this sense that the term budget is used in England and India.

Secondly the term budget has its wider meaning. In its compressive sense the budget means more than a mere estimate of revenue of the government: It includes (1) all the estimated revenues of the government: (2) all the estimated expenditure of the government. (3) enactment by the legislature (4) accounts and (5) audit. This view is held by the American writers, notably by W.I. Willoughby. According to this meaning budget is a continuous process or chain of operations.' It is in this sense that the term budget is used in the USA.

Types of Budget: Budget is of four types long-term budget, short term budget, single budget and plural budget.

1. If the budget of a state is prepared for a number of years (i.e. 5 years it is called long term budget.) This type of budget is prepared for the purpose of the strengthening of defences, extension of communications economic and industrial development, etc.
2. If the budget of a state is prepared for a short period (i.e. one or two years), it is called short term budget. This practice is adopted in some American jurisdictions. However, in modern states, the period of the budget is almost universally fixed at one year. So, the present day budget is neither long term. Nor short term, but annual.
3. If there is only one budget for the whole government, it is called single budget.
4. On the other hand, if each department of the government has separate budget, it is called plural budget. Most of the modern states have single budget, while few states (e.g. France, Germany, Switzerland and India) have two budgets. In India there are two budgets.....one is general budget and the other railway budget.

PRINCIPLES OF BUDGET MAKING

Budget is considered heart and soul of financial administration. W.F. Willougby regards budget as the central instrument of financial administration. Encyclopaedia of Social Science says: "The real significance of the budget system lies in providing for the orderly—administration of the financial affairs of a government. Since budget is such an important instrument of the financial administration, it is necessary to adopt certain principles while making it. The writers like P.K. Wattal and H.D. Smith suggest the following principles of budget making.

1. Firstly, the budget must be a balanced one. It means the total estimated revenue should be nearly equal

to the total estimated expenditure. If the estimated revenue is more than the estimated expenditure, it is called surplus budget. On the other hand, if the estimated revenue is less than the estimated expenditure, it is called the deficit budget. A surplus budget is desirable, a constant deficit budget is harmful, while a balanced budget is always good. However, there are some economists who regard deficit budget as an instrument of economic progress.

2. Secondly, the budget estimates should be on cash basis. It means the estimated revenue and expenditure should relate to the year for which the budget is prepared. It should also include the actual collection of revenues or expenditure of the budget of the previous year. This point may be explained by an example. Let us suppose that the budget is prepared for the year 1965-66. According to this principle, all the items of estimated revenue and expenditure should relate to the year-1965-66 only. If any revenue relating to 1964-65 is collected in the year 1965-66 that amount should find its place in 1965-66 budget. So also if any amount relating to 1964-65 is spent in 1965-66, that amount should find its place in the budget of 1965-66. This practice is found in England, the USA and India. The defect of this principle is that the budget does not reveal the true financial picture of that year. The budget of the reverse type is called revenue budget which is adopted in some European countries.

3. Thirdly the budget should maintain separately two items relating to recurring revenue and expenditure and occasional revenue and expenditure. The latter is called capital revenue and expenditure. The examples of capital revenue are income from loans, deposits, sale proceeds of property etc. The examples of capital expenditure are capital outlay on work, debt

payment, payment back on deposits etc. All the items of revenue and expenditure, other than capital revenue and expenditure, are called recurring items.

4. Fourthly, the budget should be gross and not net. A gross budget is one which contains all the items of estimated revenue (or receipts) on the one side and all the items of estimated expenditure on the other side. A net budget is one which shows only the net revenue (i.e. after deducting the total estimate expenditure from the total estimated revenue).

5. Fifthly, the budget estimates should be very closed. It means that the estimates prepared by the government, both of revenue and expenditure, should be, as far as possible, exact. If more revenue is received and less expenditure incurred than estimated in the budget. It is called under-estimating. If less revenue is realized and more expenditure incurred than estimated in the budget, it is called over-estimating. A good budget should avoid both because over-estimating of expenditure results in heavy taxation, while under estimating gives rise to the problems of execution. However, it is difficult to calculate exact estimating Dr. M.P. Sharma says: An absolutely exact estimating is, however, a counsel of perfection rarely realised in practice.

6. Sixthly, the budget should observe the rule of lapse. It means that all the expenditure granted in the budget should be spent by the government only during the year for which the budget is made. It cannot be transferred to any future years. In other words, if any expenditure granted remains unspent during the year, that amount lapses at the end of the year. This point may be explained by means of an example. Let us suppose that a sum of Rs. 10 lakhs is granted in the budget towards the expenditure for the year 1965-66. The government has to spend the

whole amount before the end of the year. If the government, according to the rule of lapse spends only a sum of Rs. 9 lakhs the remaining amount viz., Rs. 1 lakh lapses (or expires) at the end of the year.

7. Seventhly, the budget possess clarity. It means that budget should be prepared in such a way that it is easily understood by the common man. Especially in a state where the percentage of the educated people is very low, the budget should be very clear. The main stages of budget making should be made public. Further, a good budget is one which has flexibility. It should accommodate necessary changes in the light of changing economic situation.

PROBLEMS OF BUDGET

Budget making has certain problems. The success of any budget depends upon the extent to which these problems are satisfactorily solved. The following are the important problems of the budget.

1. The first problem is that the budget must be acceptable to the people. It is people who pay the taxes. Hence the budget must be acceptable to the tax payers and voters. If the budget is not acceptable to the voters, then, the government will face a difficult political situation during the elections.
2. The second problem of the budget is that it is not possible to forecast future civilian or military requirements of the country. So also it is not possible to forecast the revenues from the taxes because modern tax systems are sensitive to business fluctuations.
3. The third problem of the budget is that it is becoming very difficult to meet the ever-growing expenditure of the government. Demands for new services (and new expenditure) are always pushing forward in

varying degrees of readiness for action (L. Fn White). Once a member of the US Congress remarked: "Sir, there are two things that never go back: one, the increase of officers, the other the increase of their salaries. We never decrease officers; we never decrease salaries.

4. The last problem of the budget is related to the plan. A budget necessarily involves planning. A careful planning is called for at every stage in the preparation of the budget. The problem becomes more difficult in the case of budget estimates, adjustment between the revenue and expenditure.

THE PROCESS OF BUDGET MAKING

The process of budget making is continuous. There are five stages in the preparation of the budget. They are (1) preparation of the Budget estimates. (2) Review (scrutiny) of the Budget estimates; (3) Executive approval and submission in the legislature.' (4) Enactment of Budget; (5) Execution of the budget. Each stage explained hereunder.

Preparation of Budget Estimates: The first stage in the process of budget-making is the preparation of budget estimates. The responsibility for the preparation of the budget estimates falls on the executive, i.e., various ministries. The budget estimates are usually, prepared for one year. In some states (e.g. U.S.A., Italy, Sweeden) the financial year commences from Ist July and ends on the 30th of June. In the case of few states (e.g. France) the financial year commence on Ist January and closes on 31st December. The work relating the preparation of estimates starts 6 to 8 months before the commencement of the next financial year in every state. Each department of the government prepares the estimate of revenue and expenditure for the next financial year. The departments prepare the estimates either at the request of the chief executives (e.g. the U.S.A. or the Finance Ministry, (e.g., England and India). In India a request to prepare estimate is made by the Finance Ministry in September to all the Union Ministries. The budget estimates are prepared on the basis of the figure of the budget of the previous year with necessary modifications for the next year. Estimates are made separately for each major item along with necessary explanation by the departments in cases where demands are made for increased expenditure. The statement containing the explanations are called in the U.S.A. "justification sheets" In the preparation of the estimates not only the head quarters office but also field office take part. It means that department prepares the estimates on the basis of the estimation furnished by its subordinate offices.

Review (or Scrutiny) of the Budget Estimates: The second stage in the process of budget making is the scrutiny of the estimates. The various departments forward their estimates to the proper authority for the purpose of review or scrutiny. The review authority is not the same in all the countries. In the USA the final reviewing authority is vested in the Bureau of the budget (i.e. Central finance office). It was established in 1921. The Bureau is headed by a Director. It is attached to the White House as a part of the Presidential office. In England the final reviewing authority is vested in the Treasury (i.e., Ministry of Finance). The treasury is headed by Seven Lords (the Prime Minister, the Director of Exchequer and 5 Junior Lords. In India it was vested in the Ministry of Finance. The reviewing agency scrutinizes the estimates, modifies and finally approves them. In some countries (e.g., the USA) the reviewing agency provides opportunities for the departmental officials to explain reasons in support of their estimates.

Executive Approval and Submission to Parliament: The third stage in the process of budget making is the approval of the estimates by the executive. The final estimates as approved by the reviewing agency are submitted to the executive for its approval. In the USA the President approves the Budget and submits it to the Congress. In England and India the Cabinet approves the Budget and submits it to the Parliament. The executive makes all the necessary adjustment, if any, before giving it final seal of approval.

Enactment of the Budget: The fourth stage in the process of budget making is the enactment of the Budget by the legislature. The slogan of democracy is no taxation without representation. Since every budget in the modern state makes some provision for new or additional taxation, it should be approved by the representatives of the people. So the practice, to-day, is that the budget has to be passed or enacted by the legislature. At the time of enactment the legislature has the authority to modify, increase, diminish, or abandon the budget estimates submitted by the executive. There are four steps in the enactment of the budget by the legislature.

The first step is the presentation of the budget to the legislature. The executive presents the budget to the legislature for its approval. In England the budget is presented by the Chancellor of Exchequer, in India by the Minister for Finance and in the USA the President sends it to the Congress. At the time of the presentation, the Minister may deliver a speech called the budget speech which out lines the main features of the budget (e.g. India and England). In the USA the president along with the budget sends a message to the Congress called the transmitting message which contains his recommendations, statements of the expenditure of previous years etc., In India and England the budget is introduced, first, in the lower House.

The second step is the general discussion of the budget by the legislature. At this stage the members of the legislature are free to discuss the general features of the budget. A fixed time is devoted for the discussion (e.g. two or three days in India). The various committees of the legislature work activity during the period of general discussion. In the USA each House of the Congress has its Appropriation Committee consisting of the members of both parties. They play a unique and diligent role in budget making. The officials of the various departments appear before them and explain and defined their estimates. Each appropriation Committee has sub-committees. This practice has come into vogue in the USA on account of the rigid separation of powers. Such committees are not to be found in England and India.

The third step is the voting of demands. This is an important stage in the process of enacting the budget. The voting of demands means voting of expenditure part of the budget by the legislature. In England and India the lower House has the monopoly in Voting demands. All demands for grants have to be introduced only on the recommendations of the head of the state in these countries.

The legislature votes demands for grants of each department separately. A fixed time is allotted within which the various demands are voted by the Houses. In England and India 26 days are allotted for this purpose. Each demand is subject to a vote of the House. The members of the legislature may move cut motions which may or may not be approved by the legislature. In India there is a provision for supplementary grants also. Sometimes the fate of the government is also decided at this stage. If any cut motions (e.g. India and England, not the USA) are passed against the wishes of the government, it amounts to non-confidence.

The last step is the enactment of the budget. The budget of the modern state is enacted by the legislature in the form of two acts viz., (1) Appropriation Act and (2) Finance Act. All the demands for grants are enacted into an act by the legislature called the Appropriation Act. This act authorises the government to incur expenditure. All the proposals for the collection of taxes are enacted into an act by the legislature called the Finance Act. It authorises the government to raise revenue through taxation. Thus the legislature enacts these two acts the process of budget-making becomes complete. The new budget is enacted before the commencement of the new year.

Execution of the Budget: The last stage in the process of budget making is the execution of the budget. After being enacted by the legislature, the executive takes necessary steps to execute it. (1) the taxes as sanctioned by the Finance Act are collected, (2) the expenditure as sanctioned by the Appropriation Act is spent. (3) the Government cannot spend more money or raise more revenue than authorised in the budget (4) the accounts of the various departments are subject to the scrutiny by the Auditor and Comptroller General.

THE PROCESS OF BUDGET-MAKING IN INDIA

It is necessary to understand the procedure adopted in India in the preparation of the budget. There are five stages in the process of budget-making in our country. There are: (1) Preparation of the budget estimates. (2) Review (or scrutiny) of the budget estimate, (3) Executive approval and submission to the parliament, (4) Full picture of the budget on the eve of the presentation to the parliament, (5) Enactment of the budget. Each may be explained as below:

1. ***Preparation of Budget Estimates:*** The first stage in the process of budget-making in India is the preparation of budget estimates. The responsibility for the preparation of budget estimates falls on the various ministries of the Union Government. The

departments prepare estimates at the request of the Ministry of Finance. All the estimates are prepared for the financial year (i.e., from 1st April to 31st March). The work relating to the preparation of estimates starts in India 6 to 8 months before the commencement of the next financial year. Each ministry prepares estimates with the help of various department and subordinate officers under its jurisdiction.

The budget estimates are prepared by the department in a prescribed form which consists of five columns: (i) Actuals of the previous year, (ii) sanctioned estimates for the current year, (iii) revised estimates for the current year, (iv) budget estimates for the next year, (v) actuals of the current year (at the time of preparation) and (vi) actuals of the corresponding period of the previous year. If the budget is prepared for 1965-66, the previous year is 1963-64, and the current year 1964-65. The statement regarding estimates has two parts: the first relating to the existing revenue and charges; the second part relating to the fresh proposals. The estimates of each department are to be approved by the head of the department and then by the head of the Ministry.

2. ***Review (or Scrutiny) of the Budget Estimates:*** The second stage in the process of budget-making in India is the scrutiny of estimates by the reviewing authority. The scrutinizing authority in India is the Ministry of Finance. In other words, all the Ministries of the Central Government forward their budget estimates to the Ministry of Finance. The 'Budget Division' of the Ministry scrutinises the estimates of all the Ministries. The Finance Ministry may modify or revise and reduce the estimates keeping in view the economy and availability of funds. However, the Finance Ministry has nothing to do with the policy of other Ministers. As a rule no proposals for new or

increased expenditure, for any department, can be incorporated in the budget without the concurrence of the Ministry of Finance. Any difference between a Ministry and Finance Ministry is resolved at the cabinet meeting.

Regarding the power of the Finance Ministry to scrutinise, review, and control the budget estimates of the various Ministries, there are two views:

1. The first view is against such a power being given to the Finance Ministry. The critics hold that (i) It acts as a break on the progressive policies of the other Ministries; (ii) Its decisions in accepting or rejecting the new proposals of other Ministries are arbitrary; (iii) The vesting of the power of security and control over the estimates of other Ministries into one Ministry (i.e. Finance desirable to constitute an independent scrutinising agency consisting of the representatives of all the Ministers under the chairmanship of Prime Minister.
2. The Second view is in favour of such a power being given to the Finance Ministry. The people who hold this view argue that (i) There should be somebody to take care of the tax payer. Since Finance Ministry collects taxes, it should be in a position to act as a disinterested guardian of the tax payer's interest. (ii) The responsibility of raising the revenue proposed in the budget is on the shoulders of the Finance Ministry. It is its job to supply the money to all the other Ministries. Hence, it is justifiable, that the power to review and control the estimates should be in its hands.
3. Executive Approval and Submission to the Parliament: The third stage in the process of budget-making in India is that all the estimates in their final form are placed before Union Cabient. The cabinet

discusses the whole budget and, if necessary, makes necessary minor adjustments and gives its final approval. Then the whole budget is ready for presentation to the Union parliament for enactment. It now moves from Cabinet room to Parliament House.

4. Full Picture of the Budget on the Eve of the Presentation to the Parliament: The Annual Financial Statement (called budget) is laid before the Parliament towards the end of February every year. This 'Annual Financial statement 'Budget contains an estimate of all anticipated revenue and expenditure of the Union Government for the coming fiscal year. Apart from giving the estimate of revenue and expenditure the budget also contains (i) a review of the financial position of the preceding year; and (ii) proposals for financing capital expenditure. The demands for grants are shown separately for each Ministry. The budget is divided into 109 demands (i) 103 for civil expenditure and (ii) 6 for defence expenditure. (The Railway budget has 23 demands).

The estimates of expenditure shown in the budget are divided into two separate parts (ii) expenditure charged upon consolidated Fund of India; (Art. 112(2). The former i.e. the expenditure charged upon Consolidated Fund of India, includes: (Art. 112(3)(i) salaries and allowance of the President of India, Speaker and Deputy Speaker of the Lok Sabha, Chairman and Deputy Chairman of the Rajya Sabha, judges of the Supreme Court, Comptroller and Auditor General of India: (ii) the pensions payable to the judges of the Supreme Court and Federal Court; (iii) debt charges for which Government of India is liable; (iv) expenditure necessary in connection with any judgment, decree or award of any court or tribunal and (v) any other expenditure which may be included by parliament by law. All the expenditure which may be included by parliament by law. All the expenditure mentioned here is not subject to the vote of the parliament. However the parliament can discuss this item. All other expenditure is included under the second part:

The estimates of expenditure shown in the budget are of two kinds: (i) expenditure on revenue account and (ii) other expenditure.

Enactment of the Budget: The fifth stage in the process of budget-making in India is the enactment of the budget by the parliament. The constitution requires the president to cause to be laid before both the House of parliament the Annual Financial Statement every year. There are five steps in the enactment of the budget in India. Each step may be examined.

1. The first step is the presentation (or introduction) Of the budget to the parliament, the budget is first presented to Lok Sabha and then to Rajya Sabha. It is presented by the Minister for Finance) At the time of the introduction of the budget in the Lower House the Minister for Finance makes a speech usually called Budget speech which outlines the main features of the budget.

2. The second step is the general discussion of the budget by the parliament. The speaker fixes the time usually two or three days during which the members are free to discuss the general features of the budget. However the detailed discussion of the budget is not permitted at this stage. The General discussion takes place in both the house of the parliament.

3. The third step is the voting of demands for grants. This is an important step in the process of enacting the budget. The voting of demands means voting of the expenditure part of the budget by the Parliament. In this context it is necessary to remember the constitutional provisions.

According to the constitution (i) All demands for grants should be made only on the recommendation of the president (Art. 113(3) (ii) All proposals involving expenditure should be introduced in the parliament only on the recommendations of the president (iii) The charged expenditure, i.e. the expending charged on the Consolidated Fund of India should not be put to vote of the parliament (Art: 113(1) but it may be discussed. Demands are separately introduced for each Ministry by the Minister concerned. Before the demands for grant are voted there takes place a through discussion in the parliament. The Speaker fixes the time for the discussion. The demands of all the Ministries have to be passed within this period. At this stage the members may criticise or move cut motions which may or may not be approved by the legislature. It is during this period that the fate of the Government is decided. If any cut motion is passed by the lower House against the wishes of the Ministry, it amounts to no-confidence. At the end of the discussion each demand is put to vote and passed by the prescribed majority of the House. The Lok Sabha has the monopoly of power in voting demands. The Rajya Sabha has no any voice in this matter. The constitution authorised the Lok Sabha to assent or refuse to assent, to any amount specified therein. It means that the Lok Sabha has the power to reduce or refuse to pass the expenditure brought before it but not to increase. A demand, when voted duly, becomes a grant.

4. The fourth step is the voting of the taxes. There cannot take place expenditure without corresponding revenue. The principal source of revenue of the Government is taxes. Hence every budget makes provision for new or additional taxation. But the Government cannot collect taxes without the sanction of the parliament. Art 265 of the Constitution says: "No tax shall be levied or collected except by authority of law". It implies that the Parliament by law has to authorise the Government to levy and collect taxes.

However, certain taxes which are of permanent character do not come under this category. Thus all the tax proposals presented in the budget are voted by the Parliament (especially by the Lok Sabha). All the revenues of the Government are formed into Consolidation Fund of India. All proposals for taxation should be introduced in the parliament on the recommendation of the President. The Lok Sabha has the monopoly of power involving taxes.

5. The fifth and last stage is the enactment of budget. The Budget is enacted by the parliament of India in the form of two acts viz. The appropriation act and the finance act. Firstly, all the demands for grants are enacted by the Parliament into an act called the Appropriation Act. This act authorise the Government to withdraws money from the consolidated fund for meeting the expenditure. This act is passed by the parliament at the commencement of every new financial year. Secondly, all the tax proposals enacted by the parliament are embodied in another act called the Finance Atc. This act authorises the Government to raise revenue through taxation. This act is passed by the Parliament at the commencement of every new financial year.

The Appropriation Bill and Finance Bill are passed, first by the Lok Sabha and then, sent to the Rajya Sabha. The latter has to return them to the Lok Sabha within fourteen days. The assent of the President is necessary for these two Bills to become Acts.

Supplementary and Exceptional Grants: Apart from voting grants in the General budget, the parliament can vote other grants whenever required by the Government. These grants are of two kinds: Supplementary grants, and exceptional grants.

1. Supplementary Grants are those grants which are granted by the Parliament to the Government during

the financial year. Supplementary grants become necessary under three circumstances: They are (Art 115(1)): (i) If the grants sanctioned in the budget are found insufficient for any service during the year: (ii) if a need for additional expenditure upon some new service arises: (iii) if the money spent to any service during the year is in excess of the amount granted for that year. Whenever supplementary grants are necessary, a separate statement showing estimated expenditure should be presented to the Parliament. Supplementary Grants are also called the additional or excess grants.

Exceptional Grants (Art 116(1): Exceptional Grants are those grants which are granted by the parliament to the Government to meet any unforseen or sudden expenditure. The exceptional grants do not form the part of the current service of any financial year. Two methods are followed in granting exceptional grants. (1) The Parliament by law authorises the president to withdraw money from the consolidated fund of India (Art 116(1)]. The president may advance money out of the Contigency Fund of India which are to be authorised by the Parliament later on (Art 267(1)]. The exceptional grants are also called special grants.

Execution of the Budget: After enacting the budget, the next important stage is its execution. The execution of the budget is the responsibility of the executive. Finance Ministry plays a special role in this field. All the expenditure by the various Ministries has to be approved by the Finance Ministry in its capacity as the financial representative and adviser to the Government. However, due to severe criticism in the country and from the point of view of rapid comprehensive, socio-economic development, the control of the Finance Ministry has been limited in 1959. The Delegation of powers Rules, 1959 authorised Ministries to incur expenditure freely on any new scheme involving an expenditure Rs. 50 lakhs. To receive proper advice each Ministry has Financial Advisers. Inspite of this, the Finance Ministry still exercise sufficient control over the execution of the budget.

Lapsing of Budgetary Grants: Before the whole discussion can be closed it is necessary to deal with the lapsing of grants in India. It means that all the expenditure granted in the budget should be spent by the government by the end of the financial year. If any expenditure granted in the budget remains unspent during the year, that amount lapses at the end of the year. Such amount can not be transferred to any future year or years. That is why the figures of the expenditure of the government would be very high during the closing months of the financial year, especially in March. The level of monthly expenditure of the central government suddenly shoots up in March. This is well known in government circles, and even among the legislators as the March Rush (O.K. Ghosh). It is not easy to point as to who, Ministry of Finance or other Ministries, are responsible for this kind of situation. O.K. Ghosh observes;. There have been the usual recriminations about this March Rush. Executive officers have often put the blame on the Finance Department for being tardy in sanctioning expenditure. Finance Department replied black that many proposals come to late or in a half baked manner. So long as the principle of lapse exists, it is not possible to spend money more evenly and more judiciously.

BUDGET AS A TOOL OF PUBLIC ADMINISTRATION

Firstly, Budget supplies necessary finance to the State. No state can function without a government. Government is conducted by a number of civil servants called by the term Public administration. The whole administrative activity is dependent on finance. It is the wheel of the chariot of administration. Without finance there can be no administrative activity, no salaries, for the officials, no welfare programmes etc., because all these require money. As L.D. White observed: Every administrative act has its financial activities. Nothing can be done without expenditure of money... management of finance is the first responsibility of administrator. He also further said: Finance and administration cannot be divorced. Eve administrative act has its financial implication as inseparable as a man and his shadow. Since all finance of the government is supplied by the budget, it can undoubtedly be considered an essential tool of administration. Without Budget, the administration cannot have money to spend.

Budget authorises administration to assess, collect and gather the needed revenue. Administration cannot raise revenue without budgetary grants, It is in this respect that budget is a tool of administration.

Secondly, Budget gives legislative control over public funds. The revenue and expenditure of administration are controlled by the legislature. The slogan of democracy is that government should not raise revenue without the approval of the people who ultimately pay all the money. No taxation without representation is the corner stone of democracy. So all the revenue, before it is collected, must be approved by the legislature consisting of popular representatives. This is done in all the modern states including England. The U.S. and India. The legislature examines carefully all the estimates prepared by the administration with the help of its committees. The Estimates Committee in England and India, finance committees in the U.S. are the examples. This helps to secure economy, reduce waste and utilise best the national resources. It is in this respect that budget is a tool of administration.

Thirdly, Budget not only supplies necessary finance to the administration, but also authorises it to incur expenditure on various items. Mere supply of money is of no use without having authority to spend it. Budget gives this authority to the government. Every year, the legislature enacts an Appropriation Act permitting administration to spend money. This act authorises the issue of money from the treasury to meet expenditure. The budget lays down the purposes for which the money shall be devoted. If the Appropriation Act is not passed by the legislature before the commencement of the new financial year, the administration will have no money to spend on the first day of the new financial year. The administration becomes paralised.

Fourthly, Budget gives legislative control over public expenditure. Since all money is paid by the people, the legislature should act as a watchdog of public expenditure. Otherwise, the administrators may incur illegal, improper and unauthorised expenditure. Control over the expenditure prevents wastage, secures economy and desired results. The legislature which votes all grant has every right to know as to how the grants are used by the administration. This procedure is attained in all the modern states including England, U.S. and India. The Public Accounts Committee in England and India, the Congressional committee in the U.S. play an important part in securing expenditure control. Finally, at the end of the year, the legislature of these states arrange for auditing of these accounts. It is in this respect that budget is a tool of administration.

Fifthly, Budget secures the responsibility of the administration to the executive in matter of expenditure. The executive which is entrusted with the task of spending money is to have control over its officials who actually spend money. The departmental heads carefully watches as to how his subordinates are spending money. It is his responsibility to see that his staff does not spend public funds in excess of the budgetary grants. He also takes care to see that the grants are not transferred from one item to the other without the authorization. Thus the budget is a tool of administration.

Sixthly, Budget as a document of information has a great value. It is source of information to the public and the legislature. The budget speech or message which is delivered at the time of introduction in the House carries with it a valuable information. It presents an exposition of the revenues and expenditure of the government. It also furnishes information regarding the general character, purpose and amount of government expenditure, detailed data regarding the cost entailed in maintaining particular units of administration. It helps public to know the state of financial affairs of the administration, the welfare programmes that it is going to undertake, the new taxes that they have to pay, the business community eagerly awaits the budget speech of the finance minister in all the states. The budget is a tool of administration.

Seventhly, Budget has a great value as a work programme and public policy. As a work programme, budget translates into monetary terms the programme of activities. It is a statement of the various resources required to achieve these objectives. As the budget is presented by the chief executive to the legislature, it is a statement of major public policy. It gives an emphatic expression of objectives of government service. All these have profound influence upon the functioning of the whole country. Budget has an impact upon employment, production, price levels and distribution of income. The budget is a tool of administration.

Lastly, Budget as a tool of securing economy in government operation has a much value. It is an instrument of balancing of income and outgo in terms of available tax receipts. If all expenditure proposals are brought together in one place and carefully scrutinized, then some economies in operation are possible. However, budget can only focus attention upon the issue of economy, but social, economic and political circumstances determine the magnitude of government expenditure. The Budget is a tool of administration.

It is clear from the above argument that budget has an important role to play in the administration-general and financial. Willoughby describes budget as central instrument and White as an essential tool of administration.

Methods of Executive Control of Public Expenditure

The executive controls the public expenditure in India through the following agencies:

(a) The Departmental Control;

(b) Finance Ministry;

(c) Audit.

The nature and functions of each agency may be discussed as below:

1. ***The Departmental Control:*** The first agency through which the executive in India controls public expenditure is the head of the department. He watches the expenditure incurred by the officials working under him or in the offices under his jurisdiction. The various officers submit accounts every month showing the money spent by them towards various items. The total amount granted to a particular department is allotted between various items. The officers should not spend money in excess of the allotment made. Further, the amount allotted to one item cannot be transferred to another without the permission of the head. However the critics point out that department control over public expenditure is not very effective. The reason is that the receipt

and disbursements of public money take place in nearly 300 district treastures, each having sub-treasuries under its control. Hence it is not possible for the departmental head to know periodically the amount and purpose for which the public money is spent. Due to this it is not possible to keep a track of up to-date progress of expenditure either by the executive or by the Accounts authorities.

2. ***The Finance Ministry:*** The second agency through which the executive in India controls public expenditure is the Ministry of Finance. The overall control of the expenditure of various Ministries is vested in the Ministry of Finance. Till the year 1959, the Finance Ministry exercised effective control over the expenditure of the Ministries. The concurrence of the Finance Ministry was necessary for any new expenditure envisaged by the Ministries of the central Government. The various departments were required to send reports to the Finance Ministry about the expenditure incurenced by them. The ministries were required to surrender unspent balances before the close of the financial year.

However, the delegation of powers Rules, 1959, have limited the control of the Finance Ministry over the expenditure of other Ministries. These rules have authorised all the Ministries to spend the government money free on any scheme involving an expenditure of Rs. 50 lakhs. At present each Ministry consist of financial advisers who help the Ministry in the control of the expenditure against appropriation. Again in the year 1961 the central government limited the control of the Finance Ministry in the field of expenditure control. The ministries are required to make reference to the Finance Ministry only on very important matters.

Audit: The third agency through which the executve in India controls public expenditure is the Audit. Audit is defined as a systematic examination of the accounts of the revenue and expenditure. Each Ministry or Department of the Government of India maintained accounts showing all the financial transactions. The account maintained by the Ministries present a clear picture of the following:

1. total amount granted in the Budget;
2. total amount actually received;
3. total amount spent;
4. the purpose for which the amount is spent.

All these accounts of the Ministries are examined at the end of every financial year. Audit discovers illegal, irregular and improper expenditure incurred by the officials. The audit determines the correctness of the account and fixes the responsibility for illegal and improper expenditure.

In India, the audit is carried by the Comptroller and Auditor General whose appointment, salary, conditions of service and functions are governed by the constitution. He arranges for auditing the accounts of the Union and the states. At the end he prepares a report of his findings and submits it to the President of India. The report of the Comptroller and Auditor General of India brings in the light all cases of the illegal, improper, irregular, excessive expenditure and also misappropriations. The report is finally laid on the tables of the parliament.

Thus the role of the Comptroller and Auditor—General is unique in the sphere of financial administration. He takes care of the finances, ensures economy and proper use of public funds.

CHAPTER—10

Control of Public Finance

AUDIT AND ACCOUNTING

Meaning of Accounting

Accounting means keeping a systematic record of the financial transactions. It is done by all authorities—public or private-individual and organization. In the modern government accounting is the duty of the executive. An account presents clearly the facts relating to financial conditions, the amounts received from time to time and spent together with vouchers. Accounting is valuable for the following reasons:

1. It reveals the exact picture of financial position which is necessary for a government.
2. It secures responsibility of officials who are in charge of collecting and spending public funds. There can be no scope for misappropriation.
3. It gives proper control to the executive head over his subordinates, L.D. White says: "one of the principal values of an accounting system is consequently the aid it furnishes in super visiting, planing and adjusting work programmes in the light of rapidly changing economics conditions."

Meaning of Audit: Audit begins where accounting ends, Audit means examination of accounts. When accounts are maintained, all items are entered and vouchers enclosed. Such examination of accounts is called audit. The following are the definitions of audit.

1. ***R.H. Montgomery:*** "Auditing is a systematic examination of the books and records of a business or other organization in order to ascertain or verify and to report upon the facts—regarding its financial operation and result thereof.

2. ***J.C. Worth:*** Audit is the "progress of ascertaining whether the administration has spent or is spending its funds in accordance with the term of the legislative instrument which appropriated money.

Thus, audit is a name given to the work relating to the examination of accounts of the government or a private organization to determine whether expenditure is made in accordance with law.

Distinction between Accounting and Auditing: The meaning of accounting and auditing given above, reveal two differences between the two.

1. Accounting means keeping systematic accounts of financial transaction. On the other hand, auditing means examination of accounts to see whether expenditure is incured in accordance with the law passed. Audit is an act of detecting errors, frauds, misappropriations etc.
2. Accounting is the business of the executive. It is done by the officials who are in charge of financial transactions. On the other hand, auditing is the business of parliament to find out whether financial administration is carried in accordance with the law.
3. Accounting is a continuous process which runs throughout the financial year. Auditing is done at the end of the financial year. Thus, audit begins where accounting ends.

Origin and Development of Audit: We shall present of brief sketch of the origin and development of audit in modern state. Its was not in existence until the middle of the 19th century.

1. England was the earliest to introduce a systematic auditing. The Exchequer and Audit Departments Act of 1886. Created comptroller and Auditor-General. He enjoyed the office during good behaviour. He was entrusted with these functions. (1) Examination of account of the Treasury and other departments. (2) Checking of expenditure items to determine their legality (3) Making a report to the public Accounts Committee of the House of Commons.
2. In the U.S.A. there was no systematic auditing until 1921. The Treasury department Act of 1798 created a Comptroller, a Treasurer, an Auditor and a Book-Keeping Officer. The Dockery Act of 1894 determined the functions of the auditors.

The most important event in the field of Auditing in the USA is the Budget and Accounting Act of 1921. It introduced two changes:

1. A separate intuition of audit and accounts was created called "general Accounting office."
2. A Comptroller General was appointed to lead the office. He was independent of the executive and appointed for a term of 15 years. He had two functions, viz., examination of payments of officers and settlement of claims.
3. In India auditing was introduced by the Act of 1919. A systematic auditing came into vogue after the inauguration of the constitution. At present the Comptroller and Auditor—General is at the head of the Indian Audit department. He enjoys perfect independence. His appointment, tenure, conditions of service etc., are governed by the provisions of the

constitution. The functions of the Comptroller and auditor—general include examination of accounts of the Union and the State Government and submit annual reports to the President.

IMPORTANCE OF AUDIT

Audit occupies a unique place in financial administration because of the following reasons.

1. Audit determines the correctness of the accounts maintained by the government. It determines whether accounts are maintained properly or not, whether all the receipts are entered and expenditures noted, the purpose for which it is spent. Audit examines all transactions with the help of vouchers and receipts.
2. Audit acts as a check against improper and illegal spending of public funds. It examines whether money is spent in accordance with the legislative authority; whether it is spent by the officer authorised, whether funds are spent under the head for which they are allotted. Audit locates the cases of embezzelment of loss of funds. Thus audit acts as a watchdog of public expenditure. It checks improper, illegal, false, careless, erroneous expenditure. Hence it acts as a semi-judicial authority.
3. Audit ensures economy and avoids waste in public expenditure. All cases of improper and excess spending are brought into light. A report is made every year which contains all facts and figures. Audit report recommends to the government to take necessary action against the officials responsible for mismanagement of public money.

PARLIAMENTARY CONTROL OVER PUBLIC EXPENDITURE IN INDIA

Parliamentary control: It is the Parliament which votes the necessary expenditure to various Ministries of the

Government of India. So the parliament has the responsibility to see whether the money granted by it is spent by the administration economically, properly and within budget estimates. In other words, the Union Parliament has to exercise effective control over public expenditure. The parliament controls public expenditure through the following agencies:

1. The Public Accounts Committee.
2. The Estimates Committee.

These two committees are, sometimes, called the financial committees of the parliament. The nature and functions of each committee may be discussed as below:

1. ***The Public Accounts Committee:*** The first agency through which the Union Parliament controls the public expenditure is the Public Accounts Committee. This committee was created in India, for the first time in 1923. But the members of this committee were all the officials. However, the constitution of India brought about changes in the composition and functions of the committee. The organization and function of the P.A.C. are based on the British model.

The Public Accounts Committee of 22 members of which 15 are chosen from the Lok Sabha and 7 from the Rajya Sabha. (In the U.K. there is no representation from the House of Lords). The term of the members is one year. The election of the members is held on the basis of proportional representation by single transferable vote. The chairman of the P.A.C. is appointed by the Speaker. If the Deputy Speaker is a member of the P.A.C. he is ipso-facto the chairman. (The Chairmanship in the U.K. is offered to the opposition party). The chairman of the P.A.C. has a casting vote in case of a tie. The quorum is fixed at 4.

1. It scrutinises the appropriation accounts of the various Ministries of the Government of India on the basis

of the Audit report of the Comptroller and Auditor—General of India. It calls for the officials of the Ministries to explain the irregularities and improper transactions" if any, pointed out in the audit report.

2. It examines the accounts of the Ministries and finds out whether the public funds are spent legally, properly and within the budgetary limits. It scrutinises and decides whether the expenditure incurred by the officials confirms to the authority which governs it. Thus the committee conducts a post moreterm examination of the public accounts. It acts as a great check on the slackness or negligence of the administration in respect of public expenditure.

In performing these functions, the Public Accounts Committee is assisted by the Comptroller and Auditor—General of India. At the/end of the whole examination, the committee prepares a report which contains the results of the examination. The report of the Committee is laid on the table of each House of the Parliament. The significant role played by the Public Accounts Committee is well brought out by Asok Chanda. From its very inception, the Central Public Accounts Committee became a major force in the legislative control of public expenditure....it exercised enormous influence in bringing pressure to bear upon Government to enforce economy in the expenditure of public money.

Each state legislature in India has its own Public Accounts Committee performing similar functions.

1. The Estimates Committee: The second agency through which the Union Parliament controls the public expenditure is the Estimate Committee. Prior to independence there was only a Standing Finance Committee which functioned under the control of the Finance Department. The Estimates Committee of Union Parliament came into existence in the year

1950. Its role became increasingly important since 1953. It is based on the model of the British Estimates Committee.

The Estimates Committee consists of 30 members all chosen from the Lok Sabha only. The term of office is one year. The election of the members is held on the basis of the proportional representation by single transferable vote. The chairman of the Estimates Committee is appointed by the Speaker of the Lok Sabha from among the members. If the Deputy Speaker of the Lok Sabha is the member of the Estimates Committee, he will be appointed its Chairman. The following are the principal functions of the Estimates Committee.

1. It scrutinises the estimates of various Ministers and suggests necessary steps by which economy could be secured. It recommends various methods by which the cost of the administration could be brought down. It also puts forth the proposals for the purpose of eliminations of waste, best utilization of public personnel etc. It may suggest the abandonment of any policy or policies on account of which the government is incurring heavy expenditure. In the course of its work it may examine any paper or record and office.

The estimates Committee may call the officials of the ministry whose estimates are being examined to appear before it. It may call upon non-officials to tender evidence. It may undertake tours to the field establishments to examine the expenditure.

At the end of the whole work, the committee prepares a report which contains "recommendations for improving the organization, for securing economy, and for providing guidance in the presentation of the estimate. The report is laid on the table of the Lok Sabha. There have been some criticisms in recent years regarding the functions and procedures of the committee.

The Estimates committee has been doing a very valuable work since its inception. It has recommended for (1) the reorganization of the Secretariat (2) the reorganization of the state—owned industries, and (3) amalgamation of two presses viz., printing stamps and currency notes at Nasik.

Thus, the Estimates Committee has been exerting an healthy influence in the course of public expenditure. It is acting as a deterrent, against extravagance.

The Committee was established on the ground that it is acting as a fault-finding machinery.

Each state legislature has its own Estimates Committee.

OFFICE OF THE COMPTROLLER AND AUDITOR GENERAL

It is essential to study the organization and functions of the Indian Audit system at present. The Audit in India is carried on by the Indian Audit Department. It is headed by an officer called the Comptroller and Auditor—General of India. His appointment, salary, removal, powers and functions are governed by the constitution. So it is necessary to study the relevant provisions of constitution (Art 148 to 151).

1. The Comptroller and Auditor—General of India is appointment by the President of India by warrant and his hand seal. He can be removed only on the grounds of proved misbehaviour or in capacity and in the manner in which a Supreme Court judge is removed (Art. 148(1).
2. The salary and conditions of service of the comptroller and Auditor—General are to be determined by the Parliament. They cannot be altered to disadvantage during the tenure of his office (Art. 148(3)) The Act of 1953 fixed his tensure of 6 years. Salary is same as that of a judge of the Supreme Court.

3. He is prohibited to take up any office either under the Union or State Government after retirement {(Art. 148(4)}

4. His salary and allowance and pensions are to be charged upon the consolidated Fund of India (Art 148(6)} Thus it is clear that the constitution intends the Comptroller and Auditor General to be an independent and impartial officer in the discharge of his functions.

Power and Functions: The powers and functions of the Comptroller and Auditor-General of India are not clearly defined by the constitution. It leaves the matter to the Parliament to determine. Until the parliament determines the powers, he shall exercise those powers which were exercised by the Auditor General of India before the commencement of the Constitution. At present he has four powers.

1. He is responsible for maintaing the accounts of the Union and States. (Art. 149) (ii) He prescribes the form of accounts to be maintained by the Union and States with the approval of the President (Art. 150) (iii) He audits the accounts of the Union and States. At the end of the whole audit, he prepares a report of his findings and submits it to the President {Art151(1)} In the case of states the report is submitted to the Governor {Art 151(2)}(iv) An executive order of 1947 authorised the Comptroller and Auditor—General to ascertain whether the expenditure was incurred legally for the purpose for which money was allotted and by the proper authority. The reports of the Comptroller and Auditor General explain whether the officials of various departments have observed the provisions of the budget in respect of expenditure: whether the amount is spent in excess of the grants voted by the parliament whether the public funds are spent with

due authority and for proper purpose. During the audit if he comes across any cases or instances involving illegal irregular improper, unauthorized and excessive expenditure or misappropriation the Comptroller and Audit—General brings them into light. The report is finally placed on the table of the parliament (legislative in case of the states).

The office of the Comptroller and Audit-General is situated at New Delhi. He is assisted by three Deputy Comptrollers and Auditors—General and a large number of staff. There are separate sections dealing with civil order and accounts, post and telegraph audit, railway audit and defence audit. Of these the section dealing with civil audi is the biggest. The administration is decentralized. There are account officers at each state capital under the Contro of Accountants—General for the purpose of maintainin and auditing state accounts.

The foregoing discussing clearly lays down the tru importance of the role of the Comptroller and Audito General. He plays a unique role in the sphere of financia administration. The constitution accords him a distinctl important place. He takes the utmost care of nation finances. By his careful audit the Comptroller and Auditor General ensures the economy and proper use of publi funds on behalf of the parliament.

CHAPTER—11

Administrative Responsibility

MEANING OF ADMINISTRATIVE RESPONSIBILITY

'he Principal function of the administration in a state is he execution of the public policies. To perform this duty atisfactorily, the administrative agencies need some power. Vithout possessing adequate power it is not possible for he administrator to implement the state policies. But there s no guarantee that the powers, may be misused or bused. So if power is not to be abused, it must be ccompanied by some control. Especially, power in a emocratic society requires control. And the greater the ower the more need for control'. For this purpose every fficial is to be made responsible or accountable to one or nore authorities. In other words, in a state, administration nust be responsible to appropriate authorities (e.g. egislature executive or judiciary, or people) for all its ctions. This responsibility of the administration to the due uthorities is known as administrative responsibility.

L.D. White defines: "Administrative responsibility onsists of the sum total of the constitutional, statutory, dministrative and judicial rules and precedents and the stablished practices by means of which public officials may e held accountable for their official actions".

Dr. M.P. Sharma defines: "In the final analysis esponsibility means liability to give a satisfactory account of the exercise of the power of discretion vested in some authority to which it is due, failing which some kind of evil or punishment may follow".

From the definitions noted above, it is possible to note here under the essential features of administrative responsibility.

(i) Where there is duty there must be power.

(ii) Where there is power there must be control. It is followed by responsibility.

(iii) The responsibility is defined in the rules and regulations made from time to time.

(iv) The failure on the part of the administrator to be accountable leads to punishment.

THE NEED FOR ADMINISTRATIVE RESPONSIBILITY

The administrative responsibility is an important aspect of the modern state activity. It is because of two reasons which are mentioned below:

1. Firstly, man is selfish by nature: The administrator who is the main spring of new society is not free from this selfishness. So, at times, the administrator may be liable to misuse or abuse his power. It leads to all kinds of social problems which hinder the progress of the state. Therefore, it becomes necessary to bring the administrative actions under the control of the appropriate authorities. So where there is power, it should be accompanied by some form of responsibility.
2. Secondly, the importance of the administrative responsibility is very great in democracy. The success of democracy depends upon the extent of the rights and liberty enjoyed by the people. In other words, the quality of democracy is measured in terms of rights and liberty that people possess. At times the

administrators may violate or encroach upon the rights of the people. So it becomes necessary to 'protect the constitutional and other legal rights of persons against the abuse or unauthorised use of power in special cases'. This is secured by means of control and administrative responsibility.

3. Thirdly, the modern state is a welfare state. As a result, the activities of the public administration are ever growing by leaps and bounds. Increase in the activities calls for greater power and authority which, in turn, leads to centralization or bureaucracy. Hence, to check this, it becomes necessary to introduce administrative responsibility.

METHODS OF ADMINISTRATIVE RESPONSIBILITY

There are four methods (or agencies) by which the administrative responsibility is secured. They are

(i) Legislative control.

(ii) Ministerial control.

(iii) Judicial control and

(iv) Popular control.

1. Legislative control. In parliamentary system of government the legislature has the power to control, direct and supervise the administration.

(i) Firstly, the legislature exercises the control over the administration by such ways as questions, interpelations, censures, no-confidence motions etc., It initiates debates regarding the working of the administrative departments and criticizes their actions.

(ii) Secondly, the legislature controls the administration through public policy. It defines the goals, objects and aims with which the administration is to work. It lays down the

procedure by which the departments are to function. The legislature may enact a law within whose frame work the officials are to act and carry out their work. For example, in the U.S.A. legislature has the power to direct how administration shall be organized, how its duties shall be performed and what methods of procedure shall be employed.

(iii) Lastly, the legislature controls the administration through the power or purse. It sanctions expenditure, grants or with holds funds needed by the administration. It lays down the policy by which the expenditure is to be incurred by the department. It approves or disapprove the budget prepared by the administration.

2. Ministerial Control: The ministerial control over the administration is not great in presidential type of governments. The reasons is that the ministers, under this system, are the servants of the Presidents. But, in parliamentary system of government, the head of the state is nominal or titular, The real powers are exercised by the Ministers on his behalf.

(i) Firstly, the ministers are the head of the various departments. They supervise, direct and control the staff under them. They may lay down the rules of procedure governing the work of the officials.

(ii) Secondly, the Ministers control the administration by such ways as appointments, promotions, removals, disciplinary actions, Enquiriers and investigations.

(iii) Thirdly, the ministers control the administration through the power of finance. The framing of the budget. The spending of

money and maintaining accounts are done under the vigilance of the ministers. It is the cabinet or ministry that decides the nature of expenditure to be incurred by the administration. To ensure the proper use of finance, the accounts of the administration are audited every years.

3. Judicial control: Every modern democratic state established judicial control over the administration. The judiciary secures the responsibility of the administration in many ways:

(i) Firstly, judiciary controls the administration by means of Judicial review. By this, the judicial authority has the power to review all official actions. If in the opinion of the court, a particular act of the administration is contrary to the constitution or in excess of the authority, or in violation of the fundamental rights of the citizens. The court declares that act null and void.

(ii) Secondly, the judiciary Controls the administration by means of appeals. In a democratic state, the Individual has the right to appeal to the court in case he is adversely affected by the acts of administration. He can file a suit in the court for necessary damages. Thus L.D. White says that "the suit by private partis to enforce civil and criminal liability of officers remains one of the established forms of judicial controls."

(iii) Thirdly, the judiciary controls the administration by means of various remedies consisting of various writs. They are (i) Hebeas Corpus by which the court can bring out the liberation of an illegally, imprisoned individual (ii) Mandamus

by which the court on petition of a private individual, can compel the official to perform the duty specified therein. (iii) Prohibition (or injunction) by which the court can stop an official action which is likely to cause damage or loss of individual rights. (iv) Certiorari by which the superior court can order transfer of a case from an inferior court for its scrutiny or review or determination. (v) Quo Warranto by which the court can prevent an illegally appointed or elected person from functioning in that office.

4. The popular control: Democracy is based on the concept of popular sovereignty. It means all the organs of the government are, ultimately, responsible to the people. There are many ways by which the people enforce public responsibility. They are (i) Petitions, (ii) Referendum, (iii) Initiative and (iv) Recall. The best example of this is Switzerland. In this country all the laws and constitutional amendments are to be submitted to popular vote for their approval or disapproval. The voters have the power to take initiative in the formulation of bills and submit them to the Assembly.

It is clear from the above discussion that the modern state has devised a number of ways by which the administrative system is secured. All the agencies of the administrative control discussed above are to be found in many countries like Britain, the U.S.A. India etc.

METHODS OF LEGISLATIVE CONTROL

J.S. Mill in his Representative Government, has emphasized that the principle function of a representative assembly is to control administration, but not to govern. At one place, he said: "the proper duty of a representative assembly in regard to matters of administration is not to decide them by its own Vote. But to take care that the persons who have to decide them shall be the proper persons". At another place he remarked: "Instead of the function of governing, for which it is radically unfit, the proper office of a representative assembly is to watch and control the government. Hence, we shall examine how the modern legislature controls administration.

The legislature secures the responsibility of the administration in several ways. They may be explained as below:

1. ***Questions etc:*** Firstly, the legislature, in parliamentary system of government controls the administration by several means such as questions, supplementary, interpolations, adjournment motions, votes of censure and no confidence. By putting questions the legislature seeks information from government on matters of administration. "Almost any act or commission of administrative authorities, from the highest to the lowest, can be made the subject of a question. The administrative officials cannot fail to take the note of the questions and their influence over them. Hugh Gaitskell eminently remarks: Anybody who has worked in civil service department would agree with me that if there is one major thing which leads civil servants to be excessive cautions, timid, and careful to keep records. It is the fear to parliamentary questions, A.S. Rikhy: It is though question hour that government is able quickly to feel the pulse of the nation and adopt its policies and action accordingly. Questions bring to the notice of Minister many an abuse which other wise would have gone unnoticed. Attlee, the former Prime Minister of England, remarked on the importance of questions. The effect of questions to the Minister and still more Questions asked in the House is to keep the whole of the civil service on their toes". Thus the values of parliamentary questions as an instrument of control of administration has been acclaimed by several

writers as well as parliamentarians. By adopting motions and resolutions, the legislature seeks to consure the government or administration. By passing the vote of no—confidence, the legislature seeks to over throw the government. Further, the legislature initiates debates regarding the working of the administrative department and criticises their actions. The debates of house bring into light the acts of ommission or commission of the administrative authorities.

2. ***Public Policy:*** Secondly, the legislature in parliamentary democracy controls the administration through public policy. It definest he goals, objects and aims with which the administration is to work. L.D. White observes: Administrative agencies do not set their own goals, are not self directed or self-sustained, and find their authority for action in the organic action and supplementary legislation". In totalitarian state the goal of the administration is the elevation of the state. In welfare state the goal of the administration is the elevation of the individual.

3. ***Law:*** Thirdly, the legislature, in parliamentary democracy controls the administration by means of law. The law lays down the basic frame work of administrative structure, powers, duties, methods, policies and procedures for the guidance of the officials. They are to act and carry out their work within this legal frame work. This type of control is exercised by the legislature in presidential type of government also. For example in the U.S.A. The Congress has the power to direct how the administration shall be organized, how its duties shall be performed and what methods of procedure shall be employed. It creates executive departments and other commissions. The senate has considerable influence over the appointments, etc. made by the administration. This senatorial conformation acts as

an effective check against corruption, nepotism and undue centralization of power in the hands of the administration. As finer says, the government departments are virtually forty great monopolies; they need a strong force outside them to shake them up.

4. ***Legislative Committees:*** Fourthly the legislature controls the administration by means of various committees appointed by it. These committees conducts investigation into the working of administrative departments. They keep an eye and exercise continuous watchfulness over the activities of the administration. This system has acquired great importance in the USA. Both houses of the US Congress maintain standing committees. The Senate, through its investigation committees examine the working, organization and methods of various departments. Willoughby says that legislative committees can exercise administrative control through these methods.

1. Checking records reports, audit, information investigation or inquiries and determination of legality of administrative acts.

5. ***Finance.*** Lastly the legislature secures the administrative responsibility through the power of pursse. In all democratic states the legislature controls and regulates national finance. It sanctions all the expenditure of the administration. It lays down the methods by which various departments of administration have to incur expenditure. It determines the amount of revenue to be raised by the administration. Its sanction is necessary for levying new taxes and repealing old taxes. The slogan of democracy is no taxation without representation. The legislature considers, Discusses, approves and authorizes the national budget. In countries like England and USA the expenditure for war requires

legislative confirmation. The congress in the USA appoints appropriation committees before which the administrative officials appear annually to explain and defend their estimates.

Parliamentary control over administration in India. India has a parliamentary system of government. It possesses all characteristics of a parliamentary system. The chief executive. Viz., the President is a nominal authority, the real powers being exercised by the Cabinet. The ministers are the members of either House of the Union Parliament. The Parliament of India has firm control over the administration. The methods by which he union parliament enforces the administrative responsibility may be mentioned below:

1. The parliament controls administration by means of questions, supplementaries, interpolations, resolutions, debates etc. The first hour of each days sitting is devoted to questions. The Speaker allots particulars days on which particular ministries are required to answer questions. All questions are asked according to prescribed rules and with the prior permission of the Presiding officer. Though the answers to the questions are given by the ministers, they are really prepared by the administrative officials of the government. Supplementary questions are put the ministers where the answer for original questionis not satisfactory. The ministers can decline to give answers on the ground of public interest. The debates also help the parliament to secure administrative responsibility.

2. The parliament controls administration by means of purse. It is custodian of the national finance. It approves the budget at the beginning of every year. The demands of expenditure of the administration is voted by the Lok Sabha. It also sanctions revenue, special grants and supplementary grants required by the administration.

3. The parliament controls administration by means of committees. Viz. The Estimates Committee and Public Accounts Committee. The former consists of 30 members elected by the Lok Sabha from among its members on the basis of proportional representation by means of single tansferable vote. Its duty is to examine the estimates of the ministries and make a report on it. The Public Accounts Committee consists of 22 members elected on the above model. Its duty is to examine the accounts of the administrative departments after they had been audited by the Comptroller and Auditor General of India. The official of the department appear before it and explain the irregulatrities if any. At the end, the committee prepares a report to be submitted to the parliament. The accounts of the administration are audited every year by the Comptroller and Auditor General of India.

Thus, the above discussion shows, that the Union Parliament has its control over administration.

EXECUTIVE CONTROL OVER ADMINISTRATION

The parliamentary type of government consists of two executives.

1. Nominal executive and
2. Real executive

The nominal executive may consist of hereditary king as in Britain or it may consist of an elected President as in India and other states. He is the titular head of the state without any power and authority. He has no any responsibility. Legally speaking all the powers of the state belong to him. But, in fact, he does not exercise them. The real executive may consist of the cabinet. The cabinet consists of Prime Minister and other ministers. It is the real executive authority of the state exercising all powers that belong to the chief executive of the state. The ministers are the members of the legislature, have no fixed tenure and are responsible to it. In all parliamentary type of governments the executive has full control over the administration. In presidential type of governments also the chief executive enjoys similar control over the administration.

METHODS OF EXECUTIVE CONTROL

The executive secures the administrative responsibility in several ways. They may be explained as follows:

1. ***Supervision and Direction:*** The first method by which the executive controls the administration is supervision and direction. Supervision has been defined as the authoritative direction of the work of ones subordinates. Thus supervision and direction go together. In parliamentary system ministry allocates various departments among various ministers. Each ministr is the head of his department. He presides over the meetings of the departmental officials. He directs and supervises the flow of departmental business of his departmental officials. In other words, the minister carefully watches the work of the officials. If he finds out that the officials are not carrying out the administration properly or according to rules, he instructs them to discharge their duties properly. He also sees if the instructions are properly carried out or not. Thus the administration of the whole department is subject to the supervision of the minister (i.e.. Executive). The principal duty of the administration is to execute the law and enforce policies of the state. The chief Executive in every state has the principal power to direct and supervise the works of administration he USA France etc., where presidential system prevails, the chief executive supervises and directs the administration of the whole state. Thus the executive, in this respect, acts as a general manager of the administration.

Appointments and Removals: The second method by which the executive controls administrative is appointments and removals. The chief executive has the right of appointing and removing the administrative staff. He is entrusted with the task of appointing the heads of various department of the government. The practice may differ from state to state. In the U.S.A. the president makes appointments with the consent of the Senate. In Britain and India the head of the state makes appointments on the recommendation of the Cabinet. What ever may be the practice, the fact is that the power of appointment gives the executive wide power to control the administration and secure its responsibility. Besides, the executive also has the power of removing the administrative staff including the heads of the departments. The officials who violate the rules, neglect duties, practice corruption, cultivate in discipline and gross insubordination are liable to be removed or dismissed or prosecuted by the executive. Even in the USA the power of the executive to remove the officials without the consent of the state is accepted by the supreme court and most constitutional lawyers. This is a powerful weapon of controlling administration. J.S. Mill says that the civil servants should not be removed from service except for positive, proved and serious misconduct; voluntary neglect of duty or untrustworthy conduct.

2. ***Rules, orders etc.:*** The third method by which the executive controls administration is the power to make rules and regulations, issue orders, decrees, proclamations and ordinances from time to time. The president (i.e. in presidential system) or the ministers (i.e., in parliamentary system) have the power to frame rules and regulations according to which the administration is to be carried out. This power is necessary in order to ensure the proper administration of law and maintenance of peace, order, and security. All the officials of the administration are accountable to the executive for the manner in which they

perform the duties conferred upon them by law. Now and then, the chief executive of the state issues ordinances whose purpose, among others may be to make changes in or direct the administration.

3. ***Administrative reports:*** The fourth method by which the executive controls administration is the administrative reports. The chief executive (or minister) calls for annual or biennial reports from the officials. With the help of these reports, the executive head will be in a position to know the nature and amount of work turned out by the administration. He comes to know also the ommission and commission committed by the officials. This method, to a certain extent, secures the responsibility of the administrative officials.

4. ***Finance:*** The last method by which the executive controls administration is finance. The framing of budget, the spending of the money and maintaining of accounts are done under the vigilance of the ministers. It is the executive which decides the nature of the expenditure to be incurred by the administration. It arranges for the auditing of the accounts every year.

Executive Control over Administration in India

In India the executive has firm control over the administration. It employs all the methods which are discussed above to secure the administrative responsibility.

1. The President can direct, control and co-ordinate the work of administration both at the union and the states. The ministers, who are the head of the various departments, have the power of supervision and direction of the work of the officials of their respective departments.

2. The executive in India controls the administration by means of appointments and removals. The President

makes all important appointments. The heads of the departments and other officials are appointed by the political chiefs (i.e. ministers). The executive has also the power to remove any officials on the grounds of violation of rules, negligence of duties, practice of corruption, indiscipline and insubordination. It can institute enquiries, through department or commissions, into the working of the administration.

3. The executive in India controls administration by means of orders, rules, decrees, ordinances etc., The president can make rules of business for the government of India. He has the power of making rules and regulations governing the recruitment to union services. He issues ordinances necessary when the parliament is not in session.

4. The executive in India controls administration by means of reports. The officials are required to submit reports, from time to time to their political chiefs.

5. The executive in India has financial control over administration. The officials cannot raise revenue or incur expenditure without the sanction of the minister or cabinet. The budget is prepared by the officials under the guidance of the executive. The accounts maintained by the departments are carefully audited annually by the Comptroller and Auditor General of India. He makes a report at the end in which he brings into light the acts of ommission or commission by the officials.

It is by all these methods that the executive in India exercise its firm control over administration.

JUDICIAL CONTROL OVER ADMINISTRATION

Today, it is universally recognized that the administration of justice is the principal task of the modern state. A state may have a good legislature and an excellent executive, but if it does not possess an independent judicial organ, it is not worth much. According to Lord Bryce there is no better test of the excellence of a government than the efficiency of its judicial system. Garner says: "A society without legislative organs is conceivable. But a civilized state without judicial organ and machinery is hardly conceivable". To secure the judicious application of law and ensure the guarantee of order, it is necessary to possess an upright, honest and impartial judicial organ. To safeguard the rights of the people, to punish crimes, to administer justice. To protect the innocent from injury, it is necessary to possess judiciary. Thus it is clear that the functions of the judiciary in an independent state are of great importance.

To perform these functions satisfactorily, the judiciary is authorised to exercise its control over the legislature, executive and administration. We shall try to understand the various methods employeed by the judiciary to secure control over the administration.

Method of Judicial Control

The judiciary secures administrative responsibility in several ways: They may be explained as follows:

1. ***Judicial Review.*** The first method by which judiciary controls administration is judicial review, (i) By this the judiciary has the power to declare any act of the administration such as licen. Sing, delegated legislation adjudication etc. null and void if it violates the provision of the constitution which is the supreme law of the land. This power of the judiciary over the administration is essential in the interests of the people's welfare. Man is selfish by nature. Administrator who is the main spring of new society is not free from selfishness. So, at times, the administrator tends to misuse or abuse his power to harm the individuals for private reasons. Such cases

are usually difficult to prove but certainly call for judicial correction (L.D. White). In a federation the supreme court has final authority to judge the constitutionality of any administrative decision.

2. If, in the opinion of the Judiciary a particular decision or policy made by the administration is contrary to the constitution or in excess of the authority granted to it, that decision or policy can be declared null and void by the judiciary.

3. Further, in acting as a guardian of the rights of the citizens if any act or decision of the administration seeks to deny or abridge or encroach upon the civil liberties of the people, the judiciary has the power to declare that act or decision unconstitutional.

Thus, judicial review of the administrative acts has become an important weapon of securing administrative responsibility. Its practice differs rom country to country. The examples are:

1. In Britain judicial review does not extend to all administrative acts, but only to certain acts that are determined by the parliament.

2. In the USA judicial review extends to all the administrative acts. The supreme court has the power to declare any administrative act null and void if it is contrary to the constitution. It is the final court of review. Any how, the courts in the USA review the administrative acts according to the prescribed rules.

3. In France, there is a special body of law called administrative law. It determines: (1) the position and liabilities of all state officials; (ii) the civil rights of the private individual in their dealings with the public officials; (iii) the procedure by which these rights and liabilities are enforced. Accordingly in France, the ordinary judicial courts have no jurisdiction in cases

in which the administrative officials in their official capacity are involved. Such cases are tried by a special body of courts known as administrative courts presided over by the officials.

4. ***Suits and Damages:*** The second method by which judiciary controls administration is suits and damages. According to this a citizen who suffers an injury or whose right is violated by the officials sues that official in the court. It means an aggrieved individual has the right of appeal to the courts or to a higher administrative tribunal. Where the court gives decision against the official, the citizen has the right to demand damages for injury he has suffered at the hands of that officials. Thus suits and damages act as an important weapon of judicial control over administration.

5. ***Writs:*** The third method by which judiciary controls administration is the issue of various writs of Habeas corpus, mandamus, prohibition, certiorari and quowarranto. Each writ may need a brief explanation.

   (i) ***Habeas Corpus:*** It means you shall produce the body. By this writ the court can order the authorities for the immediate produce of the person in custody before it to determine the legality of his detention. This writ is thus a powerful safeguard of the liberty of person of the citizen and the subject. In the USA "the write is chiefly used in alien exclusion and deportation cases.

   (ii) ***Mandamus:*** (it means a command): By this writ the court can order authorities to perform the duty specified in the order. This writ gives the judiciary the power to compel the administration to carry out its legal duties. The

write of mandamus cannot be claimed as a matter of right. It is available against any public official.

(iii) ***Injection or prohibition:*** By this writ the court can direct an official to refrain from doing an act which is likely to cause damage or loss of individual rights. Injunction is of two kinds: Mandatory and Preventive. Prohibition can be claimed as a matter of right. It is available against judicial or quasi-judicial authority.

(iv) ***Certiorari:*** (It means 'to be certified'): By this writ the court can direct a tribunal or officer to transfer to it a case, then, pending, in which the procedure is not in accordance with the common law. Thus the aim of this writ is to review the quasi-judicial functions of the executive or administrative authorities.

(v) ***Quo-Warranto.*** (It means by what warrant or authority): By this writ the court can enquire into the legality of the claim of an official to an office. If the claim is not determined. The court can direct the official to give up the office.

Thus by all the methods explained above, the judiciary, has full control over the administration, However, there are certain limitations on judicial control. They are:

1. All the administrative actions are not subject to judicial control.
2. It cannot by itself take cognizance except on the request of somebody.
3. The judicial process is slow and cumbersome.
4. The process of judicial work i.e. above layman's knowledge.

5. It is expensive and not within the financial means of many people.

Judicial Control Over Administration in India: All the methods of judicial control discussed above are in operation in India. The courts have the power to review administrative action if they are contrary to the constitution or in excess of authority granted to it. However, the judicial review operates in our country under serious restrictions. Regarding the suits and damages, the constitution permits the citizens to sue the union or state governments. The circumstances in which the Union or State can be sued are defined by the constitution. Regarding the liability of the, action, in India the officials are exempt from personal liability for the acts done according to the constitution. They are liable personally for all the actions done by them in excess of authority or contrary to the constitution. All the writs discussed above are in operation in India. The Supreme Court and the High Courts are authorized to issue the writs of Habeas Corpus, Mandamus, prohibitions, Quowaranto and certiorari.

CHAPTER—12

Public Policy Making

MEANING OF POLICY

1. The functions of modern administration are many. They are (i) to carry out the execution of the laws of the land; (ii) to act as semi—legislative and semi-judicial authority; (iii) to assist the political executive in drawing up of the policy of the government. Of these three, the last function, vi., drawing up of the policy of the government is considered most important. It is necessary therefore, to understand the meaning of policy.

2. "Policy means a decision as to what shall be done and how, when and where. In other words, before a policy is formulated by the government, the decisions as to what, when and where a policy is to be made are taken. The task of the government becomes simple if the issue involved in the policy are simple and vice versa. Every policy made by the government carries with it a long term objective. Every policy is always based on a lot of information consisting of facts and figures. The information is gathered from various sources such as reports, statistics, enquires, statements etc.

3. Every policy made by the government is also based on careful planning. If not, it leads to a lot of

administrative problems. (i) Every policy must be consistent with the law in force. (ii) The policy of one department should not adversely affect the other, (iii) The execution of the policy must be uniform and impartial. Thus every policy needs a good preparation (iv) The words should not be ambiguous.

ROLE OF ADMINISTRATION IN POLICY-MAKING

The administration plays a vital role in the formulation of public policy in the modern state. Generally speaking, it is the function of the legislature to formulate the public policy. But it is recognised every where that legislature cannot make policy without the assistance and interference of the administration. Hence it is necessary to understand the role of public administration in making public policy.

1. Firstly, the administration supplies necessary knowledge for the formulation of policy. The legislators or ministers do not posses necessary knowledge in the sphere of the policy making. They had obtained this position because of their achievements in the general field of politics. They do not find enough time to the understand the complex issues involved in the policy—making. On the other hand, the administrative officials posses necessary knowledge of these problems because of their experience. Hence they are in a position to suggest their political chiefs the ways and means of formulating a policy. The latter simply accept the views of the former. Sir Josiah Stamp observes: I am quite clear in my mind that the official must be the mainspring of the new society suggesting, promoting and advising at every stage.

2. Secondly, the administration, in many cases, takes initiative in formulating policy. The administrative

officers, in course of their duties, come across many defects or difficulties involved in the execution of policy. They know very well whether any changes or new arrangements are to be made in a policy. In such cases, the civil servants render advice to their political chiefs in regard to the formulation of new policy. In matters where and when discretion is largely left to administration in the interest of flexibility and wherever there is discretion to do a thing in one way or another. There is some room for policy making (Dr. M.P. Sharma).

3. Thirdly, administration supplies necessary information needed in the formulation of policy. Every policy must be based on accurate and factual information. The senior officials of the administration serve as reservoirs of information for the ministers or other executives. They gather the information from various sources, viz., internal reports, records, statistics, non-official organizations, special investigations, committee reports, research etc., The officers of each department preserve the information and supply it to their political heads whenever a policy is being formulated. It is not possible for a minister or a legislator to make the policy without possessing this information.

4. Lastly, the administration chalks out a good programme necessary for the proper execution of the policy. The duty of implementing any policy rests, ultimately, on the shoulders of the administration. For this purpose, it makes necessary rules and regulations. Thus the success or failure of any new policy depends upon the programme of execution drawn by the officers.

Conclusion: Thus it is clear from the above discussion that administration plays an important part in formulating policy. However, it should be remembered that every thing cannot be done by the officials independently. They have to do their work under the over all supervision of the political executive. Hence, for the formulation of a sound policy, the co-operation between the political head and officials is essential.

Chapter—13

District Administration

NATURE OF DISTRICT ADMINISTRATION

The Unit of field administration of India is District. It is a name given to an area which is marked off for special administrative purpose. The administration of this area is known by the name District Administration. This district administration may be defined as that portion of public administration which function in the territorial limits of a district (S.S. Khera). At present there are about 320 districts in the whole country, each district having jurisdiction over an average of 1400 villages. The Indian district is a historical product. It existed in the time of Mughal Emperors under the name sarkar. Under the British rule the unit of administration was district.

The district administration in India consists a number of component parts.

1. The first component part is law and order consisting of a magistrate or judge and police. The head of the district police is the superintendent of police who is responsible for the maintenance of law and order, detection of crimes and their prevention. He is assisted by other officials like Deputy Superintendent of Police, circle inspector, a subinspector etc., The district magistrate or judge is vested with the power of administering justice and controlling jails in the district.

2. The second component part is revenue which includes government treasury. It consists of the Collector. He is assisted by Revenue Divisional Officers and Tahisildars. They are responsible for the assessment and collection of land revenue.

3. The third component element of the district administration is land reforms, records and management. This part is looked after by the Collector assisted by the Revenue Divisional Officer and Tahsildars.

4. The fourth component part of the district administration is agriculture which includes irrigation and industry. The proper management of these is the responsibility of District Agricultural office assisted by the subordinate staff. Irrigation is the charge of an executive engineer.

5. The fifth component part is supplies and transport. It is responsible for the maintenance of the supply of essential goods. It is under the control of District Officer who is assisted by divisional and taluk supply officer.

6. The other component parts of the district administration are Community Development Office (Planning Officer), Health (District Health Office), Medicine (District Medical officer), Educational (District Education Officer) and Welfare (District Welfare Office). Thus the district in India is a multipurpose administrative area. It includes a number of services working in co-ordination.

ROLE OF THE DISTRICT ADMINISTRATION IN INDIA

The district administration plays a unique role in India. The functions of the district administration may be explained as below:

1. Law and order. The first function of the district administration is the maintenance of law and order.

The principal agencies are the magistrates and the police. The prevention of crime and maintenance of law, order and peace are the responsibilities of the District Magistrate and other Magistrates. They undertake inspections and visits in the district. They make enquiries as to the law and order, crime and the work of the police. The Magistrates look also into the matters relating to prosecutions, their progress and results. The District Magistrate makes a report on law and order situation in the district. The second agency of law and order in the district is the police headed by a District Superintendent of Police. They conduct investigation, inquests arrests and order in the district is the police headed by District Superintendent of Police. They conduct investigations, inquests arrests and searches. They record information reports, complaints, statements and diaries. The police executive the writs, summons, warrants of arrests issued by the courts. It is the duty of the police to prevent injury to the public property and unlawful assembly.

2. The second function of the district administration is the collection of land revenue. As the very name suggests, the principal function of the collector during the British rule was to collect the revenue. The District officials maintain land records, assess revenue and collect it periodically. The land in the district is properly surveyed. The survey helps the authorities to classify the land into various types depending on the nature of the soil. The revenue is assessed on the basis of the soil and produce of the land. It is the responsibility of the collector and other staff to collect the revenue in full. The revenue dues are collected periodically by the Collector. In certain cases the remission of land revenue may be announced by the district authority.

3. The third function of the district administration is the improvement of agriculture. Agriculture is the most important industry of our country providing livelihood for about 70% of the people. The agricultural officials in the district supply fertilizes, seeds and scientific instruments for the improvement of agriculture. They hold responsible for the agricultural extension work, irrigation facilities etc. The district administration provides agricultural credit to the farmers and marketing facilities to enable them to buy the seeds, sell the crops and invest their money. The agricultural co-operatives are also managed by the district authorities. They are helpful for the agriculturists as they provide co-operative credit for financing agricultural operations, purchasing tractor units etc.

4. The fourth function of the district administration is to tackle the problems of health, education and industries. It is directly concerned with maintaining a constant watch on the health of the district, guarding against any threat and out break of epidemic diseases. During the period of epidemics the district health authorities under the authority of the District Health Officer make arrangements for the treatment of those who fall victims to the epidemics. The district administration is responsible for the improvement of education. In some states the primary education is the responsibility of the local bodies or panchayat institutions. The educational institutions function under the overall supervision of the District Educational officer. Further, the function of the district administration is to inspect industries. They take necessary steps to improve the working conditions, the safety and health of the workers engaged in the industries. The district labour officers have the power to supervise the working of industrial concerns. It is open to the district administration to revive the old industries and sustain rural industries.

Conclusion. It is clear from the foregoing account that the modern district administration in India undertakes not only the functions of law and order but also welfare and developmental functions. Under the British rule the District administration was mainly concerned with two things, viz., the collection of revenue and law and order. The Collector levied and collected the land revenue and other taxes. The district magistrate maintained law and order as well as administered justice. He was assisted by the police officials. But since independence the functions of the district administration have acquired new colour. At present it is the centre of the district welfare. It provides the principal points of contact between the citizen and government.

CHAPTER—14

Good Governance

Good governance is the most important issue facing the country today. It implies gearing up the government machinery to provide a responsive, transparent, clean and people—friendly administration. Good governance is also linked with the role of the state; what it can do and cannot do matching its Capability and resources to undertake the task assigned for itself. Good governance is associated with efficient and effective administration in a democratic frame work.

Meaning of Good Governance

The term 'governance' has wider meaning and implications. It means the process as well as the result of making authoritative decisions for the benefit of the society. But its conceptual difficulties begin when it is found that the term is being touted in recent years by multilateral and bilateral aid giving agencies as a part of preconditions for economic aid or as a process of reforms qualifying for economic aid.

The concept of 'good governance' device its relevance in the context of misgovernments. In many countries the democratic form of government has proved to be ineffective for checking swinging of public funds for private gains by the elected leaders as well as the bureaucrats. Misuse of power, fraud, chicanery and embezzlement of funds are systematically perpetrated by the leaders of government and their minions. Misgovernance is found all around especially in the developing countries, in rampant degree. The concept of good governance becomes attractive as a remedy against this state of affairs.

World Bank Conceptualisation

The World Bank has identified a number of aspects of good governance which has assumed significance for the developed Countries. These factors deal with political and administrative aspects, which are as follows:

(a) Political accountability, including the acceptability of political system by the people and regular elections to legitimize the exercise of political power.

(b) Freedom of association and participation by various religious, social, economic, cultural and professional groups in the process of Governance.

(c) An established legal frame work based on the rule of law and independence of judiciary to protect human rights, secure social justice and guard against exploitation and abuse of power.

(d) Bureaucratic accountability ensuring a system to monitor and control the performance of Government offices and officials in relation to quality of service, inefficiency and abuse of discretionary power. The related determinants include openness and transparency in administration.

(e) Freedom of information and expression needed for formulation of public policies, decision making, monitoring and evaluation of government performance. It also includes independent analysis of information by the professional bodies

including the universities and others needed for a civil society.

(f) A sound administrative system leading to efficiency and effectiveness. This, in turn, means the value for money and cost, effectiveness. The effectiveness includes the degree of global achievement as per the stated objectives and also the administrative system which is able to take secular and rational decisions and the system which is self propelling to take corrective measures.

(g) Co-operation between the Government and Civil Society Organizations.

It makes clear that good governance is committed to development oriented administration, aiming improvement of quality of the of the people of a nation. For a number of other experts, good governance implies presence of the Rule of law, safeguarding of basic human rights, presence of honest and efficient Govt. accountability, transparency and openess. But good governance is not simply something that government can achieve or do by itself. Good governance depends on the co-operation and an involvement of a large number of citizens and organizations. These requirements are considered not only essential for Good governance but are also important for sustainable human development. States, as the ancient Greeks said, stands for good life. It is not enough that administration is run on sound managerial lines. The equity and legitimacy aspects are as important, or perhaps more important, than good management. The governing process should provide opportunities for the people to actively participate in decision—making, and the fruits of government must be shared and not captured by an influential minority people's perception about how the governing process is going on services as the barometer of legitimacy of governance. Empowerment is thus a precondition of good governance.

PEOPLE'S PARTICIPATION AND GOOD GOVERNANCE

In a democratic system of government, the citizens and the public servants are not two separate entities. Much of the success of Public Administration depends on its capacity to enlist public participation in the administrative process. Many of our developments plans and programmes have failed due to the lack of citizens participation in them. The fifth plan stressed the need for the people's participation in planning and states. "The involvement of the people and their elected representatives is a pre-requisite for effective planning. A plan which does not take into account the people's aspirations and preferences can have no operational validity, especially since its successful implementation can be ensured only if the majority of citizens, functioning as entrepreneur decisions—makers in relation to consumption, savings, investments, etc., endorse the envisaged policies and programmes by their whole hearted participation". This shows that both democratic administration and development administration require people's participation in order to successfully achieve the goals of democratic socialism enshrined in the constitution of India.

Meaning of People's Participation

The term 'participation' varies in meaning, and content from context to context. According to a UNESCO document "participation is collective sustained activity for the purpose of achieving some common objectives, especially a more equitable distribution of the benefits of development".

Broadly speaking, the term 'people's participation' refers to the role of members of general public in influencing the activities of government. It may occur from the village to the county level. It may manifest itself in different forms. The participation may be direct, as in the community projects or it may be indirect, through elected representatives.

Hence, participation in administration refers to all those activities which indicate the people's involvement in the process of administration that is, participation in policy formulation and programme planning, implementation and evaluation of policies and programmes meant for development of particular target groups.

Problems of Peoples' Participation in India

In India people are indifferent and apathetic towards administration. Extensive empirical studies on the nature and degree of citizens participation in India have revealed that colonial legacy, social diversity, poverty and illiteracy and the peculiarity of the political process greatly restrict people's participation in the Public Administration in India. People participation demands certain preconditions. Of these, the most important are enlightened political leaders, conscientious civil servants and an informed public; all the three of which are conspicuous by their absence in the Indian scenario. But not much planned effort is visible to involve people in development processes. The system of democratic decentralization introduced in India did not really devolve power on the masses. The dominance of powerful socio-economic and political groups has alienated the common man from the national main stream. Poverty, Unemployment and inequality are still wide spread. Most of the citizens feel helpless before the mighty power of the administration and have, learnt to reconcile to the corrupt political system.

Measures to Promote People's Participation in Administration

To promote people's participation in Administration various measures need to be initiated. These my include:

constant contact of legislators with their constituents, change in the attitude of bureaucrats, competent administrative leadership, constructive role of Political parties and restructing of administration so as to make it more democratic and responsive.

In conclusion we may say that people's participation in the Administration in India must become a mass movement, because it leads to national development. If this happens, then we can say with a measure of confidence that we have good governance.

Bibliography

1. Albrow, Martin, *Bureaucracy,* London, Pall Mall, 1970.
2. Ali, Shum Shun Nisa, *Eminent Administrative Thinkers,* New Delhi, Associated Publishing House, 1984.
3. Anderson, James E., *Public Policy Making,* London. Thomas Nelson and Sons Ltd., 1975.
4. Appleby, Paul H., *Policy and Administration,* Alabama University of Alabama Press, 1957.
5. Arora, Ramesh (ed.) *Administrative Theory,* New Delhi, IIPA, 1984.
6. Awasthi A and Aroa Ramesh K. (ed.). *Bureaucracy and Development: Indian Perspectives,* New Delhi, Associated Publishing House, 1978.
7. Awasthi, A. and Maheshwari S., *Public—Administration,* Agra, Laxmi Narayan Agarawal, 1983.
8. Bhalerao, C.N., *Public Service Commissions of India:* A Study, New Delhi, Sterling, 1966.
9. Bhambhri, C.P., *Administration in a Changing Society,* Delhi, National Publishing House, 1972.
10. Bhambhri, C.P., *Bureaucracy and Politics in India,* Delhi, Vikas, 1971.
11. Bhatia, B.S. and Batra, G.S. *Public Enterprises Management,* Deep & Deep Publications Pvt. Ltd., New Delhi, 2000.
12. Bhattacharya, Mohit, *Bureaucracy and Development Administration;* New Delhi, Uppal Publishing House, 1979.
13. Burke B. John, *Bureaucratic Responsibility,* Baltimore, John Hopkins University Press, 1986.

14. Bava Noorjahan, *People's Participation in Development Administration in India,* New Delhi, Uppal Publishing House, 1984.

15. Dutta P.R., *Public Administration and the State,* New Delhi, Uppal, 1978.

16 Gladden E.N., *History of Public Administration,* London, Frank cass, 1972.

17. Goel S.L., *Advanced Public Administration,* New Delhi, sterling, 1994.

18. Goel S.L., *Personnel Administration and Management,* Sterling, New Delhi, 1993.

19. Goel S.L. *Public Administration: Theory and Practice,* New Delhi, Deep and Deep, 2003.

20. Heady, Ferrel, *Public Administration: A Comparative perspective,* New Jersey, Prentice Hall Inc. 1984.

21. Henery, Nicholas, *Public Administration and Public Affairs,* New Jersey, Prentice Hall, 1975.

22. Hill, Michael, *The Sociology of Public—Administration,* London, Deiden field and Nicolson, 1972.

23. Jain R.B., *Contemporary Issues in Indian Administration,* Delhi, Vishal Publishers, 1976.

24. Latiff, T.A.A. *Training for Management,* Delhi, Sterling, 1977.

25. Mansukhani, H.C. *Corruption and Public Services,* New Delhi, Vikas, 1979.

26. Nigro, Felix A., *Modern Public—Administration,* New York, Harper and Row, 1970.

27. Panda, Basuder, *Indian Bureaucracy:* An Inside Story; New Delhi, Uppal Publishing House, 1978.

28. Peter Self, *Administrative Theories and Politics,* London, George, Allen and Unwin, 1977.

29. Riggs, Fred W., *The Ecology of Public Administration,* Bombay, Asia Pulishing House, 1961.

30. Sharan, Parmatma, *Modern Public Administration,* Meerut, Meenakshi Prakashan, 1981.

31. Singh Narendra Kumar, *Bureaucracy: Position and Persons,* New Delhi, Abinava, Publications, 1974.

32. Smith, B.C., *Bureaucracy and Political Power,* New York, St. Martins Press, 1988.

33. Singh, Hoshiar (Ed.), *Public Service Commissions in India,* Allahabad, Kitab Mahal, 1999.

34. Sharma, M.P. *Public Administration;* (Theory and Practice), Allahabad, Kitab Muhal, 1990.

35. Thakur, Rudranand, *Elite Theory and Administrative System,* New Delhi Sterling, 1981.

36. Tripathi, P.C., *Personnel Management,* New Delhi, Sultan Chand, 1978.

37. Tyagi, A.R., *Civil Services in a Developing Society,* Delhi, Sterling Publishers, 1969.

38. Vishnoo Bhagwan and Vidya Bhushan, *Public Administration,* New Delhi, S. Chand and Co., 1990.

39. Warwick, Dehnis, *Bureacuracy,* Long man, London, 1974.

40. Wilenski, Peter, *Public Power and Public Administration,* Sydney, Hale and Iremonger, 1986.